Samba
Administrator's
Handbook

Samba Administrator's Handbook

Ed Brooksbank
George Haberberger
Lisa Doyle

M&T Books
An imprint of IDG Books Worldwide, Inc.
Foster City, CA ■ Chicago, IL ■ Indianapolis, IN ■ New York, NY

Samba Administrator's Handbook

Published by
M&T Books
An imprint of IDG Books Worldwide, Inc.
919 E. Hillsdale Blvd., Suite 400
Foster City, CA 94404
www.idgbooks.com (IDG Books Worldwide
Web site)

ISBN: 0-7645-4636-8

Printed in the United States of America

10 9 8 7 6 5 4 3 2 1

XX/RU/RR/ZZ/FC

Distributed in the United States by IDG Books
Worldwide, Inc.

Distributed by CDG Books Canada Inc. for Canada;
by Transworld Publishers Limited in the United
Kingdom; by IDG Norge Books for Norway; by IDG
Sweden Books for Sweden; by IDG Books Australia
Publishing Corporation Pty. Ltd. for Australia and
New Zealand; by TransQuest Publishers Pte Ltd. for
Singapore, Malaysia, Thailand, Indonesia, and Hong
Kong; by Gotop Information Inc. for Taiwan; by ICG
Muse, Inc. for Japan; by Intersoft for South Africa; by
Eyrolles for France; by International Thomson
Publishing for Germany, Austria and Switzerland; by
Distribuidora Cuspide for Argentina; by LR
International for Brazil; by Galileo Libros for Chile; by
Ediciones ZETA S.C.R. Ltda. for Peru; by WS
Computer Publishing Corporation, Inc., for the
Philippines; by Contemporanea de Ediciones for
Venezuela; by Express Computer Distributors for the
Caribbean and West Indies; by Micronesia Media
Distributor, Inc. for Micronesia; by Chips
Computadoras S.A. de C.V. for Mexico; by Editorial
Norma de Panama S.A. for Panama; by American
Bookshops for Finland.

For general information on IDG Books Worldwide's
books in the U.S., please call our Consumer Customer
Service department at 800-762-2974. For reseller
information, including discounts and premium sales,
please call our Reseller Customer Service department
at 800-434-3422.

For information on where to purchase IDG Books
Worldwide's books outside the U.S., please contact our
International Sales department at 317-596-5530 or fax
317-596-5692.

For consumer information on foreign language translations, please contact our Customer Service department
at 800-434-3422, fax 317-596-5692, or e-mail
rights@idgbooks.com.

For information on licensing foreign or domestic
rights, please phone +1-650-655-3109.

For sales inquiries and special prices for bulk quanti-
ties, please contact our Sales department at
650-655-3200 or write to the address above.

For information on using IDG Books Worldwide's
books in the classroom or for ordering examination
copies, please contact our Educational Sales department at 800-434-2086 or fax 317-596-5499.

For press review copies, author interviews, or other
publicity information, please contact our Public
Relations department at 650-655-3000 or fax
650-655-3299.

For authorization to photocopy items for corporate,
personal, or educational use, please contact Copyright
Clearance Center, 222 Rosewood Drive, Danvers, MA
01923, or fax 978-750-4470.

Library of Congress Cataloging-in-Publication Data
Production: Please supply CIP data. If CIP data is not
available, the book should have a Library of Congress
Catalog Card

ABOUT IDG BOOKS WORLDWIDE

Welcome to the world of IDG Books Worldwide.

IDG Books Worldwide, Inc., is a subsidiary of International Data Group, the world's largest publisher of computer-related information and the leading global provider of information services on information technology. IDG was founded more than 30 years ago by Patrick J. McGovern and now employs more than 9,000 people worldwide. IDG publishes more than 290 computer publications in over 75 countries. More than 90 million people read one or more IDG publications each month.

Launched in 1990, IDG Books Worldwide is today the #1 publisher of best-selling computer books in the United States. We are proud to have received eight awards from the Computer Press Association in recognition of editorial excellence and three from Computer Currents' First Annual Readers' Choice Awards. Our best-selling ...For Dummies® series has more than 50 million copies in print with translations in 31 languages. IDG Books Worldwide, through a joint venture with IDG's Hi-Tech Beijing, became the first U.S. publisher to publish a computer book in the People's Republic of China. In record time, IDG Books Worldwide has become the first choice for millions of readers around the world who want to learn how to better manage their businesses.

Our mission is simple: Every one of our books is designed to bring extra value and skill-building instructions to the reader. Our books are written by experts who understand and care about our readers. The knowledge base of our editorial staff comes from years of experience in publishing, education, and journalism — experience we use to produce books to carry us into the new millennium. In short, we care about books, so we attract the best people. We devote special attention to details such as audience, interior design, use of icons, and illustrations. And because we use an efficient process of authoring, editing, and desktop publishing our books electronically, we can spend more time ensuring superior content and less time on the technicalities of making books.

You can count on our commitment to deliver high-quality books at competitive prices on topics you want to read about. At IDG Books Worldwide, we continue in the IDG tradition of delivering quality for more than 30 years. You'll find no better book on a subject than one from IDG Books Worldwide.

John Kilcullen
Chairman and CEO
IDG Books Worldwide, Inc.

Steven Berkowitz
President and Publisher
IDG Books Worldwide, Inc.

*Eighth Annual
Computer Press
Awards ≥1992*

*Ninth Annual
Computer Press
Awards ≥1993*

*Tenth Annual
Computer Press
Awards ≥1994*

*Eleventh Annual
Computer Press
Awards ≥1995*

Credits

Acquisitions Editor
Laura Lewin

Development Editors
Matthew E. Lusher
Michael Koch

Technical Editor
Kevin Reichard

Copy Editors
Mildred Sanchez
Richard H. Adin

Project Coordinator
Linda Marousek

Graphics and Production Specialists
Mario Amador
Stephanie Hollier
Jude Levinson
Victor Perz-Varela
Ramses Ramirez
Dina F Quan

Quality Control Specialist
Chris Weisbart

Book Designer
Kurt Krames

Proofreading and Indexing
York Production Services

Cover Design
Deborah Reinerio

About the Authors

Ed Brooksbank has been an information technology professional for over 20 years. His current title is Senior Network Design and Development Specialist. His first exposure to UNIX was in 1989. In 1990, he downsized a mainframe for a UNIX workstation network. He has worked in the telecommunications, defense, and utilities industries as an analyst, programmer, and systems programmer.

George Haberberger has been working in the software field for nine years and in customer support for the last six years, providing support for SunOS, Netware, and Solaris printers; Macintosh, DOS, and Windows clients. He wrote user manuals for Sun-based printers and extensively revised the Mail Manager 2000 mailing list software and ZCR 2000 Zip Code encoding software manuals.

Lisa A. Doyle has been a technical editor and writer for 12 years. She has worked for McGraw-Hill, NASA, and several networking and software companies. As an independent contractor, she has written documentation for a wide range of computer subjects. She is a published author whose work includes *Basic Digital Electronics — 2nd Edition,* TAB/McGraw-Hill, Ray Ryan and Lisa Doyle, and *How to Read Schematics,* TAB/McGraw-Hill, Robert J. Traister and Anna L. Lisk (pseudonym).

Preface

Samba is a deceptively simple piece of software. It's the first solution that provides seamless integration between UNIX servers and Windows clients without having to install client software. You can share UNIX disks and printers, ensure UNIX security and reliability, and even join a Windows domain. Older UNIX servers that no longer have the horsepower for databases or scientific applications make ideal file and print servers.

If you are a UNIX or NT administrator and you want to share UNIX resources with Windows clients, this book has the information you need. This book is the only reference that you'll want or need for administering Samba file and print services. There is no introductory information, cross-references, sidebars, or screen shots. Instead, there is everything that you need to know about a topic in single chapter. This means some information might be repeated so as to save you the trouble of flipping back and forth to find all the information necessary to perform a task. Chapters are designed to be self-contained.

How This Book Is Organized

This book is organized into three parts:

- Part I: Installation and Basic Configuration
- Part II: Advanced Configuration
- Part III: Troubleshooting

Part I: Installation and Basic Configuration

Part I provides the lowdown on all issues related to installing and configuring Samba on various UNIX-based systems. Chapters 1 to 5 cover installation of server and client, configuration, and the various configuration tools.

- **Chapter 1: Server Installation** — Server installation and testing, featuring a variety of UNIX-based operating systems including Linux, Solaris, FreeBSD, and NetBSD.

- **Chapter 2: Client Installation** — Setup, configuration, and connection of a variety of client types.

- **Chapter 3: Basic Configuration Using SWAT** — A thorough and detailed explanation for using the Samba Web Administration Tool (SWAT) for configuration.

- **Chapter 4: Basic Operating System Configuration** — How to add and maintain users, groups, and printers.

- **Chapter 5: Other GUI Configuration Tools** — Using other tools such as Linuxconf, SMBEdit, and Webmin to configure your Samba parameters.

Part II: Advanced Configuration

After Samba is installed and configured, it's time to fine-tune it for your specific networking tasks. Chapters 6 to 8 cover advanced configuration topics.

- **Chapter 6: Naming Services** — Setting up and configuring naming services such as NIS, DNS, and WINS.

- **Chapter 7: Best Practices, Browsing, and Domains** — Techniques to make your server more efficient, such as backing up the server, security, and automounting user directories.

- **Chapter 8: Performance Tuning** — Hardware and software recommendations for maximizing and measuring performance.

Part III: Troubleshooting

Working with Samba on a daily basis requires knowing how to diagnose and fix problems, as well as perform the administrative and maintenance tasks that are needed to keep it running smoothly. Chapters 9 to 12 cover these issues.

- **Chapter 9: Basic Network Connectivity** — Network configuration options for Windows 95/98, Windows NT, and UNIX.

- **Chapter 10: Testing the Samba Configuration** — Various testing methods and tips to ensure that Samba runs smoothly.

- **Chapter 11: Accessing Samba** — How to check and manage shares and connections.

- **Chapter 12: Using Net Commands to Diagnose Problems** — Troubleshooting tips for networks using Windows NT servers and workstations.

Appendixes

The appendixes include helpful information such as error codes, the GNU general public license, and online resources to keep current on Samba and its associated technologies.

Keeping Current

Samba is a rapidly developing software suite. The Windows NT Primary Domain Controller code is maturing rapidly, and code for Windows 2000 is currently being added. While this book was written with reference to the latest version of Samba (2.0.5), a newer version might have been released by the time you read this. It's always a good idea to check the appropriate documentation to see what might have changed. Also, refer to the newsgroups and Web links in Appendix C, Online Resources, for up-to-date information.

Conventions Used in This Book

This book uses a number of typographic conventions to identify certain types of information. Words or characters that you're to type or enter are highlighted in **bold**. Samba commands and elements of program code, as well as URLs and e-mail addresses, appear in monospace font: for example, `http://www.samba.org` or the Samba command `smbclient \\\\laptop\\col`. Monospace font is also used to format command listings and displays of terminal window output. For example:

```
% ls -al
total 163
drwxr-xr-x 2 george wheel 512 May 31 10:39 .
```

```
drwxr-xr-x 3 root wheel 512 May 20 10:09 ..
-rw-r--r-- 1 george wheel 509 May 20 10:09 .cshrc
-rw------- 1 george wheel 235 Jun 3 19:05 .history
-rw-r--r-- 1 george wheel 561 May 20 10:09 .login
-rw-r--r-- 1 george wheel 139 May 20 10:09 .login_conf
-rw------- 1 george wheel 351 May 20 10:09 .mail_aliases
-rw-r--r-- 1 george wheel 313 May 20 10:09 .mailrc
-rw-r--r-- 1 george wheel 749 May 20 10:09 .profile
-rw------- 1 george wheel 257 May 20 10:09 .rhosts
-rw-r--r-- 1 george wheel 832 May 20 10:09 .shrc
-rwxr----- 1 george wheel 142195 May 29 22:17 libdes-
4_04b_tar.gz
```

You'll also find a number of icons throughout the text to point out special information:

Tip

Tips mark a recommendation on best practices, useful techniques, and things to make you more productive.

Caution

A Caution icon flags a warning to you of potential dangers to your code or your system.

Contents at a Glance

Contents

Part I

Installation and Basic Configuration

Chapter 1

Server Installation

Samba runs on a variety of UNIX-based operating systems including Linux, Solaris, FreeBSD, and NetBSD. If it's a new installation of Linux on a server, it's just a matter of checking a box to include Samba. If your UNIX box is already running, this book describes how to download and install Samba.

Getting the Latest Version of Samba

Samba is a rapidly evolving software suite, so it's a good practice to remain current on the newest versions. However, many of the UNIX-like operating systems have a very rapid pace of development, and their operating system CD-ROMs often have a current or nearly current version of Samba already available.

Look on your operating system CD-ROM

Most of the various Linux and BSD distributions include Samba on the OS CD-ROM. Table 1-1 shows a list of several operating systems and the versions of Samba that are included on the CD-ROMs. You can install Samba during or after the OS installation process.

Table 1-1 *OS and Samba Versions*

OS	Version	Samba Version
Red Hat Linux	6.0	2.0.3
Red Hat Linux	5.2	1.9.18p10
Caldera Open Linux	2.2	2.0.3
Caldera Open Linux	1.3	1.9.18p8
Slackware Linux	4.0	2.0.3
Slackware Linux	3.9	2.0.3
Slackware Linux	3.6	1.9.18p10
FreeBSD	3.2	2.0.3
FreeBSD	2.2.8	1.9.18p10
NetBSD	1.3.3	2.0.2

The commercial UNIX operating systems typically do not include Samba on their installation disks; fortunately, Samba is only a short download away.

Downloading the latest Samba version

The main Samba Web page is http://www.samba.org. This page includes 27 fully mirrored Web pages and 32 pages devoted to source and binaries (shown in Table 1-2). Use a mirror in your country for the fastest performance. Chapter 7 details an alternate method of downloading the latest Samba using CVS tools.

Table 1-2 *Samba Download Sites*

Country	Mirror location	Type
USA	`http://us1.Samba.org/Samba/Samba.html`	Full
USA	`http://us2.Samba.org/Samba/Samba.html`	Full
USA	`http://us3.Samba.org/Samba/Samba.html`	Full
USA	`ftp://ftp.Samba.org/pub/Samba/`	Source/binary
USA	`http://us1.Samba.org/Samba/ftp/`	Source/binary
USA	`ftp://us3.Samba.org/pub/mirrors/` `Samba.anu.edu.au/`	Source/binary
Australia	`http://au1.Samba.org/Samba/Samba.html`	Full

Australia	`http://au2.Samba.org/Samba/Samba.html`	Full
Australia	`ftp://au1.Samba.org/pub/Samba/`	Source/binary
Austria	`http://at.Samba.org/Samba/Samba.html`	Full
Austria	`ftp://gd.tuwien.ac.at/infosys/` `servers/Samba/`	Source/binary
Brazil	`ftp://ftp.ravel.ufrj.br/pub/UNIX/Samba/`	Source/binary
Canada	`http://ca.Samba.org/Samba/Samba.html`	Full
Canada	`ftp://ca.Samba.org/pub/Samba/`	Full
Costa Rica	`ftp://ftp.ucr.ac.cr/pub/UNIX/Samba`	Source/binary
Czech Rep.	`ftp://sunsite.mff.cuni.cz/Net/` `Protocols/Samba/`	Source/binary
Denmark	`http://sunsite.auc.dk/Samba/Samba.html`	Full
Denmark	`ftp://sunsite.auc.dk/pub/UNIX/` `networking/Samba/`	Source/binary
Finland	`http://fi.Samba.org/Samba/Samba.html`	Full
Finland	`ftp://fi.Samba.org/pub/Samba/`	Source/binary
France	`http://fr.Samba.org/Samba/Samba.html`	Full
France	`ftp://fr.Samba.org/pub/Samba/`	Source/binary
Germany	`http://de.Samba.org/Samba/Samba.html`	Full
Germany	`ftp://de.Samba.org/pub/mirror/Samba/`	Source/binary
Germany	`ftp://ftp.uni-trier.de/pub/UNIX/` `network/Samba/`	Source/binary
Greece	`ftp://ftp.ntua.gr/pub/net/Samba/`	Source/binary
Hong Kong	`http://hk.Samba.org/Samba/Samba.html`	Full
Hong Kong	`http://hk.Samba.org/Samba/ftp/`	Source/binary
Italy	`http://it.Samba.org/Samba/Samba.html`	Full
Italy	`ftp://it.Samba.org/pub/Samba/`	Source/binary
Italy	`ftp://volftp.tin.it/mirror/Samba/` `pub/Samba/`	Source/binary
Japan	`http://mirror.nucba.ac.jp/Samba/` `Samba.html`	Full
Japan	`ftp://mirror.nucba.ac.jp/pub/Samba/`	Source/binary
Japan	`ftp://ring.asahi-net.or.jp/pub/net/` `Samba/`	Source/binary
Japan	`ftp://ring.aist.go.jp/pub/net/Samba/`	Source/binary

Continued

Table 1-2 *Continued*

Country	Mirror location	Type
Korea	`http://kr.Samba.org/Samba/Samba.html`	Full
Korea	`ftp://CAIR-archive.kaist.ac.kr/pub/Samba/`	Source/binary
Malaysia	`http://www.twc.com.my/Samba/Samba.html`	Full
Norway	`http://www.bibsyst.no/Samba/Samba.html`	Full
Norway	`ftp://www.bibsyst.no/pub/Samba/`	Source/binary
Poland	`http://pl.Samba.org/Samba/Samba.html`	Full
Poland	`ftp://pl.Samba.org/pub/UNIX/net/Samba/`	Source/binary
Poland	`ftp://giswitch.sggw.waw.pl/pub/UNIX/Samba/`	Source/binary
Portugal	`http://pt.Samba.org/Samba/Samba.html`	Full
Portugal	`http://Samba.ist.utl.pt/Samba/Samba.html`	Full
Portugal	`ftp://pt.Samba.org/pub/mirrors/Samba`	Source/binary
Romania	`http://ro.Samba.org/Samba/Samba.html`	Full
Russia	`http://ru.Samba.org/Samba/Samba.html`	Full
Russia	`ftp://ru.Samba.org/pub/Samba`	Source/binary
Singapore	`http://sg.Samba.org/Samba/Samba.html`	Full
Singapore	`ftp://sg.Samba.org/Samba/`	Source/binary
Slovenia	`ftp://ftp.k2.net/mirrors/Samba/`	Source/binary
South Africa	`ftp://ftp.vwv.com/pub/Samba`	Source/binary
Sweden	`http://se.Samba.org/Samba/Samba.html`	Full
Sweden	`ftp://se.Samba.org/pub/Samba/`	Source/binary
Turkey	`http://tr.Samba.org/Samba/Samba.html`	Full
Turkey	`ftp://tr.Samba.org/Samba/`	Source/binary
UK	`http://uk.Samba.org/Samba/Samba.html`	Full
UK	`ftp://sunsite.org.uk/packages/Samba/`	Source/binary

Downloading binaries

While Samba is provided with the full source and make files for easy compiling, you might sometimes want to just download precompiled binaries. The binaries are uploaded by other Samba users and not necessarily by the Samba team. Table 1-3 lists the advantages and disadvantages of binary distributions.

Table 1-3 *Advantages and Disadvantages of Binaries*

Advantages	Disadvantages
Binaries are ready to run; no compiler or libraries are needed	Not all desired platforms are available.
Possibly saves time.	Not all software levels of supported platforms are available. There can be a lag between the time the latest Samba is released and when it gets compiled to a binary and uploaded.
Saves disk space.	Upload could be corrupt; you might need to download binaries from several sites to get one that installs without errors.
	No choice of compilation parameters; you might not be able to download a version that was compiled with your specific needs.

Using the Red Hat Package Manager (RPM) to Install Samba

Both Red Hat and Caldera use the Red Hat Package Manager (RPM) to make installation, removal, or the obtaining of information about software packages easy. You should almost always be able to find Samba in a RPM format, although it has the same advantages and disadvantages as a binary.

To install Samba from a Linux CD, change to the directory containing the RPMs. Type **RPM −i packagename** to install the RPM package. The following example installs the 2.0.3 version of Samba from the Red Hat CD and displays hash marks as it installs (the v and h switch).

```
RPM −ivh Samba-2.0.3-8.i386.RPM
```

RPM checks dependencies before installing, so you might need to install other packages before installing Samba.

To install a downloaded RPM, change to the directory containing the RPM and install using the same command. To learn more about RPM, check out the Red Hat web page at http://www.redhat.com or http://www.rpm.org, the group overseeing development of RPM.

Compiling Samba

For the greatest flexibility, you want to download the source and compile Samba yourself. Compiling and running Samba version 2.0 and higher is much easier than Samba version 1.9. The most recent Samba version at the download sites is called Samba-latest_tar.gz.

Compiling Samba 2.0 or higher

After downloading Samba-latest_tar.gz to an appropriate temp directory, gzip and untar it with this command string:

```
gzip —dc Samba-latest_tar.gz | tar xvf —
```

where gzip is the GNU compression utility. If you get the error

```
gzip: command not found
```

conduct a find on gzip; it might not be accessible from your path. If it's not installed on your system, it's a free download from the GNU Web page (http://www.gnu.org), or it might be on your OS CD-ROM.

Once the Samba package has been uncompressed and untarred, run the configure program to start compiling by typing

```
./configure
```

in the directory where configure was installed. If the directory named /temp has the Samba-latest_tar.gz file, then the configure program is created in /temp/Samba-2.0.3/source for the 2.0.3 version of Samba.

If you get an error about cc or gcc, the C compilers could not be found. Try to find them and include them in your search path. If they are not available, you can download the GNU C compiler gcc from the GNU Web page (http://www.gnu.org), or it could be on your OS CD-ROM.

To then compile with the default parameters, type

```
make
```

in the configure directory, and then type

```
make install
```

to install the compiled files.

If you are upgrading Samba, the old binaries should be saved and renamed with the extension .old. The `make revert` command enables you to back out of the upgrade and return to your previous version of Samba.

If you get errors about `make` not being found, such as

```
make: command not found
```

it might not be on your search path. The installation goes easier once `make` is on your search path.

Custom compilation of Samba 2.0

If you need to customize the compilation, you can add command-line parameters. The current list is available by typing ./**configure --help**. These are the `configure` command-line parameters for Samba 2.0.3, which are listed in Table 1-4. Many of them are paired, with the default option mentioned. If the options have defaults, they are indicated by square brackets.

Table 1-4 *Configuration Parameters for Samba 2.0.3*

Configuration option	Function
`--cache-file=FILE`	Cache test results in `FILE`
`--help`	Print the configure parameters
`--no-create`	Don't create output files
`--quiet, --silent`	Don't print "checking..." messages, which can print screens of text

Continued

Table 1-4 *Continued*

Configuration option	Function
`--version`	Print the version of autoconf that created the configure program
Directory and file names options	
`--prefix=PREFIX`	Install architecture-independent files in **PREFIX** directory, the default of which is /usr/local/Samba [/usr/local/Samba]
`--exec-prefix=EPREFIX`	Install architecture-dependent files in **EPREFIX**; the default should be the same as the prefix default, /usr/local/Samba [same as prefix]
`--bindir=DIR`	The user executables stored in **DIR** from **PREFIX**, the default is /usr/local/Samba/bin [**EPREFIX**/bin]
`--sbindir=DIR`	The executables for the system administrator are stored in **DIR**; the default is /usr/local/Samba/sbin [**EPREFIX**/sbin]
`--libexecdir=DIR`	The program executables for Samba stored in **DIR**; the default is /usr/local/Samba/libexec [**EPREFIX**/libexec]
`--datadir=DIR`	The read-only architecture-independent data stored in **DIR**; the default is /usr/local/Samba/share [**PREFIX**/share]
`--sysconfdir=DIR`	The directory for read-only single-machine data stored in **DIR**; the default is /usr/local/Samba/etc [**PREFIX**/etc]
`--sharedstatedir=DIR`	The modifiable architecture-independent data is stored in **DIR**; the default is /usr/local/Samba/com [**PREFIX**/com]
`--localstatedir=DIR`	The modifiable single-machine data is stored in **DIR**; the default is /usr/local/Samba/var [**PREFIX**/var]
`--libdir=DIR`	The object code libraries are stored in **DIR**; the default is /usr/local/Samba/lib [**EPREFIX**/lib]
`--includedir=DIR`	The C header files are stored in **DIR**; the default is /usr/local/Samba/include [**PREFIX**/include]
`--oldincludedir=DIR`	The C header files for non-gcc compilers stored in **DIR**; the default is /usr/include [/usr/include]
`--infodir=DIR`	The info documentation stored in **DIR**; the default is /usr/local/Samba/info [**PREFIX**/info]
`--ma ndir=DIR`	The man pages documentation stored in **DIR**; the default is /usr/local/Samba/man [**PREFIX**/man]

`--srcdir=DIR`	The source code is kept in `DIR` [`configure dir` or `..`]
`--program-prefix=PREFIX`	Prepend `PREFIX` to installed program names
`--program-suffix=SUFFIX`	Append `SUFFIX` to installed program names
`--program-transform-name=PROGRAM`	Run sed `PROGRAM` on installed program names

Host-type options

`--build=BUILD` [`BUILD=HOST`]	Configure for building on `BUILD`
`--host=HOST`	Configure for `HOST` [guessed]
`--target=TARGET`	Configure for `TARGET` [`TARGET=HOST`]

Features and packages options

`--disable-FEATURE`	Do not include `FEATURE` (same as `--enable-FEATURE=no`)
`--enable-FEATURE[=ARG]`	Include `FEATURE` [`ARG=yes`]
`--with-PACKAGE[=ARG]`	Use `PACKAGE` [`ARG=yes`]
`--without-PACKAGE`	Do not use `PACKAGE` (same as `--with-PACKAGE=no`)
`--x-includes=DIR`	X include files are in `DIR`
`--x-libraries=DIR`	X library files are in `DIR`

--enable and --with options recognized

`--enable-maintainer-mode`	Enable some make rules for maintainers
`--with-smbwrapper`	Include SMB wrapper support to give the operating system access to SMB shares
`--without-smbwrapper`	Don't include SMB wrapper support (default)
`--with-afs`	Include Andrew File System authentication (AFS) support
`--without-afs`	Don't include AFS support (default)
`--with-dfs`	Include DFS (Distributed File System) support
`--without-dfs`	Don't include DFS support (default)
`--with-krb4=base-dir`	Include Kerberos IV authentication support, using the base-dir
`--whithout-krb4`	Don't include Kerberos IV authentication support (default)

Continued

Table 1-4 *Continued*

Configuration option	Function
--with-krb5=base-dir	Include Kerberos 5 authentication support, using the base-dir
--whithout-krb5	Don't include Kerberos 5 support (default)
--with-automount	Include AUTOMOUNT support if you want to automatically send users to distributed home directories
--without-automount	Don't include AUTOMOUNT support (default)
--with-smbmount	Include SMBMOUNT (Linux only) support
--without-smbmount	Don't include SMBMOUNT support (default)
--with-ldap	Include LDAP (Lightweight Directory Access Protocol) support, which is still in the experimental stage
--without-ldap	Don't include LDAP support (default)
--with-nisplus	Include NISPLUS password database support
--without-nisplus	Don't include NISPLUS password database support (default)
--with-nisplus-home	Include NISPLUS_HOME support
--without-nisplus-home	Don't include NISPLUS_HOME support (default)
--with-ssl	Include SSL (Secure Socket Layer) support
--without-ssl	Don't include SSL support (default)
--with-sslinc=DIR	Where the SSL includes are (defaults to /usr/local/ssl)
--with-mmap	Include experimental MMAP support
--without-mmap	Don't include MMAP support (default)
--with-syslog	Include experimental SYSLOG support
--without-syslog	Don't include SYSLOG support (default)
--with-netatalk	Include experimental Netatalk support, for use with AppleTalk clients
--without-netatalk	Don't include experimental Netatalk support (default)
--with-quotas	Include experimental disk-quota support
--without-quotas	Don't include experimental disk-quota support (default)
--with-privatedir=DIR	Where to put smbpasswd (/usr/local/Samba/private)
--with-lockdir=DIR	Where to put lock files (/usr/local/Samba/var/locks)
--with-swatdir=DIR	Where to put SWAT files (/usr/local/Samba/swat), the web based GUI for Samba administration

As you can see, there is a lot to Samba that is in the experimental stage. Samba is a rapidly developing network operating system, and what is experimental at 2.0.3 might become the default at a later level. Be sure to check your parameters before you do a compile.

UNIX and UNIX-like Operating Systems

UNIX is a trademark controlled by The Open Group and typically refers to a very complex but stable and expensive multiuser, multiprocessing operating system. Many programmers are convinced that UNIX is an ideal operating system and have worked to generate UNIX-like operating systems that are free for use. In the 1990s, several of these operating systems have become available including Linux, FreeBSD, and NetBSD. Samba can run on almost any UNIX or UNIX-like system if a C compiler is available.

UNIX systems include, but are not limited to:

- Sun Solaris
- HP-UX
- IBM's AIX

UNIX-like operating systems include, but are not limited to:

- Linux
- FreeBSD
- NetBSD

Linux distributions

A narrow definition of Linux refers to the kernel that controls the operating system. Many of the other utilities and applications are provided under the terms of the GNU General Public License.

Anyone who has the desire can gather a Linux kernel and GNU applications and utilities and distribute them under the terms of the GNU General Public License. There are several organizations that are known for the Linux distributions, each tailoring their distribution to their own vision of Linux. SuSE is a very popular distribution in Europe, many Linux hackers prefer Debian, and Red Hat and Caldera take special steps to be seen as commercially viable. This book focuses on the Red Hat Linux and Caldera OpenLinux distributions because those are often the easiest distributions to place in a commercial environment.

FreeBSD/NetBSD

FreeBSD and NetBSD are two UNIX-like operating systems that were developed by some of the people that supported the Berkeley Standard Distribution of UNIX. They are peers of Linux and arguably more stable and able to run on more types of hardware.

Making sure Samba gets installed with Red Hat GNU/Linux

With Red Hat Linux 5.2 and later versions, you can specify an installation class for an easier installation. The three classes are workstation, server, and custom, as shown in Table 1-5, with custom being the same installation as Red Hat 5.1 or earlier.

Table 1-5 Installation Classes for Red Hat Linux

Class	Hardware requirements	Samba automatically installed?
Workstation	600MB of HD space	No
Server	1.7GB of HD space	Yes
Custom	at least 150MB of HD space	Varies; to ensure installation, choose SMB (Samba connectivity) under components to install, or under Individual Packages, Networking, choose Samba

Making sure Samba gets installed with Caldera OpenLinux

Caldera gives you several installation levels, some of which include Samba. Use Table 1-6 to ensure that Samba gets installed with OpenLinux 2.2.

Table 1-6 Installation for Caldera OpenLinux 2.2

Level installed?	Hardware requirements	Samba automatically
Minimal	160MB of HD space	No
Recommended	580MB of HD space	Yes
Recommended plus commercial	780MB of HD space	Yes
All	1000+MB of HD space	Yes

Use Table 1-7 to ensure that Samba gets installed with Caldera OpenLinux 1.3.

Table 1-7 Installation for Caldera OpenLinux 1.3

Level installed?	Hardware requirements	Samba automatically
Minimal	53MB of HD space	No
Minimal with X11	98MB of HD space	No
Small standard	135MB of HD space	No
Standard System	417MB of HD space	Yes
All packages	987MB of HD space	Yes

Quick and compact installation

If you are doing a quick and compact installation, include Samba by choosing Select Server and Network Services of TCPIP, NETTOOL, NETAPPL, NETSERV.

Individual series installation

If you are choosing individual series for installation, under the Network option choose preselect packages and then select Samba.

Making sure Samba gets installed with FreeBSD

None of the installation classes for FreeBSD automatically install Samba. When you get to the point where you can browse the package collection, select net and then select Samba.

Making sure Samba gets installed with NetBSD

None of the installation classes for NetBSD will automatically install Samba. After the installation, you can copy it off the distribution CD to root and untar the tgz package. This command does just that:

```
tar xzf Samba-2.0.2.tgz
```

Testing the Samba Installation

Once Samba has been installed, test that it was installed correctly. You will probably need to set up a simple configuration file for Samba, the smb.conf file, but it might have already been installed. The command to test Samba is `testparm`.

If you get an error message similar to:

```
Unable to open configuration file "/etc/smb.conf"!
```

write it down or print it out. This message tells you that Samba is looking in /etc for the configuration file smb.conf, and you need to create a simple test smb.conf in /etc. You can copy a sample one from the Samba documentation, or use this very basic one (also from the Samba documentation):

```
workgroup = MYGROUP
[home]
    guest ok = no
    read only = no
```

This sample enables connections by anyone with an account on the server. Create this file, name it smb.conf, and placed in it /etc. Then try the `testparm` command again. You should get results like:

```
Load smb config files from /etc/smb.conf
Processing section "[homes]"
Loaded services file OK.
Press enter to see a dump of your service definitions
```

Pressing Enter should show you all the parameters with which your implementation of Samba was compiled.

Starting and stopping Samba

Once you pass the `testparm` test, start Samba to check out your shares. For testing purposes, it's best to start Samba as a daemon because you might be starting and stopping it several times. System V and BSD UNIXs start Samba differently.

System V

A typical way to start Samba on a System V or System V-like system (Caldera Linux 1.1, to be specific) is to type:

```
/etc/rc.d/init.d/smb start
```

which will run smbd and nmbd as daemons. You should get feedback similar to "Starting SAMBA: smbd nmbd." There are two daemons associated with Samba: **smbd** is the service-providing daemon and **nmbd** is the browsing daemon.

On a Solaris 2.5 system, type

```
/etc/init.d/Samba start
```

To stop the daemons, type the same string but make the last parameter `stop` instead of `start`.

BSD UNIX

On a BSD UNIX platform, you need to start each daemon by hand; for instance:

```
/usr/local/sbin/smbd -D
/usr/local/sbin/nmbd -D
```

Or write the following script and make it executable (as the documentation suggests):

```
#!/bin/sh
/usr/local/sbin/smbd -D
/usr/local/sbin/nmbd -D
```

To stop the daemons, find their process number and kill it, as the following example from a FreeBSD system shows:

```
terrapin# ps -x | grep smbd
 173  ??  Ss     1:04.68 /usr/local/sbin/smbd -D
3373  ??  R      0:01.69 /usr/local/sbin/smbd -D
3374  ??  R      0:00.23 /usr/local/sbin/smbd -D
3376  p1  RV     0:00.00 grep smbd (csh)
terrapin# kill 173
terrapin# ps -x | grep nmbd
 175  ??  Ss     0:18.76 /usr/local/sbin/nmbd -D
terrapin# kill 175
terrapin# ps -x | grep smbd
3387  p1  R+     0:00.04 grep smbd
```

After finding the process numbers for smbd and nmbd and killing them, the only process left when grepping on smbd is the grep.

Checking the shares on your server using smbclient

Once Samba is running, check to see what shares are available. You can check this without leaving UNIX with the smbclient command:

```
smbclient -L hostname
```

which should list the shares available on your server, as this example shows:

```
[root@laptop col]# smbclient -L laptop
Added interface ip=192.168.11.4 bcast=192.168.11.255 nmask=255.255.255.0
```

```
Server time is Wed Jun  2 18:01:23 1999

Timezone is UTC-4.0

Password:

Domain=[WORKGROUP] OS=[UNIX] Server=[Samba 1.9.16p7]


Server=[laptop] User=[root] Workgroup=[WORKGROUP] Domain=[WORKGROUP]


        Sharename       Type        Comment

        ---------       ----        -------

        IPC$            IPC         IPC Service (Samba 1.9.16p7)

        public          Disk        Public Stuff

        root            Disk        Home Directories


This machine has a browse list:


        Server                  Comment

        ---------               -------

        LAPTOP                  Samba 1.9.16p7

        PENTIUM                 P90

        TERRAPIN                Samba 1.9.18p10


This machine has a workgroup list:


        Workgroup               Master

        ---------               -------

        WORKGROUP               PENTIUM
```

Because this particular server is running with user-level security, a password was required to show what was available. If you want to list the shares without having to enter a password, add —U%, which is a Samba variable used to indicate the user.

Checking the local client connection using smbclient

Without leaving your Linux/UNIX box, you can test the local client connectivity with the smbclient command, specifically:

```
smbclient //terrapin/george

Added interface ip=192.168.11.5 bcast=192.168.11.255 nmask=255.255.255.0

Server time is Thu Jun  3 19:25:41 1999

Timezone is UTC-4.0

Password:

Domain=[WORKGROUP] OS=[UNIX] Server=[Samba 1.9.18p10]

security=share

smb: \> ls

  .cshrc                    H      509  Thu May 20 10:09:08 1999

  .login                    H      561  Thu May 20 10:09:08 1999

  .login_conf               H      139  Thu May 20 10:09:08 1999

  .mailrc                   H      313  Thu May 20 10:09:08 1999

  .profile                  H      749  Thu May 20 10:09:08 1999

  .shrc                     H      832  Thu May 20 10:09:08 1999

  .mail_aliases             H      351  Thu May 20 10:09:08 1999

  .rhosts                   H      257  Thu May 20 10:09:08 1999

  .history                  H      235  Thu Jun  3 19:05:54 1999

  libdes-4_04b_tar.gz       A   142195  Sat May 29 22:17:26 1999

              33085 blocks of size 4096. 20195 blocks available

smb: \> exit

% ls -al

total 163

drwxr-xr-x  2 george  wheel     512 May 31 10:39 .

drwxr-xr-x  3 root    wheel     512 May 20 10:09 ..

-rw-r--r--  1 george  wheel     509 May 20 10:09 .cshrc

-rw-------  1 george  wheel     235 Jun  3 19:05 .history

-rw-r--r--  1 george  wheel     561 May 20 10:09 .login

-rw-r--r--  1 george  wheel     139 May 20 10:09 .login_conf

-rw-------  1 george  wheel     351 May 20 10:09 .mail_aliases
```

```
-rw-r--r-- 1 george  wheel      313 May 20 10:09 .mailrc
-rw-r--r-- 1 george  wheel      749 May 20 10:09 .profile
-rw------- 1 george  wheel      257 May 20 10:09 .rhosts
-rw-r--r-- 1 george  wheel      832 May 20 10:09 .shrc
-rwxr----- 1 george  wheel   142195 May 29 22:17 libdes-4_04b_tar.gz
```

If you get an error message about "Not enough '\' characters in service," check your Samba version. Versions prior to 1.9.17 only recognized DOS backslashes. You would need to escape the backslashes in UNIX, or quote them, such as `smbclient \\\\laptop\\col` or `smbclient '\\laptop\col'`.

Seeing remote clients using nmblookup

Once you can access shares locally, next check whether you can see your intended clients on the network. Do this with `nmblookup` command. First test that `nmbd` recognizes itself with:

`nmblookup hostname`

You should get back the IP address that the host is communicating with on the net. If you find that it's trying to use the wrong IP address (for example, the loopback address, 127.0.0.0), you might need to add the correct interface in the smb.conf file with the `interfaces = IP address` parameter.

Then you can test to see if `nmbd` can see a specific PC, in this case liberty, by typing

`nmblookup −B liberty`

Or have `nmblookup` poll the network

`nmblookup −d 2 "*"`

Accessing the server from a client using the net commands

The final test is to see whether a remote client can access a share on the Samba share. This is most easily tested with the `net` commands in a DOS window. At a DOS command prompt or at a /Win95/Win98/WinNT client in a DOS window, type

```
net use f: \\host\service
```

which should map the f drive to the service on host.

Automatically starting Samba

Once Samba is successfully installed, there are two ways to make it run automatically. You can run it as a daemon or have it called by inetd when requested.

Running the Samba suite using standalone daemons takes more system resources, but the response time is better. Running it from inetd means that they are only running when needed, but the performance is somewhat diminished.

For a dedicated server, running the Samba suite using standalone daemons makes the most sense. For a server that only occasionally provides Samba services, running it from inetd might make more sense.

Starting Samba as a standalone daemon

Samba has two daemons that need to be launched: smbd and nmbd. System V and BSD have different startup scripts. System V is discussed first.

System V

On a System V or System V-like system, such as Sun's Solaris 2.x or Linux, there should be a Samba script in the init.d directory. On a Solaris 2.x system, the init.d directory is located in /etc. On a Red Hat or Caldera Linux system, init.d is located in /etc/rc.d .

The Samba script should be called when the appropriate run-level is started. For almost all systems, run-level 3 is the one calling Samba. The rc3.d directory should have a script, such as S91smb, that calls Samba.

The startup scripts are called in their numeric order. Caldera has a S99skipped script that disables services. If Samba is called with the S91smb script then killed with the S99 script, it won't be running when your clients attempt to connect to it.

BSD UNIX

You need to add these lines to the /etc/rc.local file to make Samba start on boot:

```
echo " smbd" && /usr/local/sbin/smbd -D
echo " nmbd" && /usr/local/sbin/nmbd -D
```

It is somewhat simpler than System V.

Starting Samba from inetd

`Inetd` is an Internet meta-daemon. It listens on various ports for calls and launches specific services when requested. For a server that gets infrequent Samba requests, `inetd` should work fine.

First make sure `inetd` is listening for NetBIOS calls. Check the /etc/services file for the following lines

```
netbios-ns 137/udp
netbios-ssn 139/tcp
```

If they are not there, add them. Your server's Samba requests will be coming in on those ports.

 Caution

If you are using NIS or NIS+ naming services to distribute common files (i.e., password, hosts, services), you need to modify services at the master instead of the clients.

Next, edit /etc/inetd.conf to enable it to launch Samba when requested. The lines will be close to this, but you might need to check your man pages for the exact syntax, or compare it to other examples in the inetd.conf file.

```
Netbios-ssn stream tcp nowait root /usr/local/Samba/bin/smbd smbd
Netbios-ns dgram udp wait root /usr/local/Samba/bin/nmbd nmbd
```

Caution: some implementations of UNIX use netbios_ssn instead of netbios-ssn.

Finally, restart the `inetd` process by killing the process with –HUP. If `inetd` was process 3169, you kill the process by entering:

```
kill –HUP 3169
```

Chapter 2

Client Installation

This chapter guides you through the client configuration options necessary for Windows, UNIX, and even Macintosh clients to access your Samba server. It is assumed that your client machine has a network card installed and is attached to a network, but we do include a quick overview of the network interface card (NIC). It's important to check which configuration your NIC is using before setting up your network connections.

Windows 95, 98, and NT share the same GUI interface, but the steps aren't quite the same. We cover NT in a separate section to avoid confusion.

You need the names and IP addresses of a number of servers to do a client installation. You also need to know what services are used on your network. Take a moment to check the names and addresses of the servers you will use. There are several possibilities: WINS, DNS, DHCP, or perhaps you even have a default router set up on your network. You also need an IP address for your clients unless you are using the DHCP option. Once you've done that, you have all the information necessary to configure your clients following the instructions in this chapter.

Tip

If your network is not connected directly to the Internet or is connected through a proxy firewall, use the private IP addresses. The InterNIC has reserved a range of addresses in each network class for internal private use. If you don't own a range of IP addresses, you can use this set of addresses for your internal network: Class A: 10.0.0.0 through 10.255.25.255, Class B: 172.16.0.0 through 172.16.255.255 and Class C: 192.168.0.0 through 192.168.255.255.

Setting Up a Windows 95/98 Client

The differences between the two operating systems with regard to Samba networking are few but they are noted in this section.

Setting up the network interface card

The network interface is the first part of networking to install. Newer cards are Plug-and-Play–compatible, so Windows 95 usually recognizes them and correctly configures them. With older cards, you might need to get drivers from the manufacturer's Web page and manually configure the correct settings.

Plug-and-Play network cards

Most Plug-and-Play network cards work as intended: the first time the Windows PC boots after the card is installed, Windows recognizes the new hardware, finds the appropriate driver, loads it, and assigns the system resources. You may need to tell Windows where to locate the driver files (on floppy or CD-ROM) with the Have Disk option, but that should be the extent of your involvement.

Older and non–Plug-and-Play network cards

With older and non–Plug-and-Play network cards, you might need to add them to the system through the Add New Hardware control panel. You could end up having to tell Windows which drivers to use, where to find them with the Have Disk option, and even assign them IRQs and memory locations. Windows is good at alerting you to any conflicts, and a printout of your system settings (existing IRQs, DMA channels, and I/O addresses) can be most helpful.

When you install a network card in Windows 95/98, Windows also installs two network protocols: IPX/SPC and NetBEUI. Windows also installs two clients: Client for Microsoft Network and Client for Netware Networks. If you have a pure Windows (SMB) network running on TCP/IP, remove the IPX/SPX and the NetBEUI protocols, which also removes the two client components.

Tip

You can print out the device settings of the hardware installed on your Windows 95/98 PC by opening the System Control Panel, selecting the Device Manager tab, and clicking Print. This can be a big help when installing non–Plug-and-Play cards in a Windows 95/98 PC.

Setting up the TCP/IP network protocol

Samba is designed to integrate with Windows (SMB) networking on a TCP/IP network.

Adding the TCP/IP protocol

Follow these steps to add a TCP/IP network:

1. Open the Network Control Panel.
2. On the Configuration tab, click Add.
3. Select Protocol, and then click Add.
4. Select Microsoft in the left box and TCP/IP in the right box.
5. Click OK to load the TCP/IP protocol.

Configuring TCP/IP

To configure the TCP/IP properties of the Windows client, select the TCP/IP protocol in the Network menu and click Properties.

Selecting an IP address Select Obtain an IP Address Automatically if your network is using DHCP (Dynamic Host Configuration Protocol) to assign IP addresses from a pool of available ones at boot time. If your network is using static IP addressing, fill out the IP address and the desired subnet mask.

WINS configuration If your network is not using a WINS server, select Disable WINS resolution.

If your network is using a WINS server to maintain a network-wide database of IP addresses, configure it here (Samba can function as a WINS server; see Chapter 4). You can enable WINS resolution and have it point to the IP Address of the Primary and Secondary WINS server, along with the Scope ID if implemented, or you can have it handled by DHCP, if you are using DHCP.

 Caution

An improper use of the Scope ID can cause two machines on the same network segment to be unable to communicate if their Scope IDs are different. Do not use a Scope ID unless you have a very good reason.

Gateway Use the Gateway menu to add the IP address of the machine that is connecting this network to other IP networks.

DNS configuration This tab is where you disable or enable DNS (Domain Name Service). If you are using DNS, supply the host name and domain of the client, as well as the IP addresses of one or more DNS servers, and the domain suffix search order.

Bindings This tab shows the network components that are using the TCP/IP protocol. Check Client for Microsoft Networks, and check File and Printer Sharing for Microsoft Networks if you want to share this client's resources.

Advanced There is nothing to configure under the Advanced tab in TCP/IP properties (although other protocols do use it).

NetBIOS Check the option "I want to enable NetBIOS over TCP/IP"; this is what SMB is about.

Setting up the SMB client software

The final component to add for network connectivity is the SMB client, which is also known as Client for Microsoft Networks. To add the SMB client:

1. In the Network Control Panel, click Add.
2. Select Client, and then click Add.
3. Select Microsoft in the left box and Client for Microsoft Networks in the right box.
4. Click OK to load the Client for Microsoft Networks protocol.

Identifying the client

Once you have loaded the Microsoft client, set up the identification of this workstation. Select the Identification tab, give the computer a valid NetBIOS name, fill in the proper workgroup, and fill in a descriptive server name.

Working with domains

To set up the Windows client to log on to an NT domain, select the Client for Microsoft Windows and click Properties. Check the Log On to Windows NT Domain box and fill in the domain field with the desired domain.

Connecting to shares

There are several ways to make a permanent share. You can view the resource via Network Neighborhood or My Computer. Once you view the share you want, right-click on it and select Map Network Drive. You can select the drive letter, and you can choose to reconnect at the next logon to make the connection permanent.

For a temporary share, just click it in Network Neighborhood, and drop and drag files to and from it.

Finally, you can use the net commands in a command prompt to connect to shares. The syntax to map drive J: to the nancy directory on terrapin is:

```
net use J: \\terrapin\nancy
```

To end this connection, type:

```
net use J: /d
```

Connecting to printers

Connecting to printers is similar to connecting to shares unless you need to print from a DOS application. DOS applications typically need to print to a parallel port.

Using My Computer to connect to a printer To graphically connect LPT1 to the printer samsonlp on the server named terrapin, follow these steps:

1. Click My Computer.
2. Right-click the Printers folder.
3. Select Capture Printer Port.

4. Choose LPT1 for a Device.
5. Type **\\terrapin\samson** for the path name.
6. Check the Reconnect at Logon box to make it permanent.
7. Click OK to set this printer.

Using the Printer Wizard to connect to a printer You can also add a printer using the Printer Wizard. This method also enables you to choose the appropriate printer driver for the printer. To add a printer using this method, follow these steps:

1. Open the Printers Control Panel.
2. Double-click Add Printer to start the Add Printer Wizard.
3. In the Add Printer Wizard dialog box, click Next.
4. Choose Network Printer and click Next.
5. Click Browse to locate a printer, or enter the UNC path to the printer in the Network path or queue name box.
6. If you need to print from DOS applications, check the Yes box; then click Next.
7. Choose the appropriate printer driver by selecting the printer manufacturer from the left-hand box and the printer type from the right-hand box, or click Have Disk if you have a disk with a newer driver or the drivers are stored on a network disk; then click Next.
8. Choose a descriptive name for the printer in the Printer name field, and decide if this will be the default printer. Click Next.
9. Decide if you want to print a test page, and then click Finish. You will probably need to access the Windows CD-ROM to copy needed files for the installation.

Connecting to a printer using the net command Finally, you can connect to a printer using the net command in a DOS window. The following example connects LPT2 to the printer named dot on the server named deal:

```
net use LPT2: \\deal\\dot
```

Encrypted passwords

The first versions of Windows 95 used plain-text passwords. The later versions switched to encrypted passwords. If the files vredir.vxd and vnetsup.vxd, which are located in windows\system, are dated 6/2/97 or later, use encrypted passwords.

If you absolutely need to use unencrypted passwords, you can edit the Registry to enable them. Edit the following Registry key and reboot the Windows client.

```
[HKEY_LOCAL_MACHINE\System\CurrentControlset\Services\VxD\
VNETSUP] "EnablePlainTextPassword"=dword:00000001
```

Troubleshooting using the Registry

When you get an unsolvable network problem on Windows 95 — for example, everything is set up correctly in the Control Panel but you still can't get to your network — you might need to browse the Registry to see what the Windows system thinks the settings are internally. There could be a discrepancy between the internal settings and what is displayed in Control Panel.

Caution

Back up your Registry with the `cfgback` utility located on the Windows CD in \other\misc\cfgback folder before editing it. If you don't, you might be able to restore a ruined Registry with the hidden backup files, but it's safer to have done backups first.

The Registry editor shipped with Windows is regedit.exe, which is located in the Windows directory.

The information for the network adapters is located in the Net folder, one folder per adapter. Similarly, the network client software packages installed are located in the NetClient folder, one folder per client; any network services (such as file and printer sharing for Microsoft networks) are located in the NetService folder, one folder per service; and the loaded protocols are located in the NetTrans folder, one folder per protocol. The Net, NetClient, NetService, and NetTrans folders are located in:

```
HKEY_LOCAL_MACHINE\System\CurrentControlSet\Services\Class
```

The information for the Microsoft Client for Windows is located in the MSTCP folder in the following path:

`HKEY_LOCAL_MACHINE\System\CurrentControlSet\Services\VxD`

Setting Up a Windows NT 4.0 Client

Windows NT can be difficult to configure if you have to install hardware such as a network interface card. Windows NT does not support Plug and Play. Microsoft publishes a Hardware Compatibility List (HCL) that specifies tested hardware that runs under Windows NT. Before you buy any equipment for an NT system, make sure it is on the HCL.

To display a record of your system's hardware, select Programs ⇨ Administrative Tools Common ⇨ Windows NT Diagnostics. The Resources tab shows the IRQs for devices. Click Print and choose a complete report of all tabs to get a record of the entire system including your Registry settings. For more information about NT-specific details, such as installing a network card, refer to an NT manual.

There are two steps to setting up a Windows NT 4.0 client:

1. Configure the Network Control Panel.
2. Connect to shares and printers.

Configuring the Network Control Panel

Open the Network Control Panel. The five configuration tabs are:

- Identification — Fill in the Computer Name and Domain or workgroup.
- Services — Verify that Computer Browser, Workstation, and Server are listed.
- Protocols — The TCP/IP protocol must be displayed.
- Adapters — You must have a network card defined.
- Bindings — Verify that the server and workstation are bound to TCP/IP.

The following sections discuss configuration details for each tab. Finish configuring all options in all tabs before clicking OK to commit all the changes at once.

Identification

The Identification tab has two fields: Computer Name and Domain. Enter the name of your computer in the Computer Name field; don't use spaces in this field. Enter the name of your NetBIOS Domain (not your DNS domain) in the Domain field. Clicking the radio button Change displays the Identification Changes tab. Here, you can change the Computer Name and change from a domain member to a workgroup member. If you are joining a domain for the first time, you have to create a computer account in the domain. Check Create a Computer Account in the Domain and fill in the user name and password of an administrator account and then click OK. This action takes you back to the Network Identification tab; continue to Services.

Services

The Services tab has a window that displays the services that are active on your machine. The default services that should be displayed in the window are Computer Browser, NetBIOS Interface, RPC Configuration, Server, and Workstation. These services are required for Samba.

If any of these services is missing, click Add, select the service from the displayed list, check Have Disk (you need the Windows NT installation media), and click OK. Windows adds the service. If you need to add more then one service, repeat those steps. Continue with the protocol configuration.

Protocols

If the TCP/IP protocol is not displayed in the Network Protocols window, follow these steps to add it.

1. Click Add.
2. Select TCP/IP Protocol.
3. Check the Have Disk box (you will need your Windows NT installation media).
4. Click OK to load the TCP/IP protocol.

Once you have loaded the TCP/IP protocol, you have to configure it. In the Protocol tab of the Network Control Panel, highlight TCP/IP Protocol and click Properties. This brings up the Microsoft TCP/IP Properties page with four tabs:

- IP address
- DNS
- WINS address
- Routing

IP address This option has two radio button options. The first is Obtain an IP address from a DHCP server. If you have a DHCP server on your network, select this radio button. Consider using DHCP to distribute all your network information. The DHCP server can distribute the IP address, subnet mask, and default router, as well as supply the names and addresses of your WINS and DNS servers. If you are having DHCP supply all the client information, just click OK and you're done.

If you don't have a DHCP server, click the second radio button, Specify IP Address, and fill in the information in the IP address, subnet mask, and default router gateway boxes. After you've entered the addresses, don't click OK; you should configure the options under the other tabs and apply the changes all at once. Once you click OK, NT will want to reboot, so set up your DNS and WINS services before clicking OK.

DNS The DNS tab has four option boxes. Host Name is the name of your client and should match the name you entered in the Identification field. The Domain box is where you enter the name of your DNS Domain. The DNS service search order box is where you enter the IP address of your DNS server(s). Click Add and a box for the TCP/IP address appears. Fill in the TCP/IP address of the DNS server and click Add. The box Domain Suffix Search Order is for sites that have more than one DNS domain.

WINS address Again, if you are using DHCP, only fill in the DHCP address under the IP Address tab. Then your client will get the WINS and DNS server information with the lease for the IP address. If you aren't using DHCP for server information, you can enable WINS resolution by entering the IP address of the Primary and Secondary WINS servers.

There are two checkboxes on this tab: the first, Enable DNS for Windows Resolution, is an option you should *not* enable. This is not the same as enabling DNS; this option will tell your WINS server to query your DNS server when it does not know an IP address. This seems like a good idea, but it does not work out that way. If your WINS server doesn't know about a machine, it's more likely you've made a typo or the machine is not on the network at the present time. The time spent to query the DNS server is wasted, network bandwidth is wasted, and nine of ten times DNS can't help your WINS server find the address.

The other checkbox is Enable LMHOSTS Lookup. This option searches a local file called LMHOSTS for names and IP addresses. You can click the Import LMHOSTS button to import the WINS server's LMHOST file. But the question to ask yourself is "Do I want to maintain another local file?"

Routing This option is for a machine with more than one NIC; NT allows a machine with two or more NICs to be set up as a router. It's beyond the scope of this book to configure a workstation as a gateway, so for our purposes we won't check the option Enable IP Forwarding.

Adapters

The adapters tab displays your network card and its properties. It's beyond the scope of this book to go over installing an adapter in detail. If you click Add, the Select Network Adapter window appears. Highlight your adapter, click Have Disk, and click OK.

Bindings

This tab displays bindings, which are connections between your network card and the services. The services for Samba are all bound to the WINS client TCP/IP. These services are Server, Workstation, and NetBIOS Interface. These services were bound with your other configuration options.

Finally, click OK and Windows NT displays a window requesting that you reboot your computer. Click Yes.

Connecting to shares and printers

Now that the client is configured, you can access network resources. The steps to do so are very similar to Window 95/98 with a few extra options available for the NT Client.

Connecting to shares

Again, there are several ways to make a permanent share. You can view the resource via Network Neighborhood. Once you see the server you want, double-click the machine icon, right-click the share you want to access, and select Map Network Drive. You have the choice to select the drive letter. There is a box not available on Windows 95/98: the Connect As: box allows you to enter a user name other than the name of the user who is logged on. This enables you to map a network share for a user who does not have the correct security permissions. You can use this feature to map a temporary connection for a user or to map an administration drive that is only used when you are troubleshooting at that machine. The Reconnect at Login checkbox enables the machine to reconnect at the next logon to make it a permanently connected share. This is one of the advantages of SMB networking. If a share you've made permanent is not available at boot time, the client still boots up.

For a temporary share, you can just click on it in Network Neighborhood and drop and drag files to and from it.

Finally, you can use the net commands in a command-prompt window to connect to shares. The syntax to map drive J: to the nancy directory on terrapin is:

```
net use J: \\terrapin\nancy
```

To make this network share permanent:

```
net use J: \\terrapin\nancy /persistent
```

To use the net command with the new option of user name:

```
net use J: \\terrapin\adminutils /user:root
```

After entering this command, you are prompted to enter the root's password before the share takes effect. Do not use the /persistent option combined with the /user:name. The password will still be required each time this share is established.

To end this connection, type:

```
net use J: /d
```

Connecting to printers

Connecting to printers is similar to connecting to shares.

Connecting to a printer using the net command You can connect to a printer using the `net` command in a DOS window. The following example connects LPT2 to the printer named dot on the server named deal:

```
net use LPT2: \\deal\\dot
```

Use the Printer Wizard to connect NT clients to a printer To connect to the printer samson on the server named terrapin using the Printer Wizard, follow these steps:

1. Open the Printers Control Panel.

2. Double-click Add Printer.

3. Select the radio button Network Printer Server and then click Next.

4. The Connect to Printer window appears. There are two boxes to choose from. The first, labeled Printer, enables you to type the name of the server and the printer. You could type: **\\terrapin\samson** and click OK. The second box, Shared Printers, displays all of the printers shared on your network. You can click any of the displayed printers and then click OK.

5. The next dialog box asks, "Do you want your Windows-based programs to use this printer as the default printer?" Click Yes if you want all windows programs to use this printer by default, or click No if you don't, and then click Next.

6. If you are required to install a printer driver, choose the appropriate driver by selecting the printer manufacturer from the left-hand box. Select the printer type from the right-hand box, click on Have Disk if you have a disk with the latest drivers, or type the path for the drivers if they are stored on a network disk.

7. The dialog box appears that says, "The network printer has been successfully installed." Click Finish.

Setting Up a DOS Client

There's still a need for DOS network clients on Microsoft Windows networks. Some specialized programs only run in DOS and don't need to be installed on a Windows machine. You can boot a PC from a single DOS disk and then connect to a Windows network to reload a damaged system, clone a system, or even access a shared CD-ROM from a system that doesn't have a CD-ROM drive.

Obtaining the DOS client

Microsoft supplies a DOS client for Windows networks for free. You can download the two-disk set from the Microsoft FTP site `ftp://ftp.microsoft.com/bussys/Clients/MSCLIENT/`, or you can copy them from an NT server CD-ROM from \clients\msclient\disks. The two file names are DSK3-1.EXE and DSK3-2.EXE. Execute these files in separate directories to unzip their contents, then copy each set of unzipped files to a separate floppy.

Installing the DOS client

Follow these steps to install a DOS client.

1. In DOS, run the setup.exe file on the first disk.

2. In the Setup for Microsoft Network Client screen, press Enter to set up the client.

3. The next screen asks you for the directory to install the client software; the default is C:\NET.

4. The software examines your system for a while, and then displays a list of network drivers. Select your card if it is listed. If not, select the choice Network adapter not shown on list below, give the drive and path where the oemsetup.inf file for the card is located, and confirm the choice that it finds.

5. Choose between the Full Redirector (which takes more memory but allows encrypted or plain text passwords) and the Basic Redirector.

6. Now choose a user name for this setup.

7. Next is a confirmation screen that lets you change the installation settings. With the Change Names option, you can change the user name, the computer name, the workgroup name, and the domain name.

8. Selecting Change Setup Options lets you choose between the Full Redirector and the Basic Redirector. You can also choose whether you'll run the Network Client on startup or whether you are using a domain and the Net Pop Hot Key.

9. Selecting Change Network Configuration lets you change, add, and remove adapters and protocols. The NWLink protocol is usually added by default, but TCP/IP usually is not. To add TCP/IP, select Add Protocol and then TCP/IP. To remove the NWLink protocol, tab to the upper window, highlight the NWLink protocol, tab to the bottom window, and select Remove.

10. Now configure TCP/IP. Tab to the upper window and highlight TCP/IP. Tab to the lower window and select Change Settings. Select each setting that you need to change. To not use DHCP, set Disable Automatic Configuration to 1.

11. Follow the remaining prompts to insert any disks (you might need to read from any third-party network card disks, and you'll need the Microsoft client disks), and then remove them and reboot the computer when done.

Connecting the DOS client

Use the net commands with the appropriate subcommands and parameters to connect to services, log on, log off, and start and stop net services. To see a list of all the net services, type:

```
net /?
```

To see the specifics on a command, type:

```
net command /?
```

Some commands, such as net use, have so many parameters that they need to be paged, so use:

```
net use /? | more
```

Connecting to a share using the net command

Use the net use command to connect to a share and map it to a drive. This simple example mounts the Windows share on the deal server to drive h:

```
Net use H: \\deal\windows
```

Connecting to a printer using the net command

You can connect to a printer using the net use command in a DOS window. The following example connects LPT2 to the printer named dot on the server named deal:

```
net use LPT2: \\deal\\dot
```

Net commands used to configure the DOS client

This section lists the DOS configuration net commands.

net init Loads protocol and network adapter drivers without binding them to Protocol Manager. This command might be required if you are using a third-party network adapter driver. You can then bind the drivers to Protocol Manager by typing **net start netbind**. The option

```
/dynamic
```

loads the Protocol Manager dynamically. This is useful with some third-party networks, such as Banyan VINES, to resolve memory problems.

net start Starts services. Services cannot be started from a command prompt within Windows. To start the workgroup redirector you selected during setup, type **net start** without options. In general, you don't need to use any of the options. You might use the options if you need to turn on NetWare when you don't normally connect to a NetWare server at startup. The options for net start are:

/popup	This forces the pop-up interface to load into memory. Use this if the pop-up interface does not automatically get loaded when you start your computer.
/basic	Starts the basic redirector.
/full	Starts the full redirector.
/workstation	Starts the default redirector.

`/netbind`	Binds protocols and network adapter drivers.
`/netbeui`	Starts the NetBIOS interface.
`/list`	Displays a list of the services that are running.
`/yes`	Carries out the net start command without first prompting you to provide information or confirm actions.
`/verbose`	Displays information about device drivers and services as they are loaded.

To start the workgroup redirector that you specified during setup, type **net start** with no options.

net stop   Stops services or unloads the pop-up interface. Services cannot be stopped from a command prompt within Windows.

The options for `net stop` are:

`/popup`	Unloads the pop-up interface without stopping the redirector.
`/basic`	Stops the basic redirector.
`/full`	Stops the full redirector.
`/workstation`	Stops the default redirector.
`/netbeui`	Stops the NetBIOS interface.
`/yes`	Carries out the `net stop` command without first prompting you to provide information or confirm actions.

To stop the workgroup redirector, type **net stop** without options. This breaks all your connections to shared resources and removes the `net` commands from your computer's memory.

Net commands to use the network services of the DOS client

This section lists `net` commands to use the network services of the DOS client.

net logoff   Breaks the connection between your computer and the shared resources to which it is connected.

The option for `net logoff` is:

/yes	Carries out the `net logoff` command without first prompting you to provide information or confirm actions.

net logon Identifies you as a member of a workgroup.

The options for `net logon` are:

user	Specifies the name that identifies you in your workgroup.
password	The unique string of characters that authorizes you to gain access to your password-list file.
?	Specifies that you want to be prompted for your password. This is an alternative to the `password` option.
/domain	Specifies that you want to log on to a Microsoft Windows NT or LAN Manager domain.
/domain: domainname	Specifies the name of the Windows NT or LAN Manager domain you want to log on to.
/yes	Carries out the `net logon` command without first prompting you to provide information or confirm actions.
/savepw:no	Carries out the `net logon` command without prompting you to create a password-list file. Network security is better if you do not have passwords cached on local hard drives.
/disconnected	Restores persistent connections in the disconnected state, making for faster logons.

If you would rather be prompted to type your user name and password instead of specifying them in the `net logon` command line, type `net logon` without options.

net password Changes your logon password.

The options for `net password` are:

`\\computer` Specifies the Windows NT or LAN Manager server on which you want to change your password.

/DOMAIN:domainname	Specifies that you want to change your password on the Windows NT or LAN Manager domain you specified with the :domainname option.
user	Specifies your Windows NT or LAN Manager user name.
oldpassword	Specifies your current password.
newpassword	Specifies your new password.

The \\computer, /domain:name, and user options are only used for changing passwords on an NT or LAN Manager server or domain or when the Samba server is acting as an NT server or domain server.

net print Displays information about the print queue on a shared printer or controls your print jobs.

The options for net print are:

\\computer	Specifies the name of the computer whose print queue you want information about.
\\computer\printer	Specifies the name of the printer you want information about.
port	Specifies the name of the parallel (LPT) port on your computer that is connected to the printer you want information about.
job#	Specifies the number assigned to a queued print job. This has its own options: /pause, /resume, and /delete.

You can specify the /pause, /resume, and /delete options as follows:

/pause	Pauses a print job.
/resume	Restarts a print job that has been paused.
/delete	Cancels a print job.
/yes	Carries out the net print command without first prompting you to provide information or confirm actions.

When you specify the name of a computer by using the net print command, you receive information about the print queues on each of the shared printers that are connected to the computer.

net time Displays the time or synchronizes your computer's clock with the shared clock on a Microsoft Windows for Workgroups, Windows NT, or LAN Manager time server.

The options for net time are:

\\computer	Specifies the name of the computer (time server) whose time you want to check or synchronize your computer's clock with.
/workgroup	Specifies that you want to use the clock on a computer (timeserver) in another workgroup.
/workgroup:wgname	Specifies the name of the workgroup containing a computer whose clock you want to check or synchronize your computer's clock with. If there are multiple time servers in that workgroup, net time uses the first one it finds.
/set	Synchronizes your computer's clock with the clock on the computer or workgroup you specify.
/yes	Carries out the net time command without first prompting you to provide information or confirm actions.

net use Connects or disconnects your computer from a shared resource or displays information about your connections. For example:

```
net use [drive: | *] [\\computer\directory [password |
?]]
  [/persistent:yes | no] [/savepw:no] [/yes] [/no]
net use [port:] [\\computer\printer [password | ?]]
  [/persistent:yes | no] [/savepw:no] [/yes] [/no]
net use drive: | \\computer\directory /delete [/yes]
net use port: | \\computer\printer /delete [/yes]
```

```
net use * /delete [/yes]
net use /persistent:yes | no | list | save | clear [/yes]
[/no]
net use drive: | * /home
```

Definitions are:

drive
: Specifies the local drive letter you assign to a shared directory.

*
: Specifies the next available drive letter. If used with /delete, specifies to disconnect all of your connections.

port
: Specifies the parallel (LPT) port name you assign to a shared printer.

computer
: Specifies the name of the computer sharing the resource.

directory
: Specifies the name of the shared directory.

printer
: Specifies the name of the shared printer.

password
: Specifies the password for the shared resource, if any.

?
: Specifies that you want to be prompted for the password of the shared resource. You don't need to use this option unless the password is optional.

/persistent
: Specifies which connections should be restored the next time you log on to the network. It must be followed by one of these values: yes, no, list, save, or clear.

yes
: Specifies that the connection you are making and any subsequent connections should be persistent.

no
: Specifies that the connection you are making and any subsequent connections should not be persistent.

list
: Lists your persistent connections.

save
: Specifies that all current connections should be persistent.

clear
: Clears your persistent connections.

`/savepw:no`	Specifies that the password you type should not be saved in your password-list file. You need to retype the password the next time you connect to this resource. This takes an extra step but increases network security.
`/yes`	Carries out the `net use` command without first prompting you to provide information or confirm actions.
`/delete`	Breaks the specified connection to a shared resource.
`/no`	Carries out the `net use` command, responding with No automatically when you are prompted to confirm actions.
`/home`	Makes a connection to your home directory if one is specified in your LAN Manager or Windows NT user account.

To list all your connections, type **net use** without options.

To see this information one screen at a time, type the following at the command prompt:

```
net use /? | more
```

   or

```
net help use | more
```

net view Displays a list of computers in a specified workgroup or the shared resources available on a specified computer. To display a list of computers in your workgroup that share resources, type **net view** without options.

The options for `net view` are:

`/workgroup`	Specifies that you want to view the names of the computers in another workgroup that share resources.
`/workgroup:wgname`	Specifies the name of the workgroup whose computer names you want to view.
`/yes`	Carries out the `net view` command without first prompting you to provide information or confirm actions.

Net diagnostics commands with the DOS client

This section lists the net diagnostics commands for the DOS client.

net config Displays your current workgroup settings.

The option for net config is:

/yes   Carries out the net config command without first prompting you to provide information or confirm actions.

net diag Runs the Microsoft Network Diagnostics program to test the hardware connection between two computers and to display information about a single computer.

The options for net diag are:

/names   Specifies a diagnostic server name to avoid conflicts when net diag is used simultaneously by multiple users. This option works only when the network uses a NetBIOS protocol.

/status   Enables you to specify a computer about which you want network diagnostics information.

net ver Displays the type and version number of the workgroup redirector you are using. There are no options for this command.

Setting Up a UNIX Client

smbclient lets a UNIX/Linux/BSD client access an SMB share through an FTP-like interface. There are better ways to regularly access Samba shares than smbclient, but if you need to test the Samba server, smbclient is a good starting point. Also, you might need access to a storage device that can be attached only to a Windows server. smbclient works for that, too. Finally, smbclient can be used with great success in scripts.

The smbmount utility, which is included with Samba, enables Linux systems to mount an smb share as a regular file system. Samba must be compiled with the smbmount option on; the default is to have it turned off. Many precompiled versions may have had this option turned on at compile time. To check this, see if the smbmount command exists.

smbclient basics

The basic syntax for using `smbclient` to connect to a service is:

```
smbclient servicename [password] [options]
```

To connect to the setlists folder on the server helena, type:

```
smbclient //helena/setlists
```

To connect to the printer lp on the server terrapin, type:

```
smbclient //terrapin/lp
```

smbclient parameters

Many parameters can be used with `smbclient`, and the man pages should contain the latest parameters. Some of the common options are:

`-s smb.conf`

`smbclient` uses the default smb.conf configuration file for the Samba server for several parameters. This option enables you to use a different smb.conf file.

`-B IP address`

To find the IP address of the server requested, `smbclient` broadcasts NetBIOS name service requests. You can change the name of the broadcast address with this option.

`-O socket options`

This is for the TCP socket options to set on the client socket to allow you to tune `smbclient` for the local network and the smb servers. See the man pages on smb.conf and `setsocketopt` for more details.

`-R name resolve order`

This option lets you specify the order of the name resolution services when looking up the NetBIOS name of the server requested. The options are `lmhosts`, `host`, `wins`, and `bcast`.

`lmhosts`

Look up a host in the Samba lmhosts table, stored in the same directory as the smb.conf file.

`host`	Look up a host using the operating system's IP-to-host name resolution, whether via the /etc/hosts file, NIS, or DNS.
`wins`	Look up a host using the WINS server listed with the win server parameter in the smb.conf file. If there is no WINS server listed, this option is ignored.
`bcast`	Do a broadcast on the local interfaces listed in the interfaces sections of smb.conf. The broadcast won't go beyond the client's subnet, so this option is unreliable.
	If this parameter is not used, the name resolve order in the smb.conf will be used. The default name resolve order if nothing is listed, is `lmhosts, hosts, wins, bcast`.
`-M NetBIOS name`	This option enables you to send WinPopUp messages to the specified computer. After a connection occurs, type your message and end sending with a Ctrl+D. If the computer is not running WinPopUp, the message is lost with no error message returned.
	To send the message "4:45 time to go home" to the server Liberty, type:
	`echo "4:45 time to go home"	smbclient -M Liberty`
	To send the contents of the file daily.txt to Liberty, type:
	**cat daily.txt	smbclient -M Liberty**
`-i` *scope*	This sets the NetBIOS scope that `smbclient` uses to communicate with NetBIOS names. This is infrequently used and should be used with caution.
-N	This enables you to suppress the password request from `smbclient` when you are accessing a service that does not need a password.

-n NetBIOS_name	smbclient uses the local host name in upper-case as the default NetBIOS name. This option enables you to specify a different NetBIOS name.
-d *debug_level*	The debug level ranges from 0 to 10 or the letter A, with higher values logging more details. Level 0 only logs critical errors and serious warnings; level 1 is good for daily operations; levels 2 and 3 are good for debugging errors; and above level 3 generates a level of detail suitable for developers. Level A logs all debug messages.
-P	This option is no longer used in Samba 2.0. In earlier versions, it was used to specify that you were connecting to a printer share.
-p *port*	This option enables you to change the port to which the smbclient connects. The default is the well-known port for NetBIOS Session Services: 139.
-l *logfilename*	This enables you to specify a logging filename other than the one specified at compile time.
-h	This prints a usage message for the client.
-I IP_address	IP address is the address of the server to be connected to. Specify in standard "a.b.c.d" notation.
	The client normally attempts to locate a named SMB/CIFS server by looking it up via the NetBIOS name resolution mechanism in the name resolve order parameter (both previously described). Using this parameter forces the client to assume that the server is on the machine with the specified IP address, and the NetBIOS name component of the resource being connected to will be ignored.
-E	This option causes the client to write messages to the standard error stream (stderr) instead of the standard output stream.
	By default, the client writes messages to stdout (typically the user's tty).

-U *username*	This specifies the user name that the client uses to make a connection, assuming your server is not using share security levels instead of user security levels.

Some servers are fussy about the case of this name (particularly Windows for Workgroups), and some insist that it must be a valid NetBIOS name.

If no user name is supplied, it defaults to an uppercase version of the environment variable USER or LOGNAME, in that order. If no user name is supplied, and neither USER nor LOGNAME exist, the user name GUEST is used.

You can specify a password with the user name by setting the environment variable to be USER=username%password. If the USER environment variable contains a % character, everything after that is treated as a password. This avoids sending the password on the command line (where it might be visible with the ps command in some UNIX implementations). If you specify the password as part of the user name, then the -N option (suppress password prompt) is assumed.

You can also establish the password by setting up an environment variable called PASSWORD that contains the user's password. This is a potential security hole, but it enables users to script smbclient commands without having a password appear in the command line of a process listing.

Tip

Some servers (including OS/2 and Windows for Workgroups) insist on an uppercase password. These servers might reject lowercase or mixed-case passwords.

-L *NetBIOS_name*   This option enables you to look at what services are available on a server. The -I option can be used to reach hosts on a different network or if you are having NetBIOS name resolution problems.

-t *terminal_code*   This option tells smbclient how to translate characters in the filenames coming from the server. You might need this when UNIX uses different multibyte character sets than Windows does, which is a typical problem with Asian-language multibyte UNIX implementations. The terminal codes include sjis, euc, jis7, jis8, junet, hex, and cap. This feature is not fully tested and should be used with caution. This is not a complete list; check the Samba source code for the complete list.

-m *max_ protocol_level*   In Samba 2.0 and higher, smbclient always attempts to connect at the maximum protocol level the server supports; this option is ignored. It is included for backward compatibility. In versions of Samba prior to 2.0, this setting enabled you to choose the maximum protocol level to be negotiated.

-W *workgroup*   Connect to a server in a different workgroup than the default workgroup specified in the **workgroup** parameter of the smb.conf file for this connection. You might need this to connect to some servers.

-D *directory*   Mainly used with the –T *tar_options* to change to a different directory before beginning the tar operation.

-c *command_string*   Use –c to list a series of commands to be run by smbclient instead of being prompted from stdin. The command string is a semicolon-separated list of commands. This is normally used with –T and in scripts. The -N is implied by -c.

-T *tar_options*	smbclient may be used to create tar backups of all the files on an SMB/CIFS share. The secondary tar flags that can be used with this option are: c *tar_file*, I *include_expression*, X *exclude_ expression*, b *blocksize*, g, q, r, N *file_name*, a, c *tar_file* and x *tar_file*.
c *tar_file*	Create a tar file on the UNIX host from the files on the SBM/CIFS server. Follow it with the name of a tar file, tape device, or "–" for standard output. If tarring to the standard output, you must turn the log level to its lowest value, –d0, to avoid corrupting your tar file. This flag is mutually exclusive with the x flag.
x *tar_file*	Extract (restore) a local tar file back to a share. Use the –D option to restore to a different level other than the top level of the share. This must be followed by the name of the tar file, device or "–" for standard input. This option cannot be used with the c option.
I *include_expression*	Include files and directories indicated by the expression. Use it with the r option for wildcards, such as * or ?. If there are names at the end of the tar command, smbclient assumes they are file and directories to be tarred.
X exclude_ expression	Exclude the files and directories specified by the expression. Use with the r option for wildcards.
b *blocksize*	Lets you specify a block size, which must be greater than zero.
g	Perform an incremental tar and only back up files that have the archive bit set. It can only be used with the c flag.
q	Quiet mode, which keeps tar from printing diagnostics as it works.
r	Specifies that the filename globbing (wildcards) that has been compiled with smbclient should be used. If used with more than * or ?, you might experience performance problems.

N *filename*	Only files newer than the file specified will be backed up to the tar file, and it only works with the c flag.
a	Causes the archive bit to be reset when a file is backed up. Only works with the g and c flags.

The following example backs up Nancy's home directory on the server payroll and creates a tar file named nancy.tar:

```
smbclient //payroll/nancy –Tc nancy.tar
```

This example restores from the mail.tar file into the eudora directory on the server laptop:

```
sbmclient //laptop/eudora –Tx mail.tar
```

smbclient commands

After a connection is established, use FTP-like commands. The default prompt is:

```
smb:\>
```

To access file names with spaces in them, enclose the filename in double quotes.

Parameters for the following commands shown in square brackets are optional, i.e., [optional], while required ones appear in angle brackets, i.e., <required>.

? [command]

If [*command*] is specified, the ? command displays a brief help message about the command. If no command is specified, the available commands are displayed.

! [shell_command]

If [*shell_command*] is specified, the ! command executes a shell locally and runs the specified shell command. If no command is specified, a local shell runs. For example, this can be used to examine files that have been retrieved. The following looks at the first few lines of the retrieved file tapelabel.c:

```
smb: \> ! head tapelabel.c
```

And to check whether there is sufficient disk space to retrieve a file:

```
smb: \> ! df -k
```

archive [*level*]

With the level option used, `archive` [*level*] controls the behavior of the `mget` commands with respect to the archive bit on DOS/Windows files. With no level given, it returns the current value of the archive bit.

If it is used, the level can be between 0 and 3:

0   Retrieve all files regardless of the archive bit and do not change the archive bit.

1   Retrieve only files that have the archive bit set and do not change the archive bit.

2   Retrieve only files that have the archive bit set and reset the archive bit for those files.

3   Retrieve all files regardless of the archive bit and reset the archive bit.

blocksize <*blocksize*>

Specify the blocksize to be used with the `tar` command.

cancel <*jobid*>

Cancel the job with `jobid` in the print queue.

cd [*directory name*]

The `cd` command lets you change or print the current working directory. If [*directory_name*] is specified, the current working directory on the server is changed to that directory. If no directory name is specified, the current working directory on the server is printed.

del <*expression*>

The client will request that the server attempt to delete all files matching <*expression*> from the current working directory on the server.

dir [*expression*]

A list of the files matching [*expression*] in the current working directory on the server will be retrieved from the server and displayed. Dir with no expression displays all the files in the current working directory.

du

Show the space occupied by all files in the current directory.

exit | quit | q | control-D

Terminates the connection with the server and exits from smbclient.

get <*remote_file_name*> [*local_file_name*]

Copies the file called <*remote_file_name*> from the server to the machine running the client. If "local file name" was included, name the local copy [*local_file_name*]. Transfers in smbclient are binary by default unless you turn on translation. See also the lowercase command.

help [*command*]

If [*command*] is specified, the help command displays a brief help message about the command. If no command is specified, the available commands display.

lcd [*directory_name*]

If [*directory_name*] is included, the current working directory on the local machine is changed to the directory specified. If no directory name is included, the name of the current working directory on the local machine is reported.

lowercase

Toggle lowercasing of filenames for the get and mget commands. This is off by default. When lowercasing is toggled on, local filenames are converted to lowercase when using the `get` and `mget` commands, which makes for better compatibility with UNIX systems where lowercase filenames are the norm.

ls *<expression>*

A list of the files matching *<expression>* in the current working directory on the server will be retrieved from the server and displayed. `ls` with no expression displays all the files in the current working directory.

mask *<expression>*

Use `mask` to specify an expression that will be used to filter files during recursive operation of the `mget` and `mput` commands. The masks specified with the `mget` and `mput` commands act as filters for directories rather than filters for files when recursion is toggled on.

The expression specified with the mask command is needed to filter files within those directories. For example, if you specify an `mget` filter of `*1999` and a mask filter of `*.xls` and recursion toggled on, the `mget` command retrieves all files matching `*.xls` in all directories below and including all directories matching `*1999` in the current working directory.

The default value for `mask` is blank, and once the value is changed, it stays changed until changed to something else. To avoid unexpected results, it's wise to change the value of `mask` back to `*` after using the `mget` or `mput` commands.

md *<directory_name>*

Create a new directory on the server with the specified directory name if your user privileges enable you to.

mget *<expression>*

Copy all the files matching the expression from the server to the machine running `smbclient`.

When recursion is turned on, the filter supplied in the `mget` expression filters the directories, and the `mask` command would be used to filter the files.

mkdir *<directory_name>*

Create a new directory on the server with the specified directory name if your user privileges so allow.

more *<file_name>*

Retrieve the file named and display it in the smbclient session.

mput *<expression>*

Copy all the files matching the expression in the current working directory on the local machine to the current working directory on the server.

When recursion is turned on, the filter supplied in the mput expression filters the directories, and the mask command would be used to filter the files.

newer *<file_name>*

This command lets you mget files that are newer than the date of the specified file.

print *<file_name>*

This lets you print the specified file on the local machine to the printable service on the server to which smbclient has connected. This is considered obsolete and should not be used. It is kept for script compatibility. See also the printmode command.

printmode *<graphics or text>*

This command is considered obsolete in Samba 2.0 and later, but is kept for script compatibility. It sets the print mode to suit either binary data (such as graphical information) or text for all subsequent print commands.

prompt

This toggles prompting for filenames during operations of the mget and mput commands.

When prompt is toggled on, the user is prompted to confirm the transfer of each file during these commands. When prompt is toggled off, all eligible files are transferred without prompting.

put *<local_file_name>* [*remote_file_name*]

This copies the file called *<local_file_name>* in the current working directory from the machine running the smbclient to the current working directory on the server. If the remote filename parameter is included, name the remote copy [*remote_file_name*]. See the lowercase command if transferring files to a Windows server.

pwd

Prints the current working directory.

queue

If you are connected to a printable server, `queue` displays the print queue, showing the job IDs, names, sizes, and current status of each.

quit

Terminates the connection with the server and exits from `smbclient`.

rd *<directory name>*

This removes the specified directory if you have sufficient rights.

recurse

This lets you make `mget` and `mput` recurse into directories when getting or putting files. `recurse` is off by default. When recursion is toggled on, these commands process all directories in the source directory and recurse into any directories that match the filter in the command. Only files that match the filter specified using the `mask` command are retrieved. When recursion is toggled off, only the files in the current working directory on the source machine that match the filter in the `mget` or `mput` commands are copied, and any filter specified using the `mask` command is ignored.

rm *<expression>*

Removes all the files matching the expression from the current working directory on the server.

rmdir *<directory_name>*

This removes the specified directory if you have sufficient rights.

tar <c|x>[IXbgNa]

This performs a `tar` operation with the most of the same command options as the –T command. What gets backed up could be affected by the `tarmode` command. The "_" option might not work; use the command line instead.

x *tar_file*

Extract (restore) a local tar file back to a share. Use the –D option to restore to a different level other than the top level of the share. This must be followed by the name of the tar file, device, or "–" for standard input. This option can not be used with the c option.

I *include_expression*

Include files and directories indicated by the expression. Use with the r option for wildcards. If there are names at the end of the `tar` command, `smbclient` assumes that they are files and directories to be tarred.

X *exclude_expression*

excludes the files and directories specified by the expression. Use with the r option for wildcards.

b *blocksize*

lets you specify a block size, which must be greater than zero.

g

performs an incremental tar and only backs up files that have the archive bit set. Can only be used with the c flag. This affects the `tarmode` setting.

N *file_name*

backs up to the tar file only files newer than the file specified and only works with the c flag. This will affect the `tarmode` setting.

a

causes the archive bit to be reset when a file is backed up. Only works with the g and c flags.

tarmode <full|inc|reset|noreset>

changes the backup behavior of `tar` with regard to archive bits. In full mode, `tar` backs up everything regardless of the archive bit setting. In incremental mode, `tar` only backs up files with the archive bit set. In reset mode, `tar` resets the archive bit on all files it backs up if it has sufficient rights. The default for `tarmode` is full.

```
setmode <filename> <perm=[+|\-]rsha>
```

is similar to the DOS `attrib` command and is used to set file permissions. For example:

```
setmode myfile +r
```

makes myfile read-only.

Using smbmount

The `smbmount` command is a pared-down version of `smbclient` that enables a Linux system to mount an SMB share as if it were a regular file system. The version of Samba must have been compiled with `smbmount` support, which is not the default. Many precompiled distributions have `smbmount` support added; check whether the `smbmount` command exists.

Most of the `smbclient` options can be used with `smbmount`. The most useful one is the –c option to pass the mount parameters to the `smbmount` command. The following example mounts the mary share from the deal server to /home/maryg with a local UID of 123 and a local GID of 456:

```
smbmount //deal/mary —c 'mount /home/maryg —u 123 —g 456'
```

The `smbmount` command invokes `smbmnt`. The settings that can be passed to `smbmnt` from `smbmount` are:

```
-u uid, -g gid
```

A LAN Manager/SMB server does not show the file owner, but UNIX requires that each file have an owner and a group it belongs to. With -u and –g, you can tell `smbmount` which user IDs and group IDs it should assign to the files in the mounted directory.

The defaults for these values are the current uid and gid.

```
-f file mode, -d dir mode
```

Like -u and –g are used to translate owner concepts, these options are also used to translate security concepts between LAN Manager/SMB and UNIX. LAN Manager/SMB does not use UNIX file permissions, so smbmnt must be told which permissions it should assign to the mounted files and directories.

These values are specified as octal numbers. The default values are taken from the current umask, where the file mode is the current umask and the dir mode adds execute permissions where the file mode gives read permissions.

These permissions need not match the rights the server gives to us, although they cannot override the allowed rights on the server. It is best to match the rights on the server with the mounted permissions to avoid confusion.

Using smbumount

You can unmount an SMB mount using smbumount. You can only unmount SMB mountpoints that you have mounted.

Setting Up a Macintosh Client

There are several ways to enable Macintosh clients access to a Samba server. The complex way is to set up another network protocol that the Macintoshes will recognize, such as AppleTalk using Netatalk or IPX using Mars, and then map all the Samba rights to the new network protocol.

The easier way is to use software on the Macintosh that allows it to use SMB shares.

Dave is a Macintosh client that connects to SMB shares. It is available from Thursby Software Systems, http://www.thursby.com, and you can download a limited evaluation copy. This section describes how to use Dave to enable a Macintosh SMB client.

Dave's requirements

Dave requires the following hardware and software:

- Macintosh with a 68020 or higher processor
- Mac OS 7.5.x or higher with a minimum of 8MB of RAM

- Apple's MacTCP or Open Transport TCP/IP
- Network adapter

Install the network adapter if needed

Install the network adapter if your Mac needs it.

Configure TCP/IP

Configure TCP/IP on the Mac according to the instructions in the Dave manual and the section on configuring TCP/IP. You can use either Open Transport TCP/IP or MacTCP.

Configure Open Transport TCP/IP

Configure Open Transport TCP/IP as follows:

1. Select Apple Menu ⇨ Control Panels ⇨ TCP/IP.
2. Select Connect via Ethernet.
3. Select Configure manually.
4. Enter the IP address (see section on configuring TCP/IP for additional help).
5. Enter the Subnet mask.
6. Close and save.

Configure MacTCP

Configure MacTCP as follows:

1. Select Apple Menu ⇨ Control Panels ⇨ Network.
2. Select your adapter.
3. Select Apple Menu ⇨ Control Panels ⇨ MacTCP.
4. Enter the IP address.
5. Click MORE.
6. Select Obtain an IP Address Manually.
7. Click OK.

Configure Dave

Configure Dave as follows:

1. Select Apple Menu ⇨ Control Panels ⇨ NetBIOS.
2. Enter Name, organization, and license number. Click OK.
3. Enter a NetBIOS name.
4. Enter the desired workgroup.
5. Enter a description (optional).
6. Click Set and close.

Logging on with Dave

Log on to the SMB domain using the Dave Access program located under the Apple menu. Fill in the desired user, password, and domain.

Accessing shares with Dave

To mount a share, click on Access and select Mount a Volume. Fill in the server name, share name, user name, password, domain, and whether you will connect via NetBIOS or DNS or IP.

If you are more comfortable browsing for shares, use the Chooser.

Chapter 3

Basic Configuration Using SWAT

The Samba Web Administration Tool (SWAT) is a great example of a Web-based administration tool. It requires some additional configuration after you install Samba, but the results are worth the effort. SWAT is a scaled-down Web server with Common Gateway Interface (CGI) scripts. After you configure SWAT, you can log in to perform administration functions on your Samba server from any desktop with a browser. It has been installed by default with Samba since version 2.0.0. SWAT simplifies editing the smb.conf file for shares, printers, and users. SWAT even cycles the Samba daemons after you've made changes to the configuration files. SWAT also has links to HTML versions of the Samba documentation.

First Things First

Before beginning, there is one issue to consider: SWAT will rewrite your smb.conf file. It will delete all comments. It will also delete the `include=` and `copy=` options. If you are an administrator who uses configuration files as a source of documentation, you might not want to use SWAT.

To configure and start SWAT, make these changes to your system:

- Add this line to your services file:

    ```
    swat 901/tcp # Samba management tool run via inetd
    ```
- Add this line in your inetd.conf:

    ```
    Swat      streamtcp      nowait.400    root\
         /usr/local/samba/bin/swat      swat
    ```

The inet daemon or `inetd` has to be restarted for the new configuration to take effect. Use the `kill –HUP PID` (the process ID number of `inetd`) option to cycle or hang up and restart the inet daemon. Then enter the name of your server and the default port number for the SWAT page; for example, `http://terrapin:901/`. A dialog box asking for username and password displays. Log in as root or another administrator account, if you set one up for Samba. SWAT serves up the home page that links all the SWAT functions.

The top of the SWAT home page has seven buttons:

- Home
- Globals
- Shares
- Printers
- Status
- View
- Password

These seven buttons are at the top of every SWAT page so you can navigate between functions quickly. The rest of the page contains links to the html documentation. If you're new to Samba, this is the place to start. There are links for not only the essential process utilities, as well as links to the Samba introduction, to Jeremy Allison's overview "Joining an NT Domain," and to send feedback to the Samba team. On each page, there are links to the documentation for the options you can set. This is a great tool to use to manage Samba for all levels of administrators.

Global Variables Advanced View

The Globals button links to the Global Variables Basic View page. This page is set up for you to make quick, common changes to the smb.conf file. All of the options on this page and the advanced options are covered under the Global Variables Advanced View page. The Basic View page provides most functions, but the Advanced View page is the best way to become familiar with all the options contained in the smb.conf file. After the initial setup, you might never need to use the Advanced View page again.

About variable substitutions

Before describing the smb.conf file and all its options, let's review the use of variable substitutions. Many of the strings in the smb.conf file accept substitutions. Samba expands the substitution to the full name before it passes the command along to the shell or program. You can set some creative strings with these substitutions. There are examples of these substitutions throughout this chapter. Here is a list of the substitutions and the parameter that each represents:

%S   The name of the current service.

%P   The root directory of the current service.

%u   Username of the current service.

%g   Primary group name of %u.

%U   Session username (this can be different from the username that the client requested).

%G   Primary group name of %U.

%H   The home directory of the user.

%v   The Samba version.

%h   The host name on which Samba is running.

%m   The NetBIOS name of the client machine.

%L   The NetBIOS name of the server. This is useful if you are running more then one NetBIOS server under the same Samba server.

%M   The host name of the client machine.

%N   The name of your NIS home directory server. This is obtained from your NIS auto.map entry. If you have not compiled Samba with the automount option, then this value will be the same as your NetBIOS name setting.

%p   The path of the service's home directory, This is obtained from your NIS auto.map entry. The NIS auto.map entry is split up as %N:%p.

%R   The selected protocol level after protocol negotiation.

%d   The process ID of the current server process.

%a   The operating system of the remote machine (this is not quite 100 percent reliable). At this time, it recognizes Samba, Windows for Workgroups, Windows NT, and Windows 95. Others are reported as UNKNOWN.

%I   The IP address of the client machine.

%T   The current date and time.

Base options

The base options in the Advanced View define how the Samba server appears to clients, and in which workgroups and networks it appears. The base options in the Advanced View are as follows.

Workgroup

The default set at compile is `workgroup` (clicking the default button sets this option to `workgroup`). This option controls what your server will appear to be in when queried by clients.

Tip

This parameter also controls the domain name when used with the `security=domain` setting. Set this option to `workgroup = DOM` if your Samba server needs to join an NT domain.

The following example sets the workgroup to `bee-hive`:

```
workgroup        bee-hive
```

NetBIOS name

By default, Samba grabs the machine's DNS name for this option. If you are not using DNS, the field is blank. Click the Set Default button to blank out this field.

This option sets the NetBIOS name for the Samba server. The default is the same as the first component of the host's DNS name. If a machine is a browser server or logon server, this name (or the first component of the host's DNS name) is the name that these services are advertised under.

The following example sets the NetBIOS name to `sugar`:

```
netbios name       sugar
```

NetBIOS aliases

The default is an empty string or no aliases for the machine.

This option creates a group of NetBIOS names that nmbd will advertise as additional names by which the Samba server can provide services. This allows one machine to appear in browse lists under multiple names. If a machine is acting as a browse server or logon server, none of these names is advertised as either a browse server or a logon server; only the primary name of the machine is advertised with these capabilities.

The following example sets the NetBIOS aliases to honey and sweetie:

```
netbios aliases        sweetie honey
```

After you set this option, the server will respond to sugar, honey, and sweetie. This option is useful because you can test changes to your server with a different name, but don't forget that the logon and browse server services are only advertised on the primary name.

Server string

The default is the version number, as in Samba 2.0.3. In the smb.conf file, it is set with **samba %v**. The other variable substitute you can use is %h, which displays the host name of the server. This controls what text string will appear in the properties comment box and next to the IPC connection in net view. It can be any string that you want to show to your users. It also sets what appears in browse lists next to the machine name.

The following example sets the server string to Sugar – The Bee-Hive Workgroup:

```
server string         %h - The Bee-Hive Workgroup
```

Interfaces

This option enables you to set up multiple network interfaces so the Samba server can properly handle browsing on all defined interfaces. The option takes a list of IP and netmask pairs. The netmask may either be a bitmask or a bitlength.

For example, the following line:

```
interfaces = 192.168.99.24/255.255.255.0 192.168.99.124/255.255.255.0
```

configures two network interfaces with IP addresses 192.168.99.24 and 192.168.99.124. The netmasks of both interfaces is set to 255.255.255.0. You could produce an equivalent result by using:

```
interfaces = 192.168.99.24/24 192.168.99.124/24
```

The interface option accepts either format.

If this option is not set, then Samba attempts to find a primary interface but won't attempt to configure any additional interfaces. If you don't have multiple NICs, leave this option blank; Samba will find your NIC and grab the IP address and netmask, as well.

If you do have two or more NICs that you are configuring, read the bind interfaces option that follows. This option must also be set if your server is using multiple interfaces.

Bind interfaces

This global parameter enables you to limit which interfaces on a machine will serve smb requests. The file service smbd and the name service nmbd use the bind interface option in slightly different ways. Setting the bind interfaces only = yes causes nmbd to bind to ports 137 and 138 on only the interfaces listed in the interface parameter. The nmbd service also binds to the all addresses interface (0.0.0.0) on ports 137 and 138 for the purposes of reading broadcast messages. If this option is not set, then nmbd will service name requests on all of these sockets. If bind interfaces only =yes is set, then nmbd checks the source address of any packets coming in on the broadcast sockets and discards any that don't match the broadcast addresses of the interfaces in the interfaces parameter list. When unicast packets are received on the other sockets, it enables nmbd to refuse to serve names to machines that send packets that arrive through any interfaces not listed in the interface list. This is not a security method. IP source address spoofing is common knowledge and it defeats this simple check.

Setting the bind interfaces only = Yes causes smbd to bind only to the interface list given in the interfaces parameter. This restricts the networks that smbd will serve to packets coming in those interfaces. If the bind interfaces only option is set, then you must add the network address 127.0.0.1 in the interfaces parameter list. (IP address 127.0.0.1, also known as localhost, is the default address for tests and other functions for all Ethernet cards.) If you don't add this address, smbpasswd and SWAT might not work as expected.

To change a user's smb password, the smbpasswd by default connects to the localhost or the 127.0.0.1 address as an smb client to issue the password change request. If `bind interfaces only =Yes` is set, then the network address 127.0.0.1 must be added to the interfaces parameter list; otherwise smbpasswd will fail to connect in its default mode. Smbpasswd can be forced to use the primary IP interface of the local host by using its `-r remote-machine` parameter, with `remote machine` set to the IP name of the primary interface of the local host. But that's a lot more to configure than just adding the localhost IP address 127.0.0.1 to the interfaces parameter list.

The SWAT status page also tries to connect with smbd and nmbd at the address 127.0.0.1 to determine if they are running. If you use the `bind interfaces` option without adding 127.0.0.1, smbd and nmbd will always show "not running" even if they really are. This can prevent SWAT from starting, stopping, and restarting smbd and nmbd processes.

The default is:

```
bind interfaces only = No
```

To turn this option on, change the default to:

```
bind interfaces only = Yes
```

Security options

These options affect how Samba responds to clients' protocol negotiations with smbd. Each of the next 33 options work together to help protect the server and mask the differences between Windows and UNIX. The first option is set under the Base Options menu; workgroup also plays a part in security, if you are using NT domain security.

Security

Don't rely on your past experience if you've configured Samba versions before 2.0. The defaults have changed. In previous versions of Samba, the default was `security = share`. The default is now `security = user` because this is the most common setting needed when talking to Windows

95/98 and NT. If your clients have usernames that are the same as their usernames on the UNIX machine, then you will want to use `security = user`. But if the server is configured with `security = user`, it is more difficult to set up guest shares. Whichever option you choose for your network requirements, the procedure described below applies between client and server.

The server follows this procedure to determine whether it will allow a connection to a specified service. If all the steps in the procedure fail, then the connection request is rejected. Once any one of the steps passes, then the remaining steps are skipped. The steps are the same regardless of which security option you define:

1. If the client has passed a username/password pair and the Unix system's password programs validate that username/password pair, then the connection is made as that username. This includes the NT method of passing a username, along with the share request \\sugar\share1 edwardb.

2. If the client has registered a username with the system with a previous service and now supplies a correct password for that username, then the connection is allowed.

3. The client's NetBIOS name and all previous usernames are checked against the supplied password. If a match is found, then the connection is allowed.

4. If the client has previously validated a username/password pair with the server and the client has passed the validation token, then that username is used. This step is skipped if `revalidate = yes` (security option 20) is set for this service.

5. If `user = field` is used in the smb.conf file for the service, the client has supplied a password, and the password matches, then the connection is made as the username with which the password was matched. If one of the usernames in the `user =` list begins with @, then the name expands to a list of names in that group.

6. If the service is a guest service, then a connection is made as the username given in the `guest account =` for the service, irrespective of the supplied password.

There are four security option parameter settings:

- security = user
- security = share
- security=server
- security = domain

The security = user is the default security setting beginning with Samba 2.0. User-level security forces a client to log on with a valid username and password (which can be mapped using the username map parameter). Encrypted passwords (encrypt passwords security option parameter 2) can also be used in this security mode. Parameters, such as user and guest only, if set, are then applied and might change the UNIX user to use on this connection, but only after the user is successfully authenticated. The name of the resource being requested is not sent to the server until after the server has successfully authenticated the client. This is why guest shares don't work in user-level security without enabling the server to automatically map unknown users to the guest account. See map to guest security option parameter 6 for details.

The security = share setting does not require clients to log on to the server with a valid username and password before attempting to connect to a shared resource. Windows 95/98 and Windows NT clients will still send a logon request with a username but no password when talking to a security = share server. Clients send passwords for authentication on a per-share basis when they attempt to connect to the share. smbd always uses a valid UNIX user to act on behalf of the client, even in security = share level security. The smbd daemon uses several techniques to determine the correct UNIX user to use on behalf of the client. A list of possible UNIX usernames to match with the given client password is constructed using these methods:

- If the smbd parameter is set, then all the other stages are missed and only the guest account username is checked.
- If a username is sent with the share connection request, then this username (after mapping; see username map — security option number 15) is added as a potential username.
- If the client did a previous logon request, then the username sent in this smb is added as a potential username. The name of the service the client requested is also added as a potential username. The NetBIOS name of the client is added to the list as a potential username.

- If the `guest only` parameter is not set, then this list is tried with the supplied password. The first user for whom the password matches is used as the UNIX user.

- If the `guest only` parameter is set or no username can be determined, then the share is checked to determine if it is available to the guest account.

- If the share is available to the guest, then guest user account is used; otherwise, access is denied.

For the `security=server` mode, Samba tries to validate the username/password by passing it to another smb server, perhaps to an NT box. If this fails, it reverts to `security = user`, but if encrypted passwords were negotiated (if you are working with NT, you are working with encrypted passwords), then Samba cannot revert back to checking the UNIX password file. You must create a valid smbpasswd file to check users against. To generate the smbpasswd file from your /etc/passwd file, use the smbpasswd program with these shell commands:

```
cat /etc/passwd | mksmbpasswd.sh>\ /usr/local/samba/private/smbpasswd
```

If your server uses NIS, the command is:

```
ypcat passwd | mksmbpasswd.sh>\ /usr/local/samba/private/smbpasswd
```

The mksmbpasswd.sh program is in the Samba source directory. By default, the smbpasswd file is stored in /usr/local/samba/private/smbpasswd. The owner of the /usr/local/samba/private directory should be set to root and its permissions should be set to `500`, or read and execute for root only. The command is:

```
chmod 500 /usr/local/samba/private
```

The smbpasswd file inside the private directory should be owned by root and the permissions should be set to `600`, or read and write for root only. The command is:

```
chmod 600 smbpasswd
```

The client's point of view is the same for `security = server` as it is with `security = user`. These settings affect how the server deals with the authentication. Remember that the name of the resource being requested is not sent to the server until after the server has successfully authenticated the client. This is why guest shares don't work with server-level security unless you allow the server to automatically map unknown users into the guest account. See the `map to guest` security option parameter 6 for details.

The `security = domain` mode works correctly only if smbpasswd has been used to add this machine to a Windows NT domain. It expects the `encrypted passwords` parameter to be used. In this mode, Samba tries to validate the username/password by passing it to a Windows NT Primary Domain Controller or a Backup Domain Controller in exactly the same way that a Windows NT server does. From the client's point of view, `security = domain` is the same as `security = user`. As with the `security = server` setting, the name of the resource being requested is not sent to the server until the server has successfully authenticated the client. This is why guest shares don't work in domain-level security without enabling the server to automatically map unknown users into the guest account. See `map to guest` security option parameter 6 for detail.

The default is:

```
security = USER
```

To set your server to domain, change the default to:

```
security = DOMAIN
```

Encrypt passwords

This parameter sets whether encrypted passwords are negotiated with the client. Windows NT 4.0 SP3 and later and Windows 95/98 by default expect encrypted passwords unless a Registry entry is changed. Unless you have legacy applications that can only run under Windows for Workgroups or a DOS network client, set `encrypt passwords = yes`. (Do you really want to edit the Registry for each client?)

If encrypted passwords are to work correctly, smbd must either have access to a local smbpasswd file or the `security = parameter` must be set to either `server` or `domain`, which causes smbd to authenticate against another server. Again, to create a local smbpasswd file, use the smbpasswd program with these shell commands:

```
cat /etc/passwd | mksmbpasswd.sh>\ /usr/local/samba/private/smbpasswd
```

If your server uses NIS, the command is:

```
ypcat passwd | mksmbpasswd.sh>\ /usr/local/samba/private/smbpasswd
```

The mksmbpasswd.sh program is in the Samba source directory. By default, the smbpasswd file is stored in /usr/local/samba/private/smbpasswd. The owner of the /usr/local/samba/private directory should be set to root, and its permissions should be set to 500, or read and execute for root only. The command is:

```
chmod 500 /usr/local/samba/private
```

The smbpasswd file inside the private directory should be owned by root and the permissions should be set to 600, or read and write for root only. The command is:

```
chmod 600 smbpasswd
```

The default is:

```
encrypt passwords = No
```

To set encrypted passwords option to on, change the default to:

```
encrypt passwords = Yes
```

Update encrypted

This is a convenience option for administrators and users who are migrating from earlier versions of Samba or Windows clients. It enables the changeover to encrypted passwords to be made over a longer period. This parameter enables a site to migrate from plain-text password authentication to encrypted-password authentication without forcing all users to reenter their passwords via smbpasswd at the time the change is made. When all users have encrypted representations of their passwords in the smbpasswd file, this parameter should be set to off. For this parameter to work correctly, the encrypt passwords parameter must be set to no when this parameter is set to yes.

The default setting is:

```
update encrypted = No
```

To set this option to on, change the default to:

```
update encrypted = Yes
```

Use rhosts

If this global parameter is set to `yes`, it specifies that the UNIX users' .rhosts file in their home directory is to be read to find the names of hosts and users who are allowed access without specifying a password. This is a major security hole; don't use it.

The default is:

```
use rhosts = No
```

To use rhosts, change the default to:

```
use rhosts = Yes
```

Minimum password length

This parameter sets the minimum character length of plain-text passwords that smbd will accept when performing UNIX password changing.

See also UNIX password sync, passwd program, and passwd chat debug.

The default is:

```
min passwd length = 5
```

To set the minimum password length to eight characters, change the default to:

```
min passwd length = 8
```

Map to guest

This parameter is critical in security modes `user`, `server`, and `domain`. This is because in these modes, the name of the resource being requested is not sent to the server until after the server has successfully authenticated the client. There are three different values that tell smbd what to do with user login requests that don't match a valid UNIX user in some way. The three settings are:

never   Rejects user login requests with an invalid password. This is the default.

bad user   Rejects user logins with an invalid password
                        unless the username does not exist, in which case,
                        it is treated as a guest login and mapped to the
                        guest account.

bad password   Treats user logins with an invalid password as a
                        guest login and maps them to the guest account.
                        Don't use this option. If you do, it means that any
                        user incorrectly typing their password will be
                        silently logged on as a guest with the result that
                        they cannot access their files. Why? They are
                        now logged in with only guest privileges. You
                        don't want to troubleshoot what appears to be file
                        permission problems only to find the user
                        mistyped his or her password.

The default is:

```
map to guest = never
```

To set this parameter to bad user, change the default to:

```
map to guest = bad user
```

Null passwords

Allow or disallow client access to accounts that have null passwords. This
is another of the options you should not turn on.
    The default is:

```
null passwords = No
```

To set this parameter on, change the default to:

```
null passwords = Yes
```

Password server

This parameter enables you to specify the name of another smb server.
When used with security = domain or security = server options,
Samba does all its username/password validation via the remote server.
This is the option that sets the name of the password server to be used. You
must use a NetBIOS name. If the machine's NetBIOS name is different

from its Internet name, then add the name to the lmhosts file, which is stored in the same directory as the smb.conf file. The name of the password server is identified using the parameter `name resolve order` (see protocol options parameter 12) and can be resolved by any method and order described in that parameter. The password server must be a machine capable of using the LM1.2X002 or LM NT 0.12 protocol, and the server must be in user-level security mode. Don't point your Samba server at itself for password serving. This could cause a loop and lock up your server.

If you are using the `security = domain` parameter, then you must use this option to point Samba to the Primary Domain and/or Backup Domain controllers for your domain. When using `security = domain`, you can list several hosts in the `password server` option and smbd will try each one until it finds one that responds. This is useful in case your primary server goes down.

If you set the security parameter to `security = server`, then there are different restrictions. You may still list several password servers in this parameter; however, if smbd makes a connection to a password server, and the password server fails, no more users will be authenticated from this smbd. This is a restriction of the smb/CIFS protocol when in `security = server` mode and it cannot be fixed in Samba.

The default is blank:

```
password server =
```

To set this option to pass username/password validation to the NetBIOS servers sugar and terrapin, change the default to:

```
password server = sugar, terrapin
```

Smb password file

This option sets the path to the encrypted smbpasswd file. By default, the path to the smbpasswd file is compiled in Samba.

The default is:

```
smb passwd file= /usr/samba/private/smbpasswd
```

To set the smb password path to the /opt/samba/private directory, change the default to:

```
smb passwd file = /opt/samba/private/smbpasswd
```

Host equiv

Setting this global parameter specifies the name of a file to read for the names of hosts and users who are allowed access without specifying a password. Again, this is a major security hole; don't use this option. The default is blank:

```
hosts equiv =
```

To set hosts equiv to /etc/hosts.equiv, change the default to:

```
hosts equiv = /etc/hosts.equiv
```

Root directory

The server will change its root directory to the directory specified by this option on startup. Changing the root directory entry to something other than / adds an extra level of security. But every security setting comes with a price. If you use this option, it absolutely ensures that no access is given to files not in the root directory tree. This includes files needed for operation of the server. If you use this option, you will need to mirror some system files to the root directory tree. In particular, you will need to mirror files such as passwd and printcap out of the /etc directory. The full set of files that must be mirrored is operating system dependent.

The default is:

```
root directory = /
```

To set the root directory to /opt/samba/home, change the default to:

```
root directory = /opt/samba/home
```

Password program

This is the program that can be used to set UNIX user passwords. The %u parameter will be replaced with the username. The username is then checked for existence before calling the password-changing program. If the UNIX password sync parameter is set to Yes, then the UNIX password program is called with root user rights before changing the smb password in the smbpasswd file. If this UNIX password change fails, then smbd will fail to change the smb password. This is a feature, not a bug. If the UNIX `password sync` parameter is set, this parameter must use absolute paths for the programs called.

The default is:

```
passwd program = /bin/passwd
```

Password chat

This string controls the conversation that occurs between smbd and the local password program to change the user's password. The string specifies the sequence of response-receive pairs that smbd uses to determine what to send to the passwd program and what smbd will receive. This sequence is site specific and depends on what local methods are used for password control. If the expected output is not received, the password is not changed.

The string can contain the macros:

%o   old

%n   new

It can also contain these standard macros:

\n   line feed

\r   carriage return

\t   tab

\s   space

The string can also contain *, which will match any set of characters.

Double quotes can be used to collect strings with spaces in them in a single string.

The default is:

```
passwd chat = *old*password* %o\n *new*password* %n\n *new*password* %n\n

    changed
```

Here is an example of a password chat string:

```
passwd chat = "##Enter your old password##" %o\n "##Enter your new password##"

    %n\n "##Re-enter your new password##" %n\n "## Your password has been

    changed##"
```

Password chat debug

This parameter specifies whether the passwd chat script parameter runs in debug mode. In debug mode, the strings passed to and received from the passwd chat are printed in the smbd log with a debug level of 100. If you're using plain-text passwords, they can be seen in the smbd log. This option is available to help Samba administrators debug their passwd chat scripts when calling the passwd program. Turn it off after you've verified that your passwd chat string works as expected. This parameter is off by default.

The default is:

```
passwd chat debug = No
```

To turn password chat debug on, change the default to:

```
passwd chat debug = Yes
```

Username map

This parameter specifies a file containing a mapping of client usernames to Unix server usernames. This is a convenience parameter; think about the work involved in the mapping. If you are going to map all the PC usernames, why not just create the user IDs on the UNIX server? This is the place to map the NT administrator user to root if you need cross-platform administration access. You can define multiple-client usernames to one UNIX username, but is that really a good idea? You can also use a UNIX group name with the @groupname option.

File format Each line begins with a single UNIX username, followed by an =, which is followed by a list of usernames. There is a wildcard special-client name, *, which matches any name. The maximum line length is 1023 characters. There is no limit to the number of mappings. The map file is parsed line by line. If any line begins with a # or a ;, then it is ignored. For example, to map from the name admin or administrator to the UNIX name root, the format is:

```
# entry to map NT admin to root
root = admin administrator
```

You can map usernames that have spaces in them by using double quotes around the name. For example, to add a mapping for username Robert Weir to the UNIX username cheese, you would type:

```
# entry to map NT admin to root
;
root = admin administrator
# Starting terrapin user mappings
;
cheese = "Robert Weir"
```

If any line begins with an !, then the processing stops after that line if a mapping was done by the line. Otherwise, mapping continues with every line being processed. Using ! is most useful when you have a wildcard mapping line later in the file.

In the next example, after mapping root and cheese, if the user testme matches either user edwardb or georgeh, processing will cease because of the ! at the beginning of that line. If no match is found by then, the user will be mapped to guest because of the wildcard *.

```
# entry to map NT admin to root
;
root = admin administrator
# Starting terrapin user mappings
;
cheese = "Robert Weir"
;
!testme = edwardb, georgeh
guest = *
```

The default is a blank string, or no username map:

```
username map =
```

In this example, the username map is set to user.map file under /usr/local/samba/lib:

```
username map = /usr/local/samba/lib/user.map
```

Password level

Some client/server combinations have difficulty with mixed-case passwords. Most modern clients handle upper and lowercase passwords without a problem. This parameter is really a fix for the client Windows for Workgroups, which forces passwords to uppercase when using the LAN-MAN1 protocol. This parameter defines the maximum number of characters that may be uppercase in passwords. The higher the value of this parameter, the more likely it is that a mixed-case password will be matched against a single-case password. You should consider that use of this parameter reduces security and increases the time taken to process a new connection. If you are not using an old Windows for Workgroups or DOS client on your network, stick with the default, which is zero. The value of zero will cause only two attempts to be made: the password as is and the password in all lowercase.

If the password given was STRAW and the parameter was `password level = 1`, these combinations would be tried if STRAW failed:

"Straw", "straw", "sTraw", "stRaw", "strAw", "straW"

If the parameter was `password level = 2`, these combinations would be tried as well:

"STraw", "StRaw", "StraW", "sTRaw", "sTraW", "stRAw", ...

The default is:

```
password level = 0
```

In this example, the password level is set to four:

```
password level = 4
```

Username level

This parameter also helps Samba deal with legacy clients. DOS clients send an all uppercase username. By default, Samba tries all lowercase and then the username with the first letter capitalized. If after these two attempts the username was not found on the UNIX machine, then the logon fails. If the username-level parameter is set to nonzero, the behavior changes. This parameter is a number that specifies the number of uppercase combinations to try to determine the UNIX username. The higher the number, the more combinations it tries. Again, as with password level, this is both a security and a performance issue. The higher the number, the slower the discovery of usernames. This parameter can be helpful if you have strange usernames on your UNIX machine, such as WhatALongStrangeNameItIs, or if you're dealing with DOS or Windows for Workgroups clients.

The default is:

```
username level = 0
```

This example sets the username level to five passes:

```
username level = 5
```

UNIX password sync

This parameter controls whether Samba attempts to synchronize the UNIX password with the smb password. If you set UNIX password `sync = Yes`, then when the encrypted smb password in the smbpasswd file is changed, the UNIX password program is called as root. This enables the new UNIX password to be set without access to the old UNIX password.

The default is:

```
Unix password sync = No
```

To set this parameter on, change the default to:

```
Unix password sync = Yes
```

Alternate permissions

This parameter has no effect in Samba 2.0. In previous versions, it affected how the DOS read-only attribute was mapped for a file. In Samba 2.0, a file is marked read-only if the UNIX file does not have the write bit set for the owner, regardless of whether the owner of the file is the currently logged on.

Revalidate

This parameter only works with `security = share`; it is ignored if this is not the case. This parameter controls whether Samba enables a previously validated user and password pair to be used to attach to another share. The default is to enable access without revalidating. If you set `revalidate = Yes`, and then connected to \\sugar\lesh, and then tried to connect to \\sugar\hart, Samba won't automatically enable the client connection to the second share, even though it's the same username, without supplying the password.

The default is:

```
revalidate = No
```

To set this option to require revalidation for each resource, change the default to:

```
revalidate = Yes
```

Username

This is another legacy parameter for DOS and Windows for Workgroups clients. As with password level and username level, this option can be both a security loophole and performance hit. This parameter enables multiple users to be specified in a comma-delimited list. The supplied password is tested against each username in turn.

The default is blank, or no users defined:

```
username =
```

To set a list of users for Samba to try, change the default to:

```
username = straw, rubin, jack, jane, @roomers
```

Guest account

This is a username used for access to services that are specified as `guest ok`. The privileges this user has are available to any client connecting to the guest service. This user must exist in the password file but should not have a valid login. The traditional UNIX system default guest account `nobody` might not be capable of printing. You should test this by logging in as your guest user and trying to print using the system print command. If you cannot print from this account, use another account. The user account ftp is another a good choice for this parameter.

The default is specified at compile time, usually as nobody:

```
guest account = nobody
```

An example of mapping the guest account to the ftp user is:

```
guest account = ftp
```

Invalid users

This is a list of users that will not be allowed to log in to this service. The best use for this parameter is to set invalid users = administrator if you don't want cross-platform administration. This parameter also takes groups as an option.

The variables are:

+group	Check local UNIX group file
&group	Check NIS group file

These variables can also be used together:

+&group	Check local UNIX group file and then NIS group file
&+group	Check NIS group file and then local UNIX file

The third variable that checks both is:

@group	Check NIS group file and then local group file

The default is no invalid users, or blank:

```
invalid users =
```

To set the NT administrator to an invalid user, change the default to:

```
invalid users = administrator admin
```

Valid users

This parameter is a list of users that should be allowed to log in to this service. This is not required. The default is an empty string, or anyone can log in. If you define a username in both the valid users list and the invalid users list, the invalid list wins and access is denied to that user. This parameter also takes groups as an option.

The variables are:

+group   Check local UNIX group file

&group   Check NIS group file

These variables can also be used together:

+&group   Check local Unix group file and then NIS group file

&+group   Check NIS group file and then local Unix file

The third variable that checks both is:

@group   Check NIS group file and then local group file

The default is a blank string, or all users are valid:

```
Valid users =
```

To set a username phil and the wheel group (either NIS or local, whichever is found first) as the only valid users, change the default to:

```
valid users = phil, @wheel
```

Admin users

This parameter is a list of users who will be granted administrative privileges on the share. You are making this user root on shares. This is another parameter that you should not use.

The default is a blank string, or no admin users:

```
admin users =
```

This example sets the user georgeh to an admin user:

```
admin users = georgeh
```

Read list

This parameter is a list of users who are given read-only access to a service. This parameter also takes groups as an option.

The variables are:

+group   Check local Unix group file

`&group`   Check NIS group file

These variables can also be used together:

`+&group`   Check local Unix group file and then NIS group file

`&+group`   Check NIS group file and then local Unix file

The third variable that checks both is:

`@group`   Check NIS group file and then local group file

The default is an empty string, or no users are limited to read-only access:

`Read list =`

This example sets users phil and cheese to read-only access:

`read list = phil, cheese`

Write list

This parameter is a list of users that are given write and read, even if this service is set to read-only. If you define a user in both the read list and the write list, the write list wins and that user is given write access. This parameter also takes groups as an option.

The variables are:

`+group`   Check local Unix group file

`&group`   Check NIS group file

These variables can also be used together:

`+&group`   Check local Unix group file and then NIS group file

`&+group`   Check NIS group file and then local Unix file

The third variable that checks both is:

`@group`   Check NIS group file and then local group file

The default is an empty string, or no users are given write access above the set file permissions:

`write list =`

This example sets users administrator and root, plus all users in the wheel group:

```
write list = admin, root, @wheel
```

File and directory permissions

The next four parameters under Security Options configure how Samba translates security and ownership permissions between the client operating system and the Samba UNIX server.

Here is a quick refresher of UNIX octal permissions. The range of settings is 0 (no permission) to 7 (full permission). There are three sets of octal permissions applied to every file, directory, network share, or printer. The first is for the owner. The second is for members of the same group as the owner. The last is for everyone else who can log in to that server. These are referred to as owner, group, and world. The three permissions are read, write, and execute. The read permission gives the ability to read or display the file, or list the directory. The write permission gives the ability to write, edit or change the file, or create files in a directory. The execute permission gives the ability to run the file. Your system will display these permissions with an `ls` −`l`. To display the settings for smb.conf, the command is `ls` −`l smb.conf`:

```
rw-r—r-- 1 root root 648 Jun 28 08:43 smb.conf
```

This is the octal setting 644. This value was determined by concatenating the rights for the owner, group, and world from the values below.

The octal settings are:

7	Full permission
6	Permission to read and write
5	Permission to read and execute
4	Permission to read
3	Permission to write and execute
2	Permission to write
1	Permission to execute
0	No permissions

Create mask This parameter is where permissions are mapped from DOS modes to UNIX permissions. This is really a translation of client permissions to UNIX octal permissions for user, group, and world. The default value is full permission for owner and read-only permission for group and world. This parameter does not affect directory modes. There is a separate parameter for the directory mode. There is also a force create mode parameter for forcing particular permissions to be set on created files.

The default is full permission for owner and read-only for all others. This permission octet translates to 744:

```
create mask = 744
```

This example adds execute privileges for all users:

```
create mask = 755
```

Force create mode This parameter specifies the octal permissions that will be set on a file created by Samba. The default for this parameter is 000; that is, Samba gives no one access. This isn't as radical as it sounds. The owner will provide access permissions. This parameter is applied after create mask.

The default is:

```
force create mode = 000
```

This example sets permissions to full access for owner, read and execute for members of the same group, and read for everyone else:

```
force create mode = 754
```

Directory mask This parameter sets the octal modes that are used when converting DOS modes to UNIX modes when creating UNIX directories. When a directory is created, the necessary permissions are calculated. This parameter is the octal mask for the UNIX directory. The default value of this parameter provides read and execute permissions for group and world. The owner is given full access.

The default is:

```
directory mask = 755
```

This example sets permissions to full access for owner, with read and write privileges for both members of the same group and all other users:

```
directory mask = 766
```

Force directory mode   This parameter specifies the UNIX permissions that will always be set on a directory created by Samba. The default for this parameter is 000, or no permission will be added for a directory created by Samba. This operation is performed after the parameter `directory mask` is applied. Again, as with the forced `create mode` parameter, this isn't as radical as it sounds. The owner of the directory will provide access permissions.

The default is:

```
force directory mode = 000
```

This example provides full access for owner, read and execute for group, and read-only for everyone else:

```
force directory mode = 754
```

Hosts allow

This parameter is a comma-, space-, or tab-delimited list of hosts permitted to access a service. If specified in the globals section, then it applies to all services. This setting wins even when the individual service has a different setting. Name, IP address, or network/netmask pairs can specify the hosts. You can also specify by netgroup names if your system supports netgroups. The `except` keyword can be used to limit a wildcard list.

Caution

If you use the `hosts allow` parameter, you must include local-host in the string of hosts. Samba requires access to the lo-calhost interface to function as expected.

The following examples will provide some help. To allow localhost and all IP addresses in 192.168.*.* :

```
hosts allow = localhost, 192.168.*.*
```

To allow localhost and hosts that match the given network/netmask:

```
hosts allow = localhost, 192.168.99.0/255.255.255.0
```

To allow a localhost and two others by name:

```
hosts allow = localhost, terrapin, deal
```

To allow localhost and a subnet with one exception:

```
Host allow = localhost, 192.168.99.0 EXCEPT
192.168.99.222
```

If your network uses NIS netgroups, you can use them with the @ option as we've used for other options. The + and & options do not apply to this parameter. The following example enables access for the NIS group `marshotel` and `localhost`:

```
hosts allow = @marshotel, localhost
```

The default is a blank string, or all hosts are allowed access:

```
hosts allow =
```

Host deny

This parameter is the opposite of `hosts  allow`. The hosts you list here are not permitted access to services. Even if specific services have lists to override this one, this list wins and denies access to the service.

The default is a blank string, or all hosts are permitted access:

```
Hosts deny =
```

This example denies access to the 192.168.111.* subnet:

```
hosts deny = 192.168.111.*
```

Logging options

Samba does a good job of logging events and errors for diagnosing and correcting connectivity problems. As the administrator, you have a lot of leeway to decide what gets logged, and where it gets logged. You may need to increase the log level when diagnosing a tough problem, but be aware that Samba can generate copious amounts of logging data at higher logging levels.

Log level

This parameter is a synonym for debug level. The value of the parameter enables the debug level for logging to be specified in the smb.conf file.

The default is level zero:

```
debug level = 0
```

An example of setting the logging debug level to 3 is:

```
debug level = 3
```

Syslog

This parameter sets the threshold for sending messages to syslog. Messages with a debug level less than this value are sent to syslog.

The Samba debug logging levels are:

- Debug level 0 maps to syslog LOG_ERR
- Debug level 1 maps to LOG_WARNING
- Debug level 2 maps to LOG_NOTICE
- Debug level 3 maps to LOG_INFO
- All higher levels are mapped to LOG_DEBUG

The default is level 1:

```
syslog = 1
```

An example of setting the debug logging level to 3 or LOG_INFO:

```
syslog = 3
```

Syslog only

If set, this parameter sends Samba debug messages to the system syslog only, and not to the debug log files.

The default is to send debug messages to both syslog and the debug log files:

```
syslog only = No
```

To set this option on and only send debug messages to syslog, change the default to:

```
syslog only = Yes
```

Log file

This parameter overrides the default location and name of the Samba log file. The parameter accepts standard substitution. The two most commonly used are:

%m   Machine or host name

%u   User

The default set when Samba compiles is:

```
log file = /var/log/samba/log.smb
```

An example of setting the log file to /opt/log/samba/samba.log:

```
log file = /opt/log/samba/samba.log
```

This example /opt/log/samba/samba.%m would set the log file for the host deal to:

```
log file = /opt/log/samba/samba.deal
```

This is a useful option if your site uses central logging for all servers.

Max log size

This parameter sets the maximum size for the log file. The limit is set in kilobytes. Samba monitors the size. When exceeded, Samba renames the file by adding a .old extension. Setting the limit to zero actually means there is no file size limit for the log.

The default is:

```
max log size = 5000
```

An example to double the default log size:

```
max log size = 10000
```

Timestamp logs

Samba 2.0 applies timestamps to all log entries by default. This parameter enables the timestamping to be turned off. Use this option if you need to debug a problem and don't require timestamps.

The default is:

```
timestamp logs = Yes
```

An example to set timestamp off:

```
timestamp logs = No
```

Status

You should not need to set this parameter. If you set this to `status = no`, smbstatus will not be able to tell what connections are active.

The default is:

```
status = Yes
```

An example to set this parameter so that smbstatus can't tell what connections are active:

```
status = No
```

Protocol options

This section explains the network protocol options, from version and block size to the text your server will use to identify its network shares. With these parameters, you can control how your Samba server will appear as a Windows server, make some performance adjustments, and determine how Samba locates network resources.

Protocol

This parameter is the highest protocol level that is supported by the server. You don't need to set this option. The automatic negotiation phase in the smb protocol takes care of choosing the appropriate protocol.

The values are:

CORE   The first version, which is no longer in use.

COREPLUS	A more efficient stack, but still primitive.
LANMAN1	Or LAN Manager, it includes long filename support.
LANMAN2	A few more refinements on LAN Manager.
NT1	The current version of the protocol or Common Internet File System (CIFS)

The default is:

```
protocol = NT1
```

This example sets the protocol to LANMAN1:

```
protocol = LANMAN1
```

Read bpmx

This legacy parameter controls whether smbd supports the Read Block Multiplex. This is rarely used.
    The default is:

```
read bmpx = No
```

To set this option, change the default to:

```
read bmpx = Yes
```

Read raw

This parameter controls whether the server will support the raw read smb requests when transferring data to clients. If enabled, this allows reads of 65535 bytes in one packet. This can provide a major performance benefit.
    The default is:

```
read raw = Yes
```

To set this parameter off, change the default to:

```
read raw = No
```

Write raw

This parameter controls support for when clients transfer data to the server. The default is yes, to turn on optimized low level file write. Some servers may not support it, and turning it off may improve performance.

The default is:

```
write raw = Yes
```

Turning it off may improve performance on some servers:

```
write raw = No
```

NT smb support

This parameter controls whether smbd negotiates NT-specific smb support with NT clients. This is considered a developer's debugging option. However, with the present version of Samba, benchmarking reveals that Windows NT clients get better performance with this option set to no. The Samba team is investigating this "feature," so keep checking for revisions and documentation. If this option is set to no, it sets smb to the same calls that versions prior to Samba 2.0 offered.

The default is:

```
nt support = Yes
```

An example to set NT specific smb to off:

```
nt support = No
```

NT pipe support

This parameter controls whether smbd enables Windows NT clients to connect to the NT smb-specific IPC$ pipes. This is considered a developer's debugging option.

The default is:

```
nt pipe support = Yes
```

An example to turn NT–smb specific pipe support to off:

```
SMB nt pipe support = No
```

NT acl support

This is an experimental option. This parameter is set to no by default. It controls whether smbd attempts to map UNIX permissions to Windows NT access control lists.

The default is:

```
nt acl support = No
```

To turn this option on and start down the road to beta testing, change the default to:

```
nt acl support = Yes
```

Announce version

This parameter specifies the version numbers that nmbd will use to announce itself as a server. The default is 4.2. Do not change this parameter unless you have a specific need to set a Samba server as a downlevel server.

The default is:

```
announce version = 4.2
```

An example to set the version announced to 2.0:

```
announce version = 2.0
```

Announce as

This parameter specifies how nmbd announces itself to the network neighborhood browse list. The default from Samba 2.*x* and later is Windows NT. Don't change this parameter unless you have to stop Samba from appearing as an NT server. This could prevent the Samba server from participating as a browser server correctly.

The valid options are:

NT   Acts as a server for all modern Windows clients beginning with Win95.

Win95   Also acts as a server for all modern Windows clients.

The default is:

```
announce as = NT Server
```

An example to set Samba to announce as a Win95 server:

```
announce as = Win95
```

Max mux

This parameter specifies the maximum number of outstanding simultaneous smb operations that Samba allows a client. You should never need to set this parameter.

The default is:

```
max mux = 50
```

An example of lowering this threshold:

```
max mux = 35
```

Max xmit

This parameter specifies the maximum packet size negotiated by Samba. The default value is 65535, which is the maximum packet size. You might find clients get better performance with a smaller value. However, setting the value below 2048 is likely to cause problems.

The default is:

```
max xmit = 65535
```

An example to lower the maximum packet size:

```
max xmit = 16384
```

Name resolve order

This parameter specifies the naming services and the order in which the programs in the Samba suite use them. The options for this parameter use a space-separated string of name resolution options.

The options are:

Lmhosts   Looks up an IP address in the Samba server's lmhosts file.

Host   Performs a standard host name-to-IP address resolution using the UNIX system-specified method. This can be the hosts file, NIS server map, or Domain Name Service lookup. This option is operating system dependent. In Solaris, this might be controlled by the /etc/nsswitch. conf file.

Wins   Queries the Windows Internet Name Server to resolve a name to the IP address. The biggest advantage for WINS over other methods is that it is a dynamic rather than static method to resolve names. This means the WINS server listens on the network and learns the names of machines that are active. If no WINS server is specified, this method is ignored.

Bcast   Broadcast on each of the known local interfaces. Samba uses the interfaces parameter to determine the interfaces it can use. This is the least reliable of the name-resolution methods. This method depends on the target host being on a locally connected subnet.

The default is:

```
name resolve order = lmhosts host wins bcast
```

This example specifies that the local lmhosts file is to be examined first, followed by a broadcast attempt:

```
name resolve order = lmhosts bcast host
```

If both of these options fail, then the server performs a normal system hostname lookup.

Max packet

This parameter specifies the maximum packet size for Samba. The default value is 65535, which is the maximum packet size. You might find clients get better performance with a smaller value. Again, setting the value below 2048 is likely to cause problems.

The default is:

```
max xmit = 65535
```

To set the maximum packet size to one-half the default, change the default to:

```
max xmit = 32768
```

Max ttl

This parameter specifies to nmbd what the default time to live (TTL) is for NetBIOS names. This option is set in seconds. It controls the time for either a broadcast packet or a request from a WINS server. You should never need to change this parameter. The default is three days.

The default is three days in seconds:

```
max ttl = 259200
```

An example to change this option to one day in seconds:

```
max ttl = 86400
```

Max wins ttl

This parameter applies only if your Samba server is configured as a WINS server. It specifies for nmbd the maximum time to live for NetBIOS names. This parameter is set in seconds. You should never need to change this parameter.

The default is 6 days or 518,400 seconds:

```
max wins ttl = 518400
```

An example to set the time to live for NetBIOS names to 3 days or 259,200 seconds:

```
max wins ttl = 259200
```

Min wins ttl

This parameter applies only if your Samba server is configured as a WINS server. It specifies for nmbd the minimum time to live for NetBIOS names. This parameter is set in seconds. You should never need to change this parameter.

The default is 6 hours or 21,600 seconds:

```
min wins ttl = 21600
```

An example to raise the minimum time to live to 12 hours or 43,200 seconds:

```
min wins ttl = 43200
```

Time Server

Specify this parameter if nmbd advertises itself as a time server to Windows clients. This is not the standard time service and can't be used by UNIX clients.

The default is:

```
time server = No
```

To turn this service on, change the default to:

```
time server = Yes
```

Tuning options

This section is only displayed on the Global Advanced page and is for setting Samba tuning options. The options here enable you to tune your Samba server for your particular environment by determining when to disconnect idle users, what socket options to use, and what size caches to use, as well as other tuning parameters.

Change notify timeout

This parameter is one of the new NT smb requests that Samba 2.*x* supports. This new feature enables a client to tell a server to watch a particular directory for any changes and only reply to the smb request when a change has occurred. This constant scanning is resource-intensive under UNIX. To improve performance, the smbd daemon only performs such a scan on each requested directory as specified by the `change notify timeout`. This parameter is set in seconds.

The default is 60 seconds:

```
change notify timeout = 60
```

This example changes the scan time to every 10 minutes or 600 seconds:

```
change notify timeout = 600
```

Deadtime

This parameter specifies the number of minutes of inactivity before a connection is considered dead and it is disconnected. This option activates only if the number of open files is zero. It will stop a server's resources from being exhausted by a large number of inactive connections. Modern clients have an autoreconnect feature when a connection is broken. This parameter is transparent to users. It is set in minutes with a timeout between two and four minutes.

The default is a deadtime of zero and no autodisconnection will occur:

```
deadtime = 0
```

To set the deadtime to five minutes, change the default to:

```
deadtime = 5
```

Getwd cache

When this parameter is enabled, a caching algorithm reduces the time taken for some system calls. The `widelinks` parameter set under Miscellaneous Options must be set to No for this parameter to have a significant impact on performance.

The default is:

```
getwd cache = No
```

To set this parameter to on, change the default to:

```
getwd cache = Yes
```

Keepalive

This parameter specifies the value in seconds between keepalive packets. Keepalive packets tell the server whether a client is still present and responding. Most services have their own keepalive packets. This option is set in seconds. Use this option for troubleshooting.

The default is zero, or no keepalive packets are sent by the server itself:

```
keep alive = 0
```

To set the servers keepalive packets to once per minute, change the default to:

```
keep alive = 60
```

Lpq cache time

This parameter specifies how long lpq information will be cached. This prevents the `lpq` command from being called repeatedly. A separate cache is kept of the `lpq` command used by the system. The cache files are stored in /tmp. This parameter is set in seconds. A value of 0 disables caching completely.

The default is:

```
lpq cache time = 10
```

To set the cache time to one minute, change the default to:

```
lpq cache time = 60
```

Max disk size

This parameter specifies the maximum size of disks that shares report. If you set this option to 100, then all shares appear to be not larger than 100MB in size. The key word is "appear." This option does not limit the amount of data that you can put on the disk; it limits what the server tells the client when a client asks for the total disk size. This parameter is useful to work around bugs in software that can't handle very large disks.

The default is zero, or there is no maximum disk size:

```
max disk size = 0
```

To set the maximum disk size reported as 1GB, change the default to:

```
max disk size = 1000
```

Max open files

This parameter specifies the maximum number of open files for the smbd process per client. The real limit on the number of open files is set by the UNIX system per-process file limit. You should not need to change this parameter. The default is set very high because Samba uses only 1 bit per unopened file.

The default is:

```
max open files = 10000
```

This example lowers the limit to 5000 files:

```
max open files = 5000
```

Read prediction

This parameter is disabled in Samba 2.0 and might be removed at a later date. It was used to enable or disable the read prediction code.

The default is:

```
read prediction = No
```

You could set this option to on as follows, but it will have no effect:

```
read prediction = Yes
```

Read size

The parameter specifies the overlap of disk reads/writes with network reads/writes. If the amount of data being transferred is larger than this value, then the server begins writing the data before it has received the whole packet from the network. This overlapping works best when the speeds of disk and network access are similar. This parameter has had very little experimentation done to determine the optimal value. The best value varies greatly among systems. Setting this value to over 65,536 will allocate memory that will never be used because that is the maximum packet size.

The default is:

```
read size = 2048
```

This example doubles this value:

```
read size = 4096
```

Shared mem size

This parameter specifies the size of the shared memory in bytes for use between smbd processes. A large server with many files open simultaneously might need a larger value than the default. If users are reporting strange problems trying to save files, check the error messages in the smbd log. If you find errors such as `ERROR smb_shm_alloc : alloc of XX bytes failed`, you need to increase the value.

The default is 1MB of shared memory:

```
shared mem size = 1048576
```

To set the value to 5MB, change the default to:

```
shared mem size = 5242880
```

Socket options

This parameter specifies the socket options to be used when talking with clients. Socket options are controls on the networking layer of the operating systems that allow the connection to be tuned. This option is used to tune your Samba server for optimal performance on your local network. You can combine any of the supported socket options in any way you like as long as your OS allows it. However, several of the options can cause your Samba server to fail completely. If you're not a TCP/IP guru, stick with the defaults.

The socket options supported using this option are:

```
SO_KEEPALIVE
SO_REUSEADDR
SO_BROADCAST
TCP_NODELAY
IPTOS_LOWDELAY
```

```
IPTOS_THROUGHPUT
SO_SNDBUF #
SO_RCVBUF #
SO_SNDLOWAT #
SO_RCVLOWAT #
```

Those options marked with a # require an integer argument. The other options take a 1 or 0 argument to enable or disable the option. By default, they are enabled if you don't specify 1 or 0.

The following setting would increase the send buffers to 8MB (do not include any spaces before or after the second = sign):

```
socket options = SO_SNDBUF=8192
```

A pair of options to try if you are on a local network:

```
socket options = IPTOS_LOWDELAY TCP_NODELAY
```

An option to try if you are on a wide area network:

```
socket options = IPTOS_THROUGHPUT
```

The default is:

```
socket options = TCP_NODELAY
```

Stat cache size

This parameter specifies the number of entries in the static cache. This parameter does not need to be changed.

The default is:

```
stat cache size = 50
```

This example doubles the default:

```
stat cache size = 100
```

Printing options

This section is only displayed on the Global Advanced page and it is where you set the global printer options. This is the section where you would modify Samba to make the printers work with your system. You can specify the type of printing to use, the correct printer commands to use, and the location of the printcap file.

Load printers

This parameter controls whether all printers in the printcap are loaded for browsing by default.

The default is:

```
load printers = Yes
```

An example to keep printers out of the Network Neighborhood by default:

```
load printers = No
```

Printcap name

This parameter is used to override the default printcap option set when Samba compiles. It is operating system dependent. Check your system's man pages for details on the print files.

The default is:

```
printcap name = /etc/printcap
```

An example for AIX systems using qconfig:

```
printcap name = /etc/qconfig
```

Printer driver file

This parameter specifies the location of the printer driver definition file. It is used when serving drivers to Windows 95/98 clients. This option does not work with NT clients. This file is created from Windows 95/98 msprint.def files on the Windows 95/98 client system.

The default is no printer.def file created.

An example to put a printer subdirectory and a printer.def file under the install directory for Samba:

```
printer driver file = /usr/local/samba/printers/drivers.def
```

Printing

This parameter specifies how printer status information is interpreted on your system. It should be set to the printing style used by the operating system of your Samba server, for example, on a Solaris 2.5 server use SYSV. It affects the default values for these commands: `print`, `lpq`, `lppause`, `lpresume`, and `lprm`, each of which can be different depending on how printing is handled at the operating system level. The option can be set on a per-printer basis.

The commands are interpreted through the use of styles. There are eight supported styles:

BSD

AIX

LPRNG

PLP

SYSV

HPUX

QNX

SOFTQ

An example to set printing to HPUX style:

`printing = HPUX`

An example to set printing to BSD style:

`printing = BSD`

print command

This parameter specifies the command that processes a print job after it has finished spooling to a service. If you don't specify a print command, the spool files are created but not processed. The spool file name is generated automatically by the Samba server. The command specified submits the spool file to the host's printing subsystem. When specified in the Globals section, the print command is used for any printable service that does not have a print command specified. The Samba server will not remove the spool file. If the print command specified does not remove the spool file, you need to manually remove old spool files.

The print command is a text string. It passes to the UNIX system verbatim. There are two substitutions and three variables that can be used with this command. The name of the spool file is represented by either a `%s` or a `%f`. If `%s` is not preceded by a `/`, then the full path name is used for the filename. If you don't require this level of detail, use `%f` instead. All occurrences of `%f` replace the spool filename without the path. The other substitution is `%p` for the printer name. If no printer name was supplied, the `%p` is ignored. When the print job is submitted, the print command must contain at least one of these variables: `%s`, `%f`, or `%p`.

Make sure you test your printing definitions. Printing could fail on some UNIX systems if you set the guest account for Samba to use the `nobody` account. If this is the case, then change the guest account mapping to a user that can print. This is covered under the section on Security options for the guest account. Go back to this option and set the guest account in this section to the user `ftp`.

The default for this parameter depends on style specified with the `printing` option. The styles use these UNIX print commands:

For `printing = BSD, AIX, QNX, LPRNG` or `PLP`, the default command is:

```
print command = lpr -r -P%p %s
```

For `printing = SYSV` or `HPUX`, the default command is:

```
print command = lp -c -d%p %s; rm %s
```

For `printing = SOFTQ`, the default command is:

```
print command = lp -d%p -s %s; rm %s
```

You can form complex print commands because they are passed directly to the shell. Remember that the `;` is the usual separator for commands in shell scripts. You can test the command syntax in the shell before defining it in this parameter. The following example logs a print job, prints the file, and then removes it.

```
print command = echo Printing %s > /var/log/print.log; lpr -P %p %s; rm %s
```

Another method is to create a script file that contains the commands your system uses for printing and put the path and name of the script there:

```
print command = /opt/samba/bin/theprintscript %p %s
```

lpq command

This parameter specifies the command the UNIX server uses to obtain lpq printer status information. The command should be a program or a script that takes a printer name as its only parameter. There are eight styles of printer status information currently supported: BSD, AIX, LPRNG, PLP, SYSV, HPUX, QNX, and SOFTQ. See the printing option (printing =) previously in this section. If %p is given as part of the command, then the printer name is substituted. If you omit %p, it is placed at the end of the command. Use the absolute path for the lpq command, as the path might not be available to the Samba server by default.

An example for BSD-style printing:

```
lpq command = /usr/bin/lpq %p
```

An example for Solaris- and SYSV-style systems:

```
lpq command = /usr/bin/lpstat -o%p
```

lprm command

This parameter specifies the UNIX server command to delete a print job. The command should be a program or a script that can take a printer name and job number to delete the print job. Two variables are required with this command: the first is the %p for the printer name. The second is a new variable, %j, which will be replaced with the job number of the print job in the printer queue. Once again, it is good practice to include the absolute path for the lprm command, as the path might not be available to the Samba server.

An example of using the lprm command:

```
lprm command = /usr/bin/lprm -P%p %j
```

An example of the correct format for lprm for the Solaris and SYSV style:

```
lprm command = /usr/bin/cancel %p-%j
```

lppause command

This parameter specifies the command to be executed by the UNIX server to stop printing or spooling a specific print job. The command should be a program or a script that takes a printer name and job number to pause the print job. The variables required for this command are `%p` for printer and `%j` for job number. Once again, it is good practice to include the absolute path of the `lppause` command because the path might not be available to the Samba server.

Currently, defaults are defined for the SYSV, HPUX, and SOFTQ printing command styles.

The default for the SYSV style is:

```
lp -i %p-%j -H hold
```

The default for the SOFTQ style is:

```
qstat -s -j%j -h
```

The default behavior for the HPUX style includes the use of job priorities, or the –p option. Print jobs having too low of a job priority won't be sent to the printer, so setting –p0 or priority to zero pauses the print job:

```
lppause command = /usr/bin/lpalt %p-%j -p0
```

lpresume command

This parameter specifies the command used by the UNIX server to restart or continue printing or spooling a specific print job. This command should be a program or script that takes a printer name and job number to resume the print job. The variables required for this command are `%p` for printer and `%j` for job number. Again, it is good practice to include the absolute path of the `lpresume` command because the path might not be available to the Samba server.

Currently, defaults are defined for the SYSV, HPUX, and SOFTQ printing command styles.

The default for SYSV style is:

```
lp -i %p-%j -H resume
```

The default for SOFTQ style is:

```
qstat -s -j%j -r
```

The default for the HPUX style:

```
lpresume command = /usr/bin/lpalt %p-%j -p2
```

queuepause command

This parameter specifies the command used by the UNIX server to pause the specified printer queue. This command should be a program or script that takes a printer name as its parameter and stops the printer queue. If a %p is not placed in the command string, it is placed at the end of the command. Once again, it is good practice to include the absolute path for the queuepause command because the path might not be available to the Samba server.

An example for the SYSV style is:

```
queuepause command = /usr/bin/lpc stop %p
```

queueresume command

This parameter specifies the command used by the UNIX server to resume printing from the specified printer queue. This command should be a program or script that takes a printer name as its parameter and resumes printing for the specified printer queue. If a %p is not placed in the command string, it is placed at the end of the command. Once again, it is good practice to include the absolute path for the queueresume command because the path might not be available to the Samba server

An example for the SYSV style:

```
queuepause command = /usr/bin/lpc start %p
```

Printer driver location

This parameter is the client equivalent of the printer driver parameter (the third parameter of Printing Options). Printer driver location specifies for clients the location of a particular printer share. This is where the printer driver files for the automatic installation of printer drivers are located. This works for Windows 95/98 machines; NT clients cannot use this option.

The default is an empty string, that is, Samba is not set up by default to serve printer drivers for clients.

The syntax for the parameter is:

```
printer driver location = \\MACHINE\PRINTER$
```

Set MACHINE to the NetBIOS name of your Samba server. Set PRINTER$ to the share you have set up for serving printer driver files with the `printer driver` parameter.

An example using the Samba server deal and a share named HPDRVS:

```
printer driver location = \\deal\HPDRVS$
```

Filename handling

This section is only displayed on the Global Advanced page. This is where you set filename translation between UNIX and clients. The Parameters you set here determine how long filenames are displayed on your client machines.

Strip dot

This parameter specifies whether to strip trailing dots off of UNIX filenames. This can help with some CDs that have filenames ending in a single dot.

The default is:

```
strip dot = No
```

To set the option on, change the default to:

```
strip dot = Yes
```

Character set

This parameter specifies a map for smbd to use for incoming client filenames. The DOS Code can be mapped to several built-in UNIX character sets. This parameter will not work as expected unless you set the corresponding parameter `client code page`.

The built-in code page translations are:

ISO8859-1 Western European UNIX character set. The parameter `client code page` must be set to `client code page = 850`.

ISO8859-2 Eastern European UNIX character set. The parameter `client code page` must be set to `client code page = 852`.

ISO8859-5   Russian Cyrillic UNIX character set. The parameter `client code page` must be set to `client code page = 866`.

KOI8-R   Alternate mapping for Russian Cyrillic UNIX character set. The parameter `client code page` must be set to `client code page = 866`.

The default is an empty string, or no filename character translation:

```
character set =
```

An example to set the filename character translation to the Western European UNIX character set:

```
character set = ISO8859-1
```

This only works as expected when you set the corresponding parameter `client code page` to the value 850:

```
client code page = 850
```

Mangled stack

This parameter specifies the number of mangled names that should be cached in the Samba server smbd. The stack is a list of recently mangled base names and extensions if they are longer than three characters or contain uppercase characters. The default value is sufficient unless you are setting very long UNIX file and directory names. Be careful; it's possible the parameter will live up to its name and mangle long file names.

The default is:

```
mangled stack = 50
```

An example to double the memory set aside for the stack:

```
mangled stack = 100
```

Coding system

This parameter specifies how incoming Shift-JIS Japanese characters are mapped from the incoming client code page used by the client to file names on the UNIX file system. This parameter will not work as expected unless you set the corresponding parameter `client code page` to `client code page = 932`.

The options are:

`SJIS Shift-JIS`	Performs no conversion of the incoming filename.
`JIS8, J8BB, J8BH, J8@B, J8@J, J8@H`	Converts from incoming Shift-JIS to 8-bit JIS code with different shift-in, shift-out codes.
`JIS7, J7BB, J7BH, J7@B, J7@J, J7@H`	Converts from incoming Shift-JIS to 7-bit JIS code with different shift-in, shift-out codes.
`JUNET, JUBB, JUBH, JU@B, JU@J, JU@H`	Converts from incoming Shift-JIS to JUNET code with different shift-in, shift-out codes.
`EUC`	Converts an incoming Shift-JIS character to EUC code.
`HEX`	Converts an incoming Shift-JIS character to a 3-byte hex representation, i.e., `:AB`.
`CAP`	Converts an incoming Shift-JIS character to the 3-byte hex representation used by the Columbia AppleTalk Program (CAP), i.e., `:AB`. This is used for compatibility between Samba and CAP.

The default is an empty string, or no translation for Japanese characters is mapped.

```
coding system =
```

An example to set translation to Columbia AppleTalk Program is:

```
coding system = CAP
```

This will not work as expected if the corresponding parameter is not set also:

```
client code page = 932
```

Client code page

This parameter specifies for the Samba server what DOS code page the clients are using. Unless your clients have a special need for a character set, you won't need to set this option. Client code pages 437 and 850 both resolve correctly for Windows95/98 and NT clients. If you have problems, you can use the chcp command in a DOS window to determine what code page a Windows or DOS client is using. The client code page specified is dynamically loaded at startup by smbd. This parameter also uses the valid chars parameter to determine which characters are valid in filenames and whether capitalization is required. Set this parameter before you set the valid chars parameter in the smb.conf file.

Samba currently ships with these code page files:

Code Page 437	MS-DOS Latin U.S.
Code Page 737	Windows 95 Greek
Code Page 850	MS-DOS Latin 1
Code Page 852	MS-DOS Latin 2
Code Page 861	MS-DOS Icelandic
Code Page 866	MS-DOS Cyrillic
Code Page 932	MS-DOS Japanese SJIS
Code Page 936	MS-DOS Simplified Chinese
Code Page 949	MS-DOS Korean Hangul
Code Page 950	MS-DOS Traditional Chinese

The default is:

```
client code page = 850
```

An example to set the client code page to the default for Windows 95/98 and NT, the U.S. MS-DOS client code page:

```
client code page = 437
```

An example to set the client code page to MS-DOS Japanese SJIS:

```
client code page = 932
```

Remember that this will not map as expected unless you also set an option for the parameter coding system:

```
coding system = CAP
```

Matching file and directory names

The next five parameters work together to make client and server happy with the names of files and directories. The default for Samba 2.*x* uses the same semantics as a Windows NT server, which is case-insensitive, but case-preserving. Samba supports name mangling in order to allow DOS and Windows clients to use files that don't conform to the 8.3 format. The name-mangling parameters can also be set to adjust the case of 8.3 format filenames. The following options control the way mangling is done. If you need to make changes to the defaults, look at the output of the testparm program and make sure that you get the results you were expecting. All of these options can be set separately for each service. These are still the Global Options that will become the default.

Case sensitive This parameter specifies whether filenames are case sensitive. The default is that file names are not case sensitive. Samba performs a filename search and match on all passed names when this parameter is set to No.

The default is:

```
case sensitive = No
```

To set filenames to be case sensitive, change the default to:

```
case sensitive = Yes
```

Preserve case This parameter specifies whether new filenames will be created with the case that the client passes. If you set this parameter to No, then filenames are forced to be the default case.

The default is:

```
preserve case = Yes
```

An example to turn preserve case off and force filenames to the default case is:

```
preserve case = No
```

Short preserve case This parameter specifies whether new files created in uppercase and of suitable length are left as uppercase or if they are forced to be the default case. This parameter can be used in conjunction with the preserve case =Yes. It enables long filenames to retain their case, while files with short names are lowered.

The default is:

```
short preserve case = Yes
```

An example to turn short filename case preserve off:

```
short preserve case = No
```

Mangle case This parameter specifies whether names that have characters that aren't of the default case are mangled. For example, if set to Yes, then a name like Mail would be mangled.

The default is:

```
mangle case = No
```

Setting mangle case = Yes would affect files with capital letters. For example, FranklinsTower.txt would be mangled to the default case.

To turn this parameter on, change the default to:

```
mangle case = Yes
```

Mangling char This parameter specifies which character is used as the magic character in name mangling. The default is a tilde, but this can interfere with some software. You can use this option to set the mangling character to whatever you prefer.

The default is:

```
mangling char = ~
```

An example to set the mangling character to an underbar:

```
mangling char = _
```

Hide dot files

This parameter specifies whether files starting with a dot appear as hidden files. Hidden files are not displayed with the default file list commands.

The default is:

```
hide dot files = Yes
```

An example to show all files with a dot as the first character:

```
hide dot files = No
```

Delete veto files

This parameter specifies what Samba will do when attempting to delete a directory that contains one or more vetoed directories. The default setting `veto files = No` will fail for deletes if a vetoed directory contains any nonvetoed files or directories. This is the way you want Samba to behave. If this option is set to `veto files = Yes`, then Samba attempts to recursively delete any files and directories within the vetoed directory. This setting allows these directories to be transparently deleted when the parent directory is deleted. The user must have the proper permissions to perform the deletion or it will fail no matter how this parameter is set.

The default is:

```
delete veto files = No
```

An example to set delete veto files to `Yes`:

```
delete veto files = Yes
```

Veto files

This parameter is a list of files and directories that are neither visible nor accessible to your clients. However, one feature of the `veto files` parameter that is important to be aware of is this: if a directory contains nothing but files that match the veto files parameter, it is deleted. Then the veto files within that directory are automatically deleted with the directory as long as the user has UNIX permissions to do so. Also, the `case sensitive` parameter is applied to veto files. This parameter affects the performance of Samba. If you define `veto files`, Samba must check all files and directories for a match as they are scanned.

The default is a blank string, or no files and directories are set as `veto files`.

If you are setting up `veto files`, each entry in the list must be separated by a /, which allows spaces to be included. The wildcards * and ? can be used to specify multiple files or directories. Each entry must be a UNIX path, but cannot include the UNIX directory separator /.

An example to veto any files that end in .tmp or any directory that contains the word root:

```
veto files = /*.tmp/*root*/
```

Hide files

This parameter specifies a list of files or directories that are not visible but are accessible. The DOS hidden attribute is applied to any files or directories that match. Each entry in the list must be separated by a /, which allows spaces to be included. The wildcards * and ? can be used to specify multiple files or directories. Each entry must be a UNIX path, but cannot include the UNIX directory separator. Also, the `case sensitive` parameter is applied to hide files. This parameter affects the performance of Samba. If you define `hide files`, Samba must check all files and directories for a match as they are scanned.

The default is a blank string, or no files and directories are set as hidden files.

An example to hide any files that end in .log:

```
hide files = /*.log/
```

Veto oplock files

This parameter is only valid when the `oplocks` parameter is turned on for a share. It enables the Samba administrator to selectively turn off the granting of oplocks on selected files that match a wildcard list, similar to the wildcard list used in the `veto files` parameter. This parameter is useful for files that you know clients will heavily contended for.

The default is a blank string, or no files are vetoed for oplock grants.

An example to set all files ending in *.cookie for oplock:

```
veto oplock files = /*.cookie/
```

Map system

This parameter specifies whether DOS-style system files should be mapped to the UNIX group execute bit. This parameter requires that the `create mask` parameter (see Security options) be set so that the group execute bit is set on.

The default is:

```
map system = No
```

To set this parameter on, change the default to:

```
map system = Yes
```

Map hidden

This parameter specifies whether DOS-style hidden files should be mapped to the UNIX world execute bit. This parameter requires that the `create mask` parameter (see Security options) be set so that the world execute bit is set on.

The default is:

```
map hidden = No
```

To set this parameter on, change the default to:

```
map hidden = Yes
```

Map archive

This parameter specifies whether the DOS archive attribute should be mapped to the UNIX owner execute bit. The DOS archive bit is set when a file has been modified since its last backup. One motivation for this option is to keep Samba and its clients from making any file it touches from becoming executable under UNIX. This parameter requires that the `create mask` parameter (see Security options) be set so that the user execute bit is set on.

The default is:

```
map archive = Yes
```

To set this parameter off, change the default to:

```
map archive = No
```

Mangled names

This parameter specifies how your clients will see UNIX files. It determines whether UNIX files and directories that have incompatible names should be mapped to DOS-compatible names and made visible, or whether those names should simply be ignored. We set five parameters to determine how name mangling occurs. This parameter sets whether name mangling is requested. The name mangling enables a file to be copied between UNIX directories by clients while retaining the long UNIX filename. If you have files in a directory share, the same first five alphanumeric characters in the name-mangling algorithm can cause name collisions. The chance of such a clash occurring is 1 in 1300.

The default is:

```
mangled names = Yes
```

To turn off this parameter, change the default to:

```
mangled names = No
```

Mangled map

This parameter specifies a direct map of UNIX file names that are not Windows/DOS compatible. If you don't want to use the mangling of names, this option is quite useful. There are some documents with file extensions that differ between DOS and UNIX. One common example is this: Under UNIX it is common to use .html for HTML files but under Windows/DOS, .htm is the file extension used for HTML pages. In the example, we map the UNIX html to the Windows/DOS htm extension. The default is:

```
no mangled map
```

To map `html` to `htm`, you would use:

```
mangled map = (*.html *.htm)
```

Stat cache

This parameter specifies whether smbd will use a cache to speed up case-insensitive name mappings. This option is set on by default. You shouldn't change this parameter.

The default is:

```
stat cache = Yes
```

Domain options

The domain options section, which is only displayed on the Global Advanced page, is where to set the NT domain options. However, leave the options in this section set to the default. If you are going to use the NT domain features of Samba, don't use SWAT to configure them. The code is changing too fast. The record stands at 20 revisions posted in 1 day. This is not for the faint of heart, so if you are expecting a stable environment, it's not advisable to change the default settings. You are testing beta code. You can skip this section if you don't need the Samba server to join an NT domain. If you insist on trying, you must download the latest code and documentation. Chapter 6 covers the steps necessary to install and configure the version of Samba that contains the full NT domain networking functions. In the meantime, the parameters listed in this section remain in the smb.conf pending confirmation that they can be considered production code.

Domain groups

The default is a blank string:

```
domain groups =
```

Do not set this option.

Domain admin group

The default is a blank string:

```
domain groups =
```

Do not set this option.

Domain guest group

The default is a blank string:

```
domain groups =
```

Do not set this option.

Domain admin users

The default is a blank string:

```
domain groups =
```

Do not set this option.

Domain guest users

The default is a blank string:

```
domain groups =
```

Do not set this option.

Machine password timeout

This parameter is only used if the security parameter is set to the option `security = domain` under the Security option section.

This parameter specifies when smbd will change the machine account password. The parameter is expressed in seconds. The default is 1 week or 604,800 seconds. This is a standard setting for machines in a Windows NT domain.

The default is:

```
machine password timeout = 604800
```

This parameter is set to match the behavior of Windows NT systems. Do not change it.

Logon options

This section, which is only displayed on the Global Advanced page, is where to set client logon options. These parameters can be used to do a mass update of user's directories, ensure that users always have the same directories maps, and simplify user administration. These options work with all clients and are not part of the NT Domain Server code.

Add user script

This parameter is only used if the security parameter is set to either `security = domain` or `security = server` under the Security option section.

This parameter specifies the script that runs as root when called by `smbd`. This script creates the required UNIX users on demand when a user accesses the Samba server. Samba requires that a client be mapped to a valid UNIX user account when accessing files on the server. If your site uses Windows user accounts, creating these accounts again in UNIX is a tedious task. Do you have the time to create and keep the user accounts in synchronization? Put some work in this script and in the `delete user script` parameter, which is described next, and the work will be done on the fly. Every time a client login succeeds, smbd attempts to find the username in the UNIX password database. If this lookup fails and `add user script` is set, then smbd will call the script as root, expanding the %u argument to the username.

When the user is created, smbd continues on as though the UNIX user already existed. In other words, the required UNIX users are dynamically created to match the Windows client accounts. The `add user script` must be set to a full path name. It's up to you to write or locate a script for your password program. Samba can only pass one variable to the password program you specify here. That variable is the %u, which is expanded into the current session username. This username is passed by Samba to the password program, which uses it to create a UNIX user account with that name.

The default is a blank string, or no script is called:

```
add user script =
```

An example to set the script to `usercreate` under /opt/samba/bin directory:

```
add user script = /opt/samba/bin/usercreate %u
```

Delete user script

This parameter is only used if the security parameter is set to `security = domain` under the Security option section. This option will not work as expected in the `security = server` mode. Do use the `security = server` option for this parameter.

This parameter specifies the script that will be run as root when called by smbd. This script deletes UNIX users created on demand when the user accessed the Samba server. The `delete user script` must be set to a full path name. It's up to you to write or locate a script for your password program. The script is passed one argument from Samba, `%u`, which argument expands to the UNIX username created on demand for access and which is now ready to be deleted. This script deletes the given UNIX username, that is, the UNIX users that match the Windows client account are dynamically deleted when the client logs out or releases a service.

The default is a blank string, or no script is called:

```
delete user script =
```

An example to call a script `userdelete` under the /opt/samba/bin directory:

```
delete user script = /opt/samba/bin/userdelete %u
```

Logon script

This parameter is only used when Samba is set up as a logon server. This parameter specifies the file to be downloaded and run on a machine when a client successfully logs in. This parameter accepts the standard substitutions. It enables you to have separate logon scripts for each user or machine. The file must have the DOS-style line endings, such as a Carriage Return/Line Feed. Use DOS or a DOS-friendly text editor to create these scripts.

Create this file on a client machine and then ftp the file to the server. The script must be placed in the path defined by netlogon service. Do not allow write access to the netlogon share. Do not grant users write permission on the batch files. The content of the file is up to you, anything from synchronizing clocks with the time server to mounting the shares for common applications. For example:

```
NET TIME \\SUGAR /SET /YES
NET USE W: \\SUGAR\workutils
```

```
NET USE Y: \\SUGAR\datafiles
NET USE z: \\SUGAR\accounts
```

The default is a blank string, or no script is called:

```
logon script script =
```

An example to set the filename to setenv.bat:

```
logon script = setenv.bat
```

An example to make use of the standard substitution %u for user:

```
logon script = %U.bat
```

You would use this if you've created individual user login batch files:

Logon path

This parameter is only used when Samba is set up as a logon server and your clients use roaming profiles. Roaming profiles are used so that your user can log in from any of a number of similar clients and have the same work environment. This parameter specifies the home directory where roaming profiles are stored. This option takes the standard substitutions. This enables you to have separate logon scripts for each user or machine.

This option also specifies the directory from which the desktop, start menu, network neighborhood, and program folders are loaded for your Windows 95/98 client. This share and the path must be readable by the user or the preferences and directories cannot be loaded on the Windows 95/98 client. The share must be writable at least for the first login. The Windows 95/98 client will create the user.dat and other directories during the first login. After that, the directories and any of the contents can be made read-only. Do not make the user.dat file read-only. Instead, rename it to user.man and set this file to read-only. This is known as the mandatory profile.

The default is:

```
logon path = \\%N\%U\profile
```

An example to set the logon path to the server deal under the home\username directory:

```
logon path = \\DEAL\HOME\%U\PROFILE
```

Logon drive

This parameter is only used when Samba is set up as a logon server for NT workstations. This parameter specifies the local path for the home directory.

The default is a blank string, or no path is specified:

```
logon drive =
```

An example to set the home directory to drive H:

```
logon drive = h:
```

Logon home

This parameter is only used when Samba is set up as a logon server. This parameter specifies the home directory location when a Win95/98 or NT workstation logs into a Samba Primary Domain Controller (PDC). The default is set to look to the NIS maps for an NIS home directory server. This option takes the standard substitutions, enabling you to have separate logon scripts for each user or machine.

The default is set to look for the NIS maps for the session username:

```
logon home = "\\%N\%U"
```

An example to hard code the server name but still use substitutions for the session username:

```
logon home = "\\deal\%U"
```

Domain logons

This parameter specifies whether the Samba server will serve Windows 95/98 clients their workgroup domain logons. Win95/98 domain logons are not the same as Windows NT domain logons.

The default is:

```
domain logons = No
```

To turn Windows 95/98 domain logons on, change the default to:

```
domain logons = Yes
```

Browse options

Browse options can be used to determine how your Samba server acts as a Windows network browser. By setting the parameters, you can have your Samba win browser elections and become the local master browser, supplying network resource information to all clients, or have it lose all browser elections, or have it win against some operating systems and lose against others.

OS level

This parameter specifies what level Samba advertises for browse elections. This parameter determines whether nmbd can become a local master browser for the workgroup. The default is set to lose elections to Windows machines.

The default is:

```
os level = 0
```

An example of a setting that will win against all Windows servers:

```
os level = 65
```

lm announce

This parameter specifies whether nmbd will produce Lanman announce broadcasts that are needed by OS/2 clients. If this setting is set to `false`, OS/2 clients will not be capable of seeing the Samba server in their browse list. This parameter has three values:

`true`   Listens and responds to Lanman announce broadcasts.

`auto`   Responds if Lanman announce broadcasts are detected on the network.

`false`   Does not respond to Lanman announce broadcasts.

The default setting listens for and then responds to Lanman announce broadcasts:

```
lm announce = auto
```

An example to set Samba to never respond to Lanman announce broadcasts:

```
lm announce = false
```

lm interval

If you set the preceding parameter `lm announce` to either `true` or `auto`, this parameter sets the frequency of broadcasts. If this parameter is set to zero, then no Lanman announcements occur. This overrides the setting of the `lm announce` parameter. The parameter is set in seconds.

The default is:

```
lm interval = 60
```

To triple the time between Lanman announce broadcasts, change the default to:

```
lm interval = 180
```

Preferred master

This parameter specifies whether nmbd becomes a preferred master browser for its workgroup. If this parameter is set to `preferred master = Yes`, then nmbd forces a master browser election on startup. By default, it has a slight advantage in winning the election. The `OS level` parameter previously discussed is another place where you can tilt the election in your Samba server's favor. If you set preferred master to `Yes`, you should also set the `domain master = Yes`. Using these three settings together—preferred master = Yes, domain master = Yes, and os level = 65—ensures that nmbd can become a domain master.

This option can be a performance bottleneck if there are several hosts that are set to be preferred master browsers on the same subnet. It doesn't matter whether the servers are Samba, NT, or Windows 95/98 machines—if it's configured to be the master browser, it periodically attempts to become the local master browser. The result is unnecessary broadcast traffic and slower browsing.

The default is:

```
preferred master = No
```

An example to set the Samba server to become the preferred master browser:

```
preferred master = Yes
```

Local master

This parameter specifies whether nmbd will participate in elections to become the local master browser on a subnet. If this parameter is set to `local master = No`, nmbd will not attempt to become a local master browser on a subnet. The server will also lose in all browsing elections. If you set this value to `local master = No`, nmbd will never become a local master browser.

The default is:

```
local master = Yes
```

To turn this option off, change the default to:

```
local master = No
```

Domain master

This parameter specifies whether nmbd will enable wide area network (WAN) browse list collation. This option tells nmbd whether to claim a special, domain-specific NetBIOS name. This NetBIOS name identifies the server as a domain master browser for its given workgroup. Other local master browsers in the same workgroup on broadcast-isolated subnets give this nmbd their local browse lists. These local master browsers then ask smbd for the browse list of the WAN. Browser clients receive the domain-wide browse list from their local master browser. If you are part of a network with Windows NT domain servers, leave this option set to the default. Windows NT Primary Domain Controllers expect to be able to claim this workgroup-specific, special NetBIOS name. If the Samba server takes the NetBIOS name before the Windows NT PDC, then cross-subnet browsing will behave strangely and could even fail.

The default is:

```
domain master = No
```

An example to set this option on:

```
domain master = Yes
```

Browse list

This parameter is the opposite of the domain master = parameter. It specifies whether smbd will serve a browse list to a domain master browser building a wide-area browse list. The Samba server receives information about other servers during this exchange.

The default is:

```
browse list = Yes
```

You should never need to turn this off.

WINS options

The WINS section is where you determine how Samba interacts with any WINS servers, or whether it will become a WINS server.

DNS proxy

This parameter only works if Samba is configured as a WINS server. It specifies whether nmbd will forward name requests to the domain name server when a name isn't found in its WINS database. This is not a great idea unless you have no other way for some clients to get DNS information This is not a performance issue because nmbd spawns a second copy of itself to do the DNS name-lookup requests. The issue is this: If a client is looking for WINS information on your network, how likely is it that your DNS server will know the answer? This parameter will pass a maximum of 15 characters.

The default is:

```
dns proxy = Yes
```

To turn this parameter off and not pass client requests to the DNS server, change the default to:

```
dns proxy = No
```

WINS proxy

This parameter specifies whether nmbd will respond to broadcast name queries on behalf of other hosts. Just as in real life, it's never a good idea to answer for someone else. Setting this parameter to `wins proxy = Yes` could help you troubleshoot network problems. If you can't get services to work without this parameter set to `on`, double-check your settings.

The default is:

```
wins proxy = No
```

An example to turn on WINS proxy:

```
wins proxy = Yes
```

WINS server

This parameter specifies the IP address or DNS name of the WINS server with which nmbd will register. You should have a WINS server defined if you have subnets on your network. Samba must point to a WINS server when subnets are present or browsing will not work correctly. If you have a WINS server on your network, set this parameter to the WINS server's IP address. Even though you can use the DNS name for this option, don't. It can be a performance bottleneck and could even fail. Use the IP address.

The default is a blank string, or no WINS server:

```
wins server =
```

An example to set a WINS server to 192.168.99.24:

```
wins server = 192.168.99.24
```

WINS support

This parameter specifies whether the nmbd process in Samba acts as a WINS server. This should never be set to `Yes` on more than one machine in your network. You should only need to set this to `Yes` if you have a subnetted network and you need a particular nmbd to be your WINS server.

The default is:

```
wins support = No
```

An example to set this option on is:

```
wins support = Yes
```

Locking options

This section, which is only displayed on the Global Advanced page, is where you set the Samba lock options. You can increase your Samba server's performance by setting these parameters correctly.

Kernel oplocks

This parameter is currently only supported by the IRIX OS. This parameter specifies whether kernel-based oplocks will be used. In short, kernel oplocks support allows Samba oplocks to be broken whenever a local UNIX process or NFS operation accesses a file that smbd has oplocked. This parameter defaults to the correct setting based on the system binaries. Linux and FreeBSD developers are both working on implementing kernel oplocks.

The default for IRIX systems is:

```
kernel oplocks = Yes
```

The default for all other systems is:

```
kernel oplocks = No
```

Locking

This parameter specifies whether locking will be performed by the server in response to lock requests from the client. This parameter is useful only to developers. Don't change this option from the default. Setting this option to `locking` = `No` will cause all lock and unlock requests to appear to succeed. However, the server is doing no real locking. If you disable locking either here globally or in a specific service, the lack of locking will result in data corruption.

The default is:

```
locking = Yes
```

An example of something really unwise to do:

```
locking = No
```

OLE locking compatibility

This parameter specifies whether a byte range lock manipulation will be turned on. This is done to give compatibility for OLE applications. The Windows OLE locking can cause certain UNIX lock managers to crash or cause other problems. The default setting enables Samba to get between your OLE application lock requests and the UNIX lock manager. If you set this parameter to `ole locking compatibility = No`, you are trusting your UNIX lock manager to handle this locking request correctly.

The default is:

```
ole locking compatibility = Yes
```

An example to send OLE application lock request on to the UNIX lock manager:

```
ole locking compatibility = No
```

Oplocks

This parameter specifies whether smbd will issue oplocks to file open requests on shares. Using oplocks can speed up access to files on the Samba server. It enables the clients to cache files locally. It is the default for Windows NT servers. Oplocks can be turned off on certain files on a per-share basis. The parameter to do this is the **veto oplock files** that is set under File Handling Options.

The default is:

```
oplocks = Yes
```

To set this option off, change the default to:

```
oplocks = No
```

Strict locking

This parameter specifies how the server handles file locking. When this parameter is set to Yes, the server checks every read and write access for file locks. Access is denied if a lock is present. When this parameter is set to No, the server does file lock checks only at the client's request. This is the default, which provides the best performance.

The default is:

```
strict locking = No
```

To turn this setting on, change the default to:

```
strict locking = Yes
```

Share modes

This parameter specifies whether share modes are used during a file open. These are client modes used to gain exclusive read or write access. If you set this parameter to No, Windows applications will fail. UNIX does not support these open modes. They are simulated in shared memory or through file locks under some flavors of UNIX. This parameter is enabled by default and provides full share compatibility.

The default is:

```
share modes = Yes
```

There is no reason to set this parameter to No.

Miscellaneous options

This section, which is only displayed on the Global Advanced page, is a mixture of parameters. Some of the parameters are used to configure smb.conf for your particular system, while others enable the Samba server to be seen in remote networks. Still others determine what users see when they connect to the Samba server. The options are as follows.

Smbrun

This parameter specifies the full path for the smbrun binary. This defaults to the value used in the makefile. If Samba is installed correctly, you will not need to change this parameter. The default is set in the makefile.f

An example to set the smbrun path to /usr/local/samba/bin:

```
smbrun = /usr/local/samba/bin/smbrun
```

An example to set the smbrun path to /opt/samba/bin:

```
smbrun = /opt/samba/bin/smbrun
```

Preload

This parameter is a list of services that the server automatically adds to the browse lists. This is most useful for home directories or printer services that would otherwise not be visible. The services are space separated.

The default is a blank string, or no services are loaded automatically:

```
preload =
```

This example loads the shares for the server sugar and makes a printer named sparc_printer available:

```
preload = sugar sparc_printer
```

Lock dir

This parameter specifies the directory where lock files will be placed. Lock files are used by Samba to implement the `max connections` parameter.

The default creates a directory called samba under /tmp:

```
lock dir = /tmp/samba
```

An example to place this directory under /var/samba/locks:

```
lock dir = /var/samba/locks
```

Default service

This parameter specifies the name of a service that will be connected if the requested service is not found. There is no default value for this parameter. If this parameter is not given, attempting to connect to a nonexistent service results in an error.

Typically, the default service is a guest-OK, read-only service. Also, the apparent service name will be changed to equal that of the requested service. This is very useful because it enables you to use macros such as `%S` to make a wildcard service.

Any _ characters in the name of the service used in the `default ser-vice` parameter will be mapped to a /.

The default is a blank string, or no service will be substituted if the requested service is not available. The client receives an error message when the request fails:

```
default service =
```

An example of setting the default service named access_tmp:

```
default service = access_tmp
```

Message command

This parameter specifies the command to run when the server receives a WinPopup-style message. The command specified delivers the message. How it delivers the message depends on the services you run on your server. You can make this command send mail, pop open an edit program with the message in it, or even just delete it. The messages are delivered as the global guest user. If you come up with a method that works well for your network, forward a copy of your solution to the Samba team. This command takes the standard substitutions, except that `%u` will not work. These three substitutions apply to all messages:

`%s`   The filename containing the message

`%t`   The destination to which the message was sent (probably the server name)

`%f`   Who the message is from

The default is a blank string, or no message command. Samba will report an error when a client tries to send a WinPopup message:

```
message command =
```

An example to send the message through the shell into an xedit session and then erase the message:

```
message command = csh -c 'xedit %s;rm %s' &
```

The **&** at the end of the command string puts this series of commands to the background. This is done to prevent the client from freezing while waiting for the command to complete.

Here's a way of sending the messages as mail to root:

```
message command = /bin/mail -s /
'message from %f on %m' root < %s; rm %s
```

This example just silently deletes the message:

```
message command = rm %s
```

Dfree command

This parameter should only be used on systems where a problem occurs with the UNIX system's internal disk space calculations. The symptom is the error `Abort, Retry, Ignore` at the end of each directory listing. This problem has been documented only with Ultrix systems. This parameter is not set by default. Don't set it without researching the current bug fixes for this problem.

The default is a blank string, or there is no command substituted for the disk-free system command:

```
dfree command =
```

An example to call a script called dfree from the directory /opt/samba/bin:

```
dfree command = /opt/samba/bin/dfree
```

Valid chars

This parameter specifies additional characters that are to be considered valid by the server in filenames. This is useful for national character sets such as if you need to use the ü or Å. The option takes a list of characters, either in integer or character form using space separators. If you put a colon between two characters, they will be taken for a lowercase:uppercase pair. For this parameter to work as expected, it must be set after the `client code page` parameter. This is the default in the samba.conf file. If the `client code page` parameter is set after the `valid chars` parameter, the settings will be overwritten. See more about the settings for the `client code page` parameter in the Filename Handling section.

It is difficult to correctly produce a `valid chars` line for a particular system. A program has been added to the Samba distribution to help automate the process. The program, called `validchars`, automatically produces a complete `valid chars` line for a given client system. The program, examples with a .oout extension, and the source code are located in the examples/validchar subdirectory of the samba directory. This program was written by tino@augsburg.net.

The default is a blank string, or no additional valid characters are mapped to the client code page:

```
valid chars =
```

Remote announce

This parameter specifies whether nmbd periodically announces itself to the specified IP addresses, even across subnets, and can include a workgroup name. If the workgroup name is not included, then it defaults to the setting of the workgroup parameter. This was the first parameter set under Base Options. This parameter is useful if you need your Samba server to share resources with a remote workgroup. This setting adds another method for the browse propagation rules under Samba. The remote workgroup can be anywhere as long as you can send IP packets to it. If the network connections are stable, try setting this parameter to the IP addresses of known browse masters for the remote workgroup.

The default is a blank string, or no remote announcements:

```
remote announce =
```

An example to configure nmbd to announce itself to the two IP addresses using the workgroup names QandA and ENGINEERS:

```
remote announce = 192.168.99.24/QandA
192.168.100.124/ENGINEERS
```

Remote browse sync

This parameter only works with other Samba servers. This parameter specifies whether nmbd will request synchronization of browse lists with the master browser of another Samba server on a remote segment. This option enables a server to gain browse lists for multiple workgroups across routed networks. It only works with other Samba servers. This parameter will work as expected as long as Samba can send IP packets to the server specified for synchronization.

The default is an empty string, or no other Samba servers are identified for remote browse synchronization:

```
remote browse sync =
```

An example that would configure Samba to try to synchronize browse list with Samba servers on IP addresses 192.168.99.24 and 192.168.100.100:

```
remote browse sync = 192.168.99.24 192.168.100.100
```

When you specify addresses for this parameter, Samba sends the packets. No validation is attempted in any way.

Socket address

This parameter specifies the address that Samba listens on for connections. This parameter is used to configure multiple virtual interfaces on one server. Each Samba server specified can have a different configuration.

The default is 0.0.0.0, or Samba will listen and accept connections on any address:

```
socket address = 0.0.0.0
```

An example to set the socket address to IP address 198.168.99.124:

```
socket address = 192.168.99.124
```

Homedir map

This parameter only works if you are using NIS home directories. This parameter also requires that Samba is configured as a login server and the nis homedir parameter is set to Y (which maps to True for the nis homedir parameter in the smb.conf file) (nis homedir is discussed later in this section after the time offset and unix realname parameters).

This parameter specifies the NIS map that the server will use to locate the user's home directory. This parameter uses the SUN auto.home file format to extract directory information.

The default is:

```
homedir map = auto.home
```

Time offset

This parameter specifies a setting in minutes to add to the normal GMT to local time conversion. This is a legacy setting for old clients that can't handle daylight savings time (DST) correctly.

The default is zero, or time is not offset for your clients:

```
time offset = 0
```

An example if you had clients that couldn't handle DST:

```
time offset = 60
```

UNIX realname

This parameter only works if you are using the UNIX password file for your clients. It specifies whether Samba will supply the realname field from the UNIX password file to the client.

The default is the client is not supplied the realname field:

```
unix realname = No
```

An example to supply the realname field for the UNIX password file:

```
unix realname = Yes
```

nis homedir

This parameter requires that the Samba server be configured as a login server. The NIS server should also be configured as a Samba server when you are integrating Samba and NIS. Doing so helps avoid possible performance bottlenecks and enables clients to talk directly with the NIS server when mapping their home directories.

The parameter specifies whether Samba will use NIS home directories, even if the home directories reside on another server. Samba consults the

NIS map specified in the `homedir map` parameter and returns the home directories based on the NIS map listed there.

The default is `No`, or NIS maps are not searched by default, this maps to a value of False for the `nis homedir` parameter in the smb.conf file:

```
nis homedir = No
```

An example to set this parameter on and search the NIS map for a client's home directory information:

nis homedir = YesWide links

This parameter specifies whether the Samba server is to follow links in the UNIX file system. It sets access only to areas that are outside the directory tree being exported. This parameter is for the paranoid system administrator. If your permissions are correct, setting this option to `Yes` will not break your system's security.

The default is set to enable Samba to follow links outside the directory tree exported:

```
wide links = Yes
```

To turn this option off, change the default to:

```
 wide links = No
```

Follow symlinks

This parameter specifies whether smbd will follow symbolic links. If this parameter is set to `No`, the user receives an error when the file or directory they attempt to access is a symbolic link. This option not only stops users from following symbolic links, it also prevents them from making symbolic links. It could be a useful security tool if your users are linking to server files on their home directories.

The default is `Yes`, which means that Samba follows symbolic links:

```
follow symlinks = Yes
```

This example turns the parameter off and prevents Samba from following symbolic links:

```
follow symlinks = No
```

Delete read-only

This parameter specifies whether DOS read-only files can be deleted. This parameter enables the UNIX file permissions to override the DOS file-level control. It has been suggested that this parameter can be useful for running applications such as a revision control system. There could be a situation where UNIX file ownership prevents changing file permissions and DOS semantics prevent deletion of a read-only file.

The default is set to No, or read-only files will not be deleted:

```
delete readonly = No
```

To set this parameter to on and enable the deletion of DOS read-only files, change the default to:

```
delete readonly = Yes
```

DOS filetimes

This parameter specifies whether smbd will use DOS or POSIX standards for file timestamping. The DOS/Windows standard is that if a user can write to a file, the timestamp can be changed. The POSIX standard is that only the owner of the file or root may change the timestamp. Samba is set to the POSIX standard by default. Setting this option to Yes enables smbd to change the file timestamp as DOS requires.

The default is set to No, or only the owner and root can change timestamps:

```
dos filetimes = No
```

An example to set Samba to the DOS/Windows standard and enable any user who can write to a file to change the timestamp:

```
dos filetimes = Yes
```

DOS filetime resolution

This parameter is used to resolve problems that occur when using the DOS/Windows FAT file system. The finest granularity the FAT file system can use for time resolution is two seconds. This can cause some compatibility problems when using some products such as the Microsoft Visual

Programming Languages with Samba shares. The problem occurs when oplocks are enabled on a share (oplocks are discussed in the Locking options section). If oplocks are enabled on a share, then Microsoft Visual Programming Language will use two different time-reading calls to check whether a file has changed since the last read. The first call uses a one-second granularity. The other uses a two-second granularity. The two-second call rounds any odd second down. So, when a file has a timestamp of an odd number of seconds, the two timestamps do not match. When this occurs, the Microsoft Visual Programming Language always reports the file has changed.

When this parameter is set to `Yes` on a share, Samba rounds the reported time down to the nearest even two-second boundary. When the two timestamps are set to match through this parameter, the Microsoft Visual Programming Language is happy and reports file creation time correctly for revisions.

The default is No, or file creation times do not get rounded:

```
dos filetime resolution = No
```

An example to set this option to `Yes` and perform file creation time rounding to fool some products such as Microsoft Visual Programming Languages:

```
dos filetime resolution = Yes
```

Fake directory create times

This parameter also fudges directory creation times for compatibility with Microsoft Visual Programming Languages using Samba shares. Even the newer file systems, such as NTFS and Windows VFAT file systems, keep a create time that is not the same as the UNIX ctime, or status change time. Samba by default reports the earliest of the various times UNIX does keep. This can cause the compiler to rebuild objects that have not changed. Setting this parameter for a share causes Samba to always report midnight 1-1-1980 as the create time for directories.

The default is `No`, or Samba reports the UNIX create times:

```
fake directory create times = No
```

To set this parameter to `Yes` and make Samba shares report a create time compatible with Microsoft Visual Programming compilers using Samba shares, change the default to:

```
fake directory create times = Yes
```

Panic action

This parameter is for Samba developers. It calls a system command when either smbd or nmbd crashes. It's used to notify the developer that his or her change failed.

The default is an empty string, or no panic action is set. Don't worry — your users will tell you when services crash:

```
panic action =
```

An example to send a mail message to root when a Samba service crashes:

```
panic action = /bin/mail -s 'Samba Server %L needs help!'
root < %s; rm %s
```

Share Parameters Advanced View

The Shares button links to the Create and Delete Share Page. If you input something into the drop-down box, SWAT creates a share with that name (think of it as a feature). Picking any of the three buttons — Choose Share, Delete Share, or Create Share — takes you to the Share Parameter Options page. The Share Parameter Options page adds three buttons below the Choose, Delete, and Create Share buttons: Commit Changes, Reset Values, and Advanced View. Click Advanced View to display all parameters including all the Basic Parameters. This section covers the parameters in the Advanced View. After becoming familiar with Samba, you might only need to set subsequent parameters on the Basic View Page, but you should be familiar with all the parameters under the Advanced View Page first.

Base options

The Base options section is where you set the comment for the share, and where you set the path the share will access.

Comment

This parameter defines the text field visible next to a share when a client displays the shares on the server.

The default is a blank string, or no comment is displayed for the share:

```
comment =
```

An example to set a comment to display with the share:

```
comment = Plans to take over the world tonight
```

Path

This parameter specifies the directory accessed for the service. If you were configuring print services, this would be the spool directory. This path is based on the root directory set under Global Variables, Security Options. This parameter accepts standard substitutions. Two substitutions useful for this parameter are:

%u   The UNIX username the client is using on this connection

%m   The NetBIOS name of the machine

The default is a blank string. If you set your root directory to the root file system or /, the blank string defaults to the root file system.

```
path =
```

If you define your root directory as root directory = /opt/samba and you define:

```
path = /printer/spoolfiles
```

then the service would look for /opt/samba/printer/spoolfiles as the directory for the print service.

Security options

The Security options section is where you set up the allowed or denied users and groups, and the rights they have to the share. It is also the place where you set up guest access to a share.

Revalidate

This parameter only works with `security = share`; it is ignored if this is not the case. This parameter controls whether Samba enables a previously validated user and password pair to be used to attach to another share. The default is to enable access without revalidating. If you set `revalidate = Yes` and then connect to \\sugar\lesh and then tried to connect to \\sugar\hart, Samba won't automatically enable the client connection to the second share, even though it's the same username, without supplying the password.

The default is:

```
revalidate = No
```

To set this option to require revalidation for each resource:

```
revalidate = Yes
```

Username

This is a legacy parameter for DOS and Windows for Workgroups clients. It can be both a security loophole and performance hit. This parameter enables multiple users to be specified in a comma-delimited list. This parameter does not restrict who can log in. It supplies the Samba server with usernames that might correspond to the supplied password. This parameter accepts group options, but searching though the groups database can be slow and some clients might timeout during the search. The supplied password is tested against each username in turn.

The group substitutions are:

`@username`	Check first in the NIS netgroups, then in the Unix groups database
`+username`	Check only in the Unix groups database
`&username`	Check only in the NIS netgroups database

The default is blank, or no users defined:

```
username =
```

An example to set a list of users for Samba to try:

```
username = straw, rubin, jack, jane, @roomers
```

Guest account

This is a username used for access to services that are specified as `guest` `ok`. The privileges this user has are available to any client connecting to the guest service. This user must exist in the password file, but should not have a valid login. The traditional UNIX system default guest account `nobody` might not be capable of printing. You should test this by logging in as your guest user and trying to print using the system print command. If you cannot print from this account, use another account. The user account `ftp` is another a good choice for this parameter.

The default is specified at compile time, usually `nobody`.

```
guest account = nobody
```

An example to map the guest account to the ftp user:

```
guest account = ftp
```

Invalid users

This is a list of users that are not allowed to log in to this service. The best use for this parameter is to set `invalid users = administrator` if you don't want cross-platform administration. This parameter also takes groups as an option.

The variables are:

+group	Check local UNIX group file
&group	Check NIS group file

These variables can also be used together:

+&group	Check local UNIX group file and then NIS group file
&+group	Check NIS group file and then local UNIX file

The third variable that checks both is:

`@group`   Check NIS group file and then local group file

The default is no invalid users, or blank:

```
invalid users =
```

To set the NT administrator to an invalid user, change the default to:

```
invalid users = administrator admin
```

Valid users

This parameter is a list of users that should be allowed to log in to this service. It is not required. The default is an empty string, or anyone can log in. If you define a username in both the valid users list and the invalid users list, the invalid list wins, and that user is denied access. This parameter also takes groups as an option.

The variables are:

`+group`   Check local UNIX group file

`&group`   Check NIS group file

These variables can also be used together:

`+&group`   Check local UNIX group file and then NIS group file

`&+group`   Check NIS group file and then local UNIX file

The third variable that checks both is:

`@group`   Check NIS group file and then local group file

The default is a blank string, or all users are valid.

```
valid users =
```

To set a username phil and the wheel group (either NIS or local, whichever it finds first) as the only valid users, change the default to:

```
valid users = phil, @wheel
```

Admin users

This parameter is a list of users who are granted administrative privileges on the share. You are making this user root on shares.

The default is a blank string, or no admin users:

```
admin users =
```

An example to set a user georgeh to be an admin user:

```
admin users = georgeh
```

Read list

This parameter is a list of users who get read-only access to a service. This parameter also takes groups as an option.

The variables are:

+group	Check local UNIX group file
&group	Check NIS group file

These variables can also be used together:

+&group	Check local UNIX group file and then NIS group file
&+group	Check NIS group file and then local UNIX file

The third variable that checks both is:

@group	Check NIS group file and then local group file

The default is an empty string, or no users are limited to read-only access.

An example to set users phil and cheese to read-only access:

```
read list = phil, cheese
```

Write list

This parameter is a list of users that are given write and read privileges, even if this service is set to read-only. If you define a user in both the read list and the write list, the write list wins and that user is given write access. This parameter also takes groups as an option.

The variables are:

+group	Check local UNIX group file
&group	Check NIS7 group file

These variables can also be used together:

`+&group`	Check local UNIX group file and then NIS group file
`&+group`	Check NIS group file and then local UNIX file

The third variable that checks both is:

`@group`	Check NIS group file and then local group file

The default is an empty string, or no users are given write access above the set file permissions.

```
write list =
```

An example to set users administrator and root, plus all users in the wheel group:

```
write list = admin, root, @wheel
```

Force user

This parameter specifies a UNIX username assigned as the default user for all who connect to the service. This is both a blessing and a curse. Samba implements the forced username after a connection has been established. Clients still need a valid username and password. All file actions performed during that session are logged to the forced username. Plan carefully if you use this parameter.

The default is a blank string, or no forced user:

```
force user =
```

An example to force the username for file operations on this share to cheese:

```
force user = cheese
```

Do not force the username for file operations on this share to root.

Force group

This parameter specifies a UNIX group name assigned as the default primary group for all users who connect to the service. This parameter is a blessing for sharing files because it forces a service to use the group specified for the permissions. It's a quick and easy way to set permissions if you have large base of clients to support.

The default is a blank string, or no forced group:

```
force group =
```

An example to set the `force group` to samba_group:

```
force group = samba_group
```

Read-only

This parameter specifies whether a share is read-only. You must set this parameter to `No` if you want to make the share available for writing.

The default is `Yes`, or the share is read-only:

```
read-only = Yes
```

An example to make the share available for writing:

```
read-only = No
```

Create mask

This parameter is where permissions are mapped from DOS modes to UNIX permissions. This is really a translation of client permissions to UNIX octal permissions for user, group, and world. The default value is full permissions for owner and read-only permission for group and world. This parameter does not affect directory modes. There is a separate parameter for the directory mode. There is also a `force create mode` parameter for forcing particular permissions to be set on created files.

The default is full permission for owner and read-only for all others. This permission octet translates to 744:

```
create mask = 744
```

An example to add executing privilege for all users:

```
create mask = 755
```

Force create mode

This parameter specifies the octal permissions that will be set on a file created by Samba. The default for this parameter is 000, or no access is given anyone by Samba. This isn't as radical as it sounds. The owner provides access permissions. This parameter is applied after `create mask`.

The default is:

```
force create mode = 000
```

An example to set permissions to full access for owner, read and execute for members of the same group, and read for everyone else:

```
force create mode = 754
```

Directory mask

This parameter sets the octal modes that are used when converting DOS modes to UNIX modes when creating UNIX directories. When a directory is created, the necessary permissions are calculated. This parameter is the octal mask for the UNIX directory. The default value of this parameter provides read and execute permissions for group and world. The owner is given full access.

The default is:

```
directory mask = 755
```

An example to set permissions to full access for owner and read and write privileges for members of the same group and all other users:

```
directory mask = 766
```

Force directory mode

This parameter specifies the UNIX permissions that will always be set on a directory created by Samba. The default for this parameter is 000, or no permissions will be added for a directory created by Samba. This operation occurs after applying the parameter `directory mask`. Again, as with the forced `create mode` parameter, this isn't as radical as it sounds. The owner of the directory provides access permissions.

The default is:

```
force directory mode = 000
```

An example to provide full access for owner, read and execute for group, and read-only for everyone else:

```
force directory mode = 754
```

Guest only

This parameter will not work if guest access is not allowed on a Global Level setting and if the next parameter is guest ok = No. Setting this parameter to guest only = No does not disable guest access.

The default is that the guest account is not the only user account that is enabled to access the share:

```
guest only = No
```

An example to set the share permissions so only guest user account access is enabled for this share:

```
guest only = Yes
```

Guest ok

This parameter specifies whether a share can be accessed by the guest user account. The default is set to No, or the share requires a valid username and password to connect:

```
guest ok = No
```

An example to allow guest access to the share:

```
guest ok = Yes
```

Only user

This parameter specifies whether only the user accounts listed in the user = parameter are granted access rights to the share.

The default is No, or the client's username and password are passed along to another security check:

```
only user = No
```

An example to set this option to Yes, or only users specifically listed in the user = parameter are granted access rights to the share:

```
only user = Yes
```

Hosts allow

This parameter is a comma-, space-, or tab-delimited list of hosts permitted to access the share. If this is specified in the Global Variables section, then it applies to all services. The Global setting wins even when the individual service has a different setting. Name, IP address, or network/netmask pairs can specify the hosts. You can also specify by NIS netgroup names if your system supports NIS netgroups. You can use the except keyword to limit a wildcard list.

Caution

If you use the hosts allow parameter, you must include local-host in the string of hosts. Samba requires access to the local-host interface to function as expected.

The default is a blank string, or all hosts are allowed access:

```
hosts allow =
```

The following examples provide some help in using this parameter. An example to allow localhost and all IP addresses in 192.168.*.* :

```
hosts allow = localhost, 192.168.*.*
```

An example to allow localhost and hosts that match the given network/netmask:

```
hosts allow = localhost, 192.168.99.0/255.255.255.0
```

An example to allow a localhost and two others by name:

```
hosts allow = localhost, terrapin, deal
```

An example to allow localhost and a subnet with one exception:

```
Host allow = localhost, 192.168.99.0 EXCEPT
192.168.99.222
```

If your network uses NIS netgroups, you can use those with the @ option as we've used for other options. The + and & options do not apply to this parameter. The following example enables access for a NIS group marshotel and localhost.

```
hosts allow = @marshotel, localhost
```

Hosts deny

This parameter is the opposite of `hosts allow`. The hosts you list here are not permitted access to services. If this is specified in the Global Variable section also, the value in the Global section wins over the specific share setting specified here.

The default is a blank string, or no hosts are denied access.

An example to deny the 192.168.111.* subnet:

```
hosts deny = 192.168.111.*
```

Logging options

The Logging options section of SWAT defines only one parameter at the moment, the status parameter.

Status

You should not need to set this parameter. If you set this to `status` = No, smbstatus will not be able to tell if the service is active.

The default is:

```
status = Yes
```

An example to set this parameter so smbstatus can't tell whether the connection is active:

```
status = No
```

Tuning options

This section defines a few share-related parameters that can influence your Samba server's performance. A good setting for a parameter can increase performance, while a poor setting can decrease performance.

Max connections

This parameter specifies the number of simultaneous connections allowed for a service. The default value of zero means an unlimited number of connections can be made to the share. Any value specified that is greater than zero results in connections that are refused when the number of connections to the service that are already open is equal to your setting. Samba uses record lock files to implement this feature. The lock files are stored in the directory specified by the `lock directory` parameter. The `lock directory` parameter is set under the Global Variables ⇨ Miscellaneous Options.

The default is zero, or there is no limit for the maximum number of connections for this share:

```
max connections = 0
```

An example to set the maximum number of connections for this share to 100, or the 101st simultaneous request for access to this share will be refused:

```
max connections = 100
```

Strict sync

This parameter is used to compensate for the difference between what Windows clients think of as a sync and what UNIX systems believe is a sync. A UNIX sync call forces the process to be suspended until all outstanding data in the kernel disk buffers has been stored in the specified storage area. This is very slow. In ancient days, it was necessary to ensure data validity. The default setting enables smbd to ignore the Windows client applications requests for a sync call. There is a possibility of losing data if your server crashes. This is a very slim chance based on typical UNIX server performance. The default parameter also fixes performance problems reported with the new Windows Explorer for Windows 98.

The default is No, or UNIX sync does not take place at the client's request:

```
strict sync = No
```

Setting `strict sync` to `Yes` will cause performance problems for your server. Only use it as a troubleshooting tool:

```
strict sync = Yes
```

Sync always

This parameter has no effect if the `strict sync` parameter is set to `no`.

This parameter specifies if writes should always be written to disk storage before the write call returns. The default setting enables the server to be guided by the client's request with each write call. If this parameter is set to `Yes`, every write is followed by an `fsync()` call to force the data to be written to disk.

The default is:

```
sync always = No
```

An example to set this parameter on (this has no effect if you've set `strict sync = no`):

```
sync always = Yes
```

Filename handling

The Filename Handling section lets you specify how your Samba will handle filenames, and how it will present filenames to users accessing shares from different clients. The parameters here also let you hide some files for protection.

Default case

This parameter specifies the default case of all files and directories created by clients on your Samba server. The setting you choose here is passed to the parameters `mangle case`, `preserve case`, and `short preserve case`, which were described earlier in this chapter.

The default is lowercase for all files and directories created by clients under the Samba server:

```
default case = lower
```

An example to set your files and directories to all uppercase:

```
default case = upper
```

Case sensitive

This parameter specifies whether filenames are case sensitive. The default is filenames are not case sensitive. Samba performs a filename search and matches all passed names when this parameter is set to No.

The default is:

```
case sensitive = No
```

An example to set filenames to be case sensitive:

```
case sensitive = Yes
```

Preserve case

This parameter specifies whether new filenames will be created with the case that the client passes. If you set this parameter to No, then filenames are forced to the default case.

The default is:

```
preserve case = Yes
```

An example to turn preserve case off and force filenames to the default case:

```
preserve case = No
```

Short preserve

This parameter specifies whether new files created in uppercase and of suitable length are left as uppercase or if they are forced to be the default case. This parameter can be used in conjunction with the `preserve case`

=Yes. This enables long filenames to retain their case, while files with short names are lowercased.

The default is:

```
short preserve case = Yes
```

An example to turn short filename case preserve off:

```
short preserve case = No
```

Mangle case

This parameter specifies whether filenames of existing files are mangling to the default case. This is done for legacy clients that might choke on a mixed-case filename.

The default is No, or existing filenames are passed to clients in their original case even if mixed:

```
mangle case = No
```

An example to turn mangle case on and send all filenames as the default case:

```
mangle case = Yes
```

Mangling char

This parameter specifies which character is used as the magic character in name mangling. The default is a tilde, but this can interfere with some software. You can use this option to set the mangling character to whatever you prefer.

The default is:

```
mangling char = ~
```

An example to set the mangling character to an underbar:

```
mangling char = _
```

Hide dot files

This parameter specifies whether files starting with a dot appear as hidden files. Hidden files are not displayed with the default file list commands.

The default is:

```
hide dot files = Yes
```

An example to show all files with a dot as the first character:

```
hide dot files = No
```

Delete veto files

This parameter specifies what Samba will do when it attempts to delete a directory that contains one or more vetoed directories. The default setting `veto files = No` will fail for deletes if a vetoed directory contains any nonvetoed files or directories. This is how you want Samba to behave. If this option is set to `veto files = Yes`, then Samba attempts to recursively delete any files and directories within the vetoed directory. This setting enables these directories to be transparently deleted when the parent directory is deleted. The user must have the proper permissions to perform the deletion or it will fail no matter how this parameter is set.

The default is:

```
delete veto files = No
```

An example to set delete veto files to **Yes**:

```
delete veto files = Yes
```

Veto files

This parameter is a list of files and directories that are neither visible nor accessible to your clients. However, one feature of the `veto files` parameter that is important to be aware of is that if a directory contains nothing but files that match the veto files parameter, the directory is deleted. Then the veto files within that directory are automatically deleted with the directory as long as the user has UNIX permissions to do so. Also, the `case sensitive` parameter applies to veto files. This parameter affects the performance of Samba. If you define `veto files`, Samba must check all files and directories for a match as they are scanned.

The default is a blank string, or no files and directories are set as `veto files`.

If you are setting up `veto files`, each entry in the list must be separated by a /, which allows spaces to be included. The wildcards * and ? can be used to specify multiple files or directories. Each entry must be a UNIX path, but cannot include the UNIX directory separator /.

An example to veto any files that end in .tmp or any directory that contains the word root:

```
veto files = /*.tmp/*root*/
```

Hide files

This parameter specifies a list of files or directories that are not visible but which are accessible. The DOS hidden attribute is applied to any files or directories that match. Each entry in the list must be separated by a /, which allows spaces to be included. The wildcards * and ? can be used to specify multiple files or directories. Each entry must be a UNIX path, but cannot include the UNIX directory separator. Also, the `case sensitive` parameter applies to hide files. This parameter affects the performance of Samba. If you define `hide files`, Samba must check all files and directories for a match as they are scanned.

The default is a blank string, or no files and directories are set as hidden files.

An example to hide any files that end in .log:

```
hide files = /*.log/
```

Veto oplock files

This parameter is only valid when the `oplocks` parameter is turned on for a share. It enables the Samba administrator to selectively turn off the granting of oplocks on selected files that match a wildcard list, similar to the wildcard list used in the `veto files` parameter. This parameter is useful for files that clients will heavily contend for.

The default is a blank string, or no files are vetoed for oplock grants.

An example to set all files ending in *.cookie for oplock:

```
veto oplock files = /*.cookie/
```

Map system

This parameter specifies whether DOS-style system files should be mapped to the UNIX group execute bit. This parameter requires that the `create mask` parameter (see Security options) be set so that the group execute bit is set on.

The default is:

```
map system = No
```

An example to set this parameter on:

```
map system = Yes
```

Map hidden

This parameter specifies whether DOS-style hidden files should be mapped to the UNIX world execute bit. This parameter requires that the `create mask` parameter be set under Global Parameters, Security Options so that the world execute bit is set on.

The default is:

```
map hidden = No
```

An example to set this parameter on:

```
map hidden = Yes
```

Map archive

This parameter specifies whether the DOS archive attribute should be mapped to the UNIX owner execute bit. The DOS archive bit is set when a file has been modified since its last backup. One motivation for this option is to keep Samba and its clients from making any file it touches from becoming executable under UNIX. This parameter requires that the `create mask` parameter under Global Variables, Security Options be set so that the user execute bit is set on.

The default is:

```
map archive = Yes
```

An example to set this parameter off:

```
map archive = No
```

Mangled names

This parameter specifies how your clients will see UNIX files. It determines whether UNIX files and directories that have incompatible names should be mapped to DOS-compatible names and made visible, or if those names should simply be ignored. Five parameters are set to determine how name mangling occurs. Set this parameter if name mangling is requested. The name mangling enables a file to be copied between UNIX directories by clients while retaining the long UNIX filename. If you have files in a directory share, the same first five alphanumeric characters in the name-mangling algorithm can cause name collisions. The chance of such a clash occurring is very slim.

The default is:

```
mangled names = Yes
```

An example to turn off this parameter:

```
mangled names = No
```

Mangled map

This parameter specifies a direct map of UNIX file names that are not Windows/DOS compatible. If you don't want to use name mangling, this option is quite useful. There are some documents with file extensions that differ between DOS and UNIX. For example, under UNIX it is common to use `.html` for HTML files, whereas under Windows/DOS, `.htm` is the file extension used for HTML. In the example, the UNIX `html` is mapped to the Windows/DOS `htm` extension.

The default is:

```
no mangled map
```

To map html to htm, you would use:

```
mangled map = (*.html *.htm)
```

Browse option

The Browse Option section only defines one parameter at the moment, the browseable parameter.

Browseable

This parameter specifies whether the share is visible in the list of available shares in a net view and in the browse list. This parameter does not make a share unavailable, only invisible, by default. The default is that all shares are available for browsing.

The default is:

```
browseable = Yes
```

An example to set a share to be invisible in the net view and browse list:

```
browseable = No
```

Locking options

The Locking options section lets you specify the file-locking options that Samba will use. You can increase your server's performance with proper use of locking options.

Blocking locks

This parameter specifies whether smbd can lock files requested by a client using a byte-range lock on a region of an open file. The request also has a time limit associated with it. When this parameter is set to Yes and the lock range requested cannot be satisfied, Samba versions 2.0 and later internally queue the lock request. Samba then attempts periodically to obtain the lock until the timeout period expires. If this parameter is set to No, then Samba 2.0 behaves as previous versions of Samba (1.9 and before) — the lock request fails immediately when the lock range cannot be satisfied. If you use this parameter, it can be set on a per-share basis.

The default is `Yes`, or Samba will use a byte-range lock:

```
blocking locks = Yes
```

An example to turn this option off, implementing Samba behavior prior to version 2.0:

```
blocking locks = No
```

Fake oplocks

This parameter is outdated. Samba has implemented real oplocks, which you set under Global Parameters, Locking Options. One use for `fake oplocks` is on read-only file systems or file systems dedicated to one client. In these two cases, using `fake oplocks` could provide a performance improvement. If you use this option for services that are accessed by multiple clients, data will be corrupted. Don't take the chance — leave this option set to `No`.

This option is disabled by default:

```
fake oplocks = No
```

An example to turn this option on:

```
fake oplocks = Yes
```

Locking

This parameter specifies whether the server will perform locking in response to lock requests from the client. This parameter is useful only to developers. Don't change this option from the default. Setting this option to `locking = No` causes all lock and unlock requests to appear to succeed. However, the server is doing no real locking. If you disable locking either here or globally, the lack of locking results in data corruption.

The default is:

```
locking = Yes
```

Oplocks

This parameter specifies whether smbd issues oplocks to file-open requests on shares. Using oplocks can speed up access to files on the Samba server. It enables clients to cache files locally. It is the default for Windows NT servers. Oplocks can be turned off on certain files on a per-share basis. The parameter to do this is the `veto oplock files` in File Handling Options.

The default is:

```
oplocks = Yes
```

An example to set this option off:

```
oplocks = No
```

Strict locking

This parameter specifies how the server handles file locking. When this parameter is set to `Yes`, the server checks every read and write access for file locks. Access is denied if there is a lock present. When this parameter is set to `No`, the server does file lock checks only at the client's request. This is the default and provides the best performance.

The default is:

```
strict locking = No
```

An example to turn this setting on:

```
strict locking = Yes
```

Share modes

This parameter specifies whether share modes will be used when opening a file. These are client modes used to gain exclusive read or write access. If you set this parameter to `No`, Windows applications will fail. UNIX does not support these open modes. They are simulated in shared memory or through file locks under some flavors of UNIX. This parameter is enabled by default and provides full share compatibility.

The default is:

```
share modes = Yes
```

There is no reason to set this parameter to No.

Miscellaneous options

The Miscellaneous options section is where you can customize shares for users by using **exec** and **postexec** commands and magic scripts. It also tells how to customize which files are available in a share.

Exec

This parameter (also known as **preexec**) specifies the name of a script or scripts to run when the client connects to a service. The script runs with the user ID of the current session user. This is the place to work magic for your clients, or you can do even simple things such as generating a custom log message when a user connects.

The default is an empty string, or no scripts are run:

```
exec =
```

An example to pass a message to a log file at connection time:

```
exec = echo 'At %T %u connected to %S' /
> /opt/samba/connect.log
```

Postexec

This parameter specifies the name of a script or scripts to run when the client disconnects from a service. The script runs with the user ID of the current session user. The command can be run as the root on some systems. This is useful if you need to dismount file systems after terminating a connection.

The default is a blank string, or no scripts are run:

```
postexec =
```

An example to post the disconnect time for your user's session:

```
exec = echo 'At %T %u disconnected from %S' /
> /opt/samba/connect.log
```

Root preexec

This parameter is the root-user version of exec and preexec. It allows root to run scripts necessary for the user environment. The most common use is to mount file systems.

The default is a blank string, or no scripts are run by root at the service startup:

```
root preexec =
```

An example to use the root preexec parameter to issue a mount command:

```
root preexec = /bin/mount —ro /cdrom
```

Root postexec

This parameter is the root user version of postexec. It enables root to run scripts when the user disconnects from the service. The most common use is to unmount file systems.

The default is a blank string, or no scripts are run by root at the service startup:

```
root preexec =
```

An example to use the root preexec parameter to issue a mount command:

```
root preexec = /bin/unmount /cdrom
```

Available

This parameter specifies whether a service is available. If you set this parameter to No, then all attempts to connect to the service will fail. The failures are logged.

The default is set to Yes, or the service is available:

```
available = Yes
```

Setting this parameter to No turns off the service and prevents connections:

```
available = No
```

Volume

This parameter specifies an override of the volume label returned for a share. This can be useful for CD-ROMs shared from the Samba server when Windows or DOS installation programs insist on a particular volume label.

The default is the name of the share.

An example to set your CD-ROM share to D:

```
volume = D:
```

Fstype

This parameter specifies the type of file system a share reports when a client queries the file system type. This parameter only sets what Samba tells the client. It does not change the file system structure.

The default is NTFS for compatibility with Windows NT:

```
fstype = NTFS
```

An example to set the reported file system type to FAT:

```
fstype = FAT
```

Set directory

This parameter is used with Digital Pathworks clients. It specifies whether a client can use the `setdir` command to change directories.

The default is `No` because most clients are not Digital Pathworks clients:

```
set directory = No
```

An example to set this option to `Yes` for your Digital Pathworks clients:

```
set directory = Yes
```

Wide links

This parameter specifies whether the Samba server will follow links in the UNIX file system. It sets access only to areas that are outside the directory tree being exported. This parameter is for the paranoid system administrator. If your permissions are correct, setting this option to Yes will not break your system's security.

The default is set to allow Samba to follow links outside the directory tree exported:

```
wide links = Yes
```

An example to turn this option off:

```
wide links = No
```

Follow symlinks

This parameter specifies whether smbd follows symbolic links. If this parameter is set to No, the user gets an error if the file or directory they attempt to access is a symbolic link. This option not only stops users from following symbolic links, it also prevents them from making symbolic links. It could be a useful security tool if your users are linking to server files on their home directories.

The default is Yes, where Samba follows symbolic links:

```
follow symlinks = Yes
```

An example to turn the parameter off and prevent Samba from following symbolic links:

```
follow symlinks = No
```

Dont descend

This is not a security parameter; rather, it is a parameter of convenience. This parameter affects the listing of directories, not access to them. If a user has permission, the user can still write or delete to the directories specified. You can specify more then one directory, separated by commas.

The default is a blank string, or no directories are pruned for display:

```
dont descend =
```

An example to set the /proc and /dev directories to appear empty when displayed by clients:

```
dont descend = /proc,/dev
```

Magic script

The next two parameters `magic script` and `magic output` are experimental. Use them with caution until they become more fully supported. The default is a blank string, or no `magic script` executes:

```
magic script =
```

Magic output

This parameter contains the output generated by `magic script`. Avoid using these parameters because they are experimental. Find another solution to your problem.

The default is a blank string, or no output file is specified for the magic script:

```
magic output =
```

Delete readonly

This parameter specifies whether DOS read-only files can be deleted. It enables the UNIX file permissions to override the DOS file-level control. It has been suggested that this parameter can be useful for running applications such as a revision control system. There could be a situation where UNIX file ownership prevents changing file permissions and DOS semantics prevent deletion of a read-only file.

The default is set to No, or read-only files will not be deleted:

```
delete readonly = No
```

An example to set this parameter to on and allow the deletion of DOS read-only files:

```
delete readonly = Yes
```

DOS filetimes

This parameter specifies whether smbd will use DOS or POSIX standards for file timestamping. The DOS/Windows standard is that if a user can write to a file, the timestamp can changed. The POSIX standard is that only the owner of the file or root may change the timestamp. Samba is set to the POSIX standard by default. Setting this option to `Yes` enables smbd to change the file timestamp as DOS requires.

The default is set to `No`, or only the owner and root can change timestamps:

```
dos filetimes = No
```

An example to set Samba to the DOS/Windows standard and enable any user who can write to a file to change the timestamp:

```
dos filetimes = Yes
```

DOS filetime resolution

This parameter is used to resolve problems that can occur when using the DOS/Windows FAT file system. The finest granularity the FAT file system can use for time resolution is two seconds. This can cause some compatibility problems when using some products, such as the Microsoft Visual Programming Languages, with Samba shares. The problem occurs when oplocks are enabled on a share (oplocks are discussed in the Locking options section). If oplocks are enabled on a share, then Microsoft Visual Programming Language will use two different time-reading calls to check whether a file has changed since the last read. The first call uses a one-second granularity. The other uses a two-second granularity. The two-second call rounds any odd second down. So, when a file has a timestamp of an odd number of seconds, the two timestamps do not match. When this occurs, the Microsoft Visual Programming Language always reports the file has changed.

When this parameter is set to `Yes` on a share, Samba rounds the reported time down to the nearest even two-second boundary. When the two timestamps are set to match through this parameter, the Microsoft Visual Programming Language is happy and reports file creation time correctly for revisions.

The default is `No`, or file creation times are not rounded:

```
dos filetime resolution = No
```

An example to set this option to `Yes` and perform file creation-time rounding to fool some products, such as Microsoft Visual Programming Languages:

```
dos filetime resolution = Yes
```

Fake directory create times

This parameter also fudges directory creation times for compatibility with Microsoft Visual Programming Languages using Samba shares. Even the newer file systems, such as NTFS and Windows VFAT, keep a creation time that is not the same as the UNIX ctime, or status change time. Samba by default reports the earliest of the various times UNIX does keep. This can cause the compiler to rebuild objects that have not changed. Setting this parameter for a share causes Samba to always report midnight 1-1-1980 as the creation time for directories.

The default is No, or Samba reports the UNIX creation times:

```
fake directory create times = No
```

An example to set this parameter to Yes and make Samba shares report a create time compatible with Microsoft Visual Programming compilers using Samba shares:

```
fake directory create times = Yes
```

Printer Parameters Advanced View

The Printers button links to the Create and Delete Printer Page. If you type anything in the drop-down box, SWAT creates a printer with that name. Picking any of the three buttons — Choose Printer, Delete Printer, or Create Printer — takes you to the Printer Parameter Options page. The Printer Parameter Options page adds three buttons below the Choose, Delete, and Create Printer buttons: Commit Changes, Reset Values, and Advanced View. The options are as follows.

Base options

The Base options section is where you set the comment for the printers and where you set the path that the share will access.

Comment

This parameter specifies a text field that is visible next to a share when a client queries the server. This parameter is for the share level comment. The section Global Variables, Base Options describes how to set the string that is displayed next to the machine name with the server string parameter.

The default is a blank string, or no comment is displayed with the service:

```
comment =
```

An example of a comment:

```
comment = Home Directories served up by Samba
```

Path

This parameter is based on the root directory, if one was set under Global Variables ➪ Security Options. It specifies the directory that a given user can access. If it's a print service, this is where the print data spools before being submitted for printing. This service accepts variable substitutions; the two most common variable substitutions are:

%u   UNIX username that the client is using on this connection

%m   NetBIOS name of the machine from which the client connects

The default is blank string:

```
path =
```

An example to set the path to the home directory follows. If your root directory path was set to /opt/samba, the service would look for /opt/samba/home:

```
path = /home
```

Security options

The Security options section lets you give guest access to printers, as well as determine which hosts are allowed access and which hosts are denied access.

Guest account

This is a username used for access to services that are specified as `guest ok`. The privileges this user has are available to any client connecting to the guest service. This user must exist in the password file but should not have a valid login. The traditional UNIX system default guest account `nobody` might not be capable of printing. You should test this by logging in as your guest user and trying to print using the system print command. If you cannot print from this account, use another account. The user account `ftp` is another a good choice for this parameter.

The default is specified at compile time, usually `nobody`:

```
guest account = nobody
```

An example to map the guest account to the `ftp` user:

```
guest account = ftp
```

Guest ok

This parameter specifies whether the guest account can access the service.

The default is `No`, or the guest account is not allowed to access the service:

```
guest ok = No
```

An example to enable the guest account access:

```
guest ok = Yes
```

Hosts allow

This parameter is a comma-, space-, or tab-delimited list of hosts permitted to access a service. If specified in the globals section, then it applies to all services. This setting wins even when the individual service has a different setting. Name, IP address, or network/netmask pairs can specify the hosts. You can also specify by netgroup names if your system supports netgroups. You can use the `except` keyword to limit a wildcard list.

Caution

If you use the hosts allow parameter, you must include local-host in the string of hosts. Samba requires access to the local-host interface to function as expected.

The following examples provide some help in using this parameter. To allow localhost and all IP addresses in 192.168.*.* :

```
hosts allow = localhost, 192.168.*.*
```

To allow localhost and hosts that match the given network/netmask:

```
hosts allow = localhost, 192.168.99.0/255.255.255.0
```

To allow a localhost and two others by name:

```
hosts allow = localhost, terrapin, deal
```

To allow localhost and a subnet with one exception:

```
Host allow = localhost, 192.168.99.0 EXCEPT
192.168.99.222
```

If your network uses NIS netgroups, you can use those with the @ option as we've used for other options. The + and & options do not apply to this parameter. The following example enables access for a NIS group marshotel and localhost.

```
hosts allow = @marshotel, localhost
```

The default is a blank string, or all hosts are allowed access.

Host deny

This parameter is the opposite of hosts allow. The hosts you list here are not permitted access to services. Even if specific services have lists to override this one, this list wins and denies access to the service.

The default is a blank string, or no hosts are denied access.

An example to deny the 192.168.111.* subnet:

```
hosts deny = 192.168.111.*
```

Logging options

The Logging options section of SWAT defines only one parameter at the moment, the status parameter.

Status

You should not need to set this parameter. If you set it to `status` = no, smbstatus will not be able to tell what connections are active.

The default is:

```
status = Yes
```

An example to set this parameter so smbstatus can't tell which connections are active:

```
status = No
```

Tuning options

The Tuning options section of the Printers page has only one parameter at the moment, the `min print space` parameter.

Min print space

This parameter specifies the minimum amount of free disk space that must be available so that a user can spool a print job. A value of 0 means there is no limit on the print spool space. This parameter is specified in kilobytes.

The default is zero, which means a user has no limits on disk space:

```
min print space = 0
```

An example to set a small minimum of disk space:

```
min print space = 2000
```

Printing options

The Printing options section is where you modify Samba to make the printers work with your system. You can specify the type of printer to use, the correct printer commands to use, and the location of the printcap file.

Print ok

This parameter specifies whether clients may open, write to, and submit spool files on the directory specified for the service.

The default is No, but the print service will still accept files spooled for print. This just prevents clients from accessing the files directly:

```
print ok = No
```

An example to allow a client access to spool files:

```
print ok = Yes
```

PostScript

This parameter forces a printer to interpret the print files as PostScript. This is done by adding a %! to the start of print output. This is most useful when you have lots of PCs that persist in putting a Ctrl+D at the start of print jobs, which confuses your PostScript printer.

The default is:

```
postscript = No
```

To force a printer to interpret the print files as PostScript:

```
postscript = Yes
```

Printing

This parameter specifies how printer status information is interpreted on your system. The option can be set on a per-printer basis. It affects the default values for these commands: print, lpq, lppause, lpresume, and lprm.

The commands are interpreted through the use of styles. There are eight supported styles:

BSD
AIX
LPRNG
PLP
SYSV

HPUX

QNX

SOFTQ

An example to set printing to HPUX style:

```
printing = HPUX
```

An example to set printing to BSD style:

```
printing = BSD
```

print command

This parameter specifies the command that processes a print job after it has finished spooling to a service. If you don't specify a print command, the spool files are created but not processed. The spool file name is generated automatically by the Samba server. The command specified submits the spool file to the host's printing subsystem. When specified in the Globals section, the `print` command is used for any printable service that does not have a print command specified. The Samba server will not remove the spool file. If the print command specified does not remove the spool file, you need to manually remove old spool files.

The `print` command is a text string. It passes to the UNIX system verbatim. There are two substitutions and three variables that can be used with this command. Either a `%s` or a `%f` represents the name of the spool file. If `%s` is not preceded by a /, then the full path name is used for the filename. If you don't require this level of detail, use `%f` instead. All occurrences of `%f` replace the spool filename without the path. The other substitution is `%p` for the printer name. If no printer name was supplied, the `%p` is ignored. When the print job is submitted, the `print` command must contain at least one of the variables `%s`, `%f`, or `%p`.

Make sure you test your printing definitions. Printing could fail on some UNIX systems if you set the guest account for Samba to use the `nobody` account. If the Samba guest account is set to use `nobody` account, then change the guest account mapping to a user that can print. See Security options for the guest account. Return to this option and set the guest account to the user `ftp`.

The default for this parameter depends on the style specified with the `printing` option. The following is a list of the UNIX print commands that are used by the styles:

For `printing = BSD, AIX, QNX, LPRNG,` or `PLP`, the default command is:

```
print command = lpr -r -P%p %s
```

For `printing = SYSV` or `HPUX`, the default command is:

```
print command = lp -c -d%p %s; rm %s
```

For `printing = SOFTQ`, the default command is:

```
print command = lp -d%p -s %s; rm %s
```

You can form complex print commands because they are passed directly to the shell. Remember that the `;` is the usual separator for commands in shell scripts. You can test the command syntax in the shell before defining it in this parameter. The following example logs a print job, prints the file, and then removes it.

```
print command = echo Printing %s > /var/log/print.log;
lpr -P %p %s; rm %s
```

Another method is to create a script file that contains the commands your system uses for printing, and put the path and name of the script there:

```
print command = /opt/samba/bin/theprintscript %p %s
```

lpq command

This parameter specifies the command the UNIX server uses to obtain lpq printer status information. The command should be a program or a script that takes a printer name as its only parameter. There are eight styles of printer status information currently supported: BSD, AIX, LPRNG, PLP, SYSV, HPUX, QNX, and SOFTQ. See the `printing` option (`printing =`) previously in this chapter. If a %p is given as part of the command, then the printer name is substituted. If you omit `%p`, it is placed at the end of the command. Use the absolute path for the `lpq` command because the path might not be available to the Samba server by default.

An example for BSD-style printing:

```
lpq command = /usr/bin/lpq %p
```

An example for Solaris- and SYSV-style systems:

```
lpq command = /usr/bin/lpstat -o%p
```

lprm command

This parameter specifies the command by the UNIX server to delete a print job. The command should be a program or a script that can take a printer name and job number to delete the print job. Two variables are required with this command: the first is the %p for the printer name. The second is a new variable, %j, which is replaced with the job number of the print job in the printer queue. Once again, it is good practice to include the absolute path for the lprm command because the path might not be available to the Samba server.

An simple example of using the lprm command:

```
lprm command = /usr/bin/lprm -P%p %j
```

An example of using the lprm command for Solaris- and SYSV–style systems:

```
lprm command = /usr/bin/cancel %p-%j
```

lppause command

This parameter specifies the command to be executed by the UNIX server to stop the printing or spooling of a specific print job. The command should be a program or a script that takes a printer name and job number to pause the print job. The variables required for this command are %p for printer and %j for job number. Once again, it is good practice to include the absolute path of the lppause command because the path might not be available to the Samba server.

Currently, defaults are defined for the SYSV, HPUX, and SOFTQ styles.

The default for the SYSV style is:

```
lp -i %p-%j -H hold
```

The default for SOFTQ style is:

```
qstat -s -j%j -h
```

The default behavior for the HPUX style includes the use of job priorities, or the –p option. Print jobs with too low of a job priority won't be sent to the printer, so setting –p0, or priority to zero, pauses the print job:

```
lppause command = /usr/bin/lpalt %p-%j -p0
```

lpresume command

This parameter specifies the command used by the UNIX server to restart or continue printing or spooling a specific print job. This command should be a program or script that takes a printer name and job number to resume the print job. The variables required for this command are %p for printer and %j for job number. Again, it is good practice to include the absolute path of the lpresume command because the path might not be available to the Samba server.

Currently, defaults are defined for the SYSV, HPUX, and SOFTQ styles.

The default for SYSV style is:

```
lp -i %p-%j -H resume
```

The default for SOFTQ style is:

```
qstat -s -j%j -r
```

The default for the HPUX style:

```
lpresume command = /usr/bin/lpalt %p-%j -p2
```

queuepause command

This parameter specifies the command used by the UNIX server to pause the specified printer queue. This command should be a program or script that takes a printer name as its parameter and stops the printer queue. If a %p is not placed in the command string, it is placed at the end of the command. Once again, it is good practice to include the absolute path for the queuepause command because the path might not be available to the Samba server.

An example for the SYSV style:

```
queuepause command = /usr/bin/lpc stop %p
```

queueresume command

This parameter specifies the command used by the UNIX server to resume printing from the specified printer queue. This command should be a program or script that takes a printer name as its parameter and resumes printing for the specified printer queue. If a `%p` is not placed in the command string, it is placed at the end of the command. Once again, it is good practice to include the absolute path for the `queueresume` command because the path might not be available to the Samba server

An example for the SYSV style:

```
queuepause command = /usr/bin/lpc start %p
```

Printer name

This parameter is synonymous with `printer`.

Printer driver

This option enables you to control the string that clients receive when they ask the server for the printer driver associated with a printer. If you are using Windows 95 or Windows NT, you can use this to automate the setup of printers on your system.

Set this parameter to the exact string (case-sensitive) that describes the appropriate printer driver for your system. If you don't know the exact string to use, first try it with no `printer driver` option set; the client will give you a list of drivers. Select the appropriate strings from the provided list after you have chosen the printer manufacturer.

See also `printer driver file`.

Printer driver location

This parameter is the client equivalent of the printer driver parameter (the third parameter of Printing options). `Printer driver location` specifies for clients the location of a particular printer share. This is where the printer driver files for the automatic installation of printer drivers are located. This works for Windows 95/98 machines; NT clients cannot use this option.

The default is an empty string, or Samba is not set up by default to serve printer drivers for clients.

The syntax for the parameter is:

```
printer driver location = \\MACHINE\PRINTER$
```

Set MACHINE to the NetBIOS name of your Samba server. Set PRINTER$ to the share you have set up for serving printer driver files with the `printer driver` parameter.

An example for the Samba server deal and a share named HPDRVS:

```
printer driver location = \\deal\HPDRVS$
```

Browse option

The Browse Option section only defines one parameter at the moment, the `browseable` parameter.

Browseable

This parameter specifies whether the share is visible in the list of available shares in a net view and in the browse list. This parameter does not make a share unavailable, only invisible, by default. The default is all shares are available for browsing.

The default is:

```
browseable = Yes
```

An example to set a share to be invisible in the net view and browse list:

```
browseable = No
```

Miscellaneous options

The Miscellaneous options section is where you can customize printers for users by using **exec** and **postexec** commands.

Exec

This parameter, also known as `preexec`, specifies the name of a script or scripts to run when the client connects to a service. The script runs with the user ID of the current session user. This is the place to work magic for your clients or even do simple things such as sending a custom message to the log when a user spools a print job.

The default is an empty string, or no scripts are run:

```
exec =
```

An example to pass a message to a log file at connection time:

```
exec = echo 'At %T %u printed to %S' /
> /opt/samba/print.log
```

Postexec

This parameter specifies the name of a script or scripts to run when the client disconnects from a service. The script runs with the user ID of the current session user. The command may be run as the root on some systems. This is useful if you need to dismount file systems after terminating a connection.

The default is a blank string, or no scripts are run:

```
postexec =
```

An example to post the disconnect time for your user's session:

```
exec = echo 'At %T %u completed printing from %S' /
> /opt/samba/print.log
```

Root preexec

This parameter is the root-user version of `exec` and `preexec`. It allows root to run scripts necessary for the user environment. The most common use is to mount file systems. You could use it to set up some print queues with some scripting.

The default is a blank string, or no scripts are run by root at the service startup:

```
root preexec =
```

An example to use the `root preexec` parameter to issue a `mount` command:

```
root preexec = /bin/mount —ro /cdrom
```

Root postexec

This parameter is the root user version of `postexec`. It enables root to run scripts when the user disconnects from the service. The most common use is to unmount file systems. You could use it to make sure spool files are deleted.

The default is a blank string, or no scripts are run by root at the service startup:

```
root preexec =
```

An example to use the `root preexec` parameter to delete all files in the tmp directory:

```
root preexec = rm /tmp/*
```

Available

This parameter specifies whether a service is available. If you set this parameter to No, then all attempts to connect to the service will fail. The failures are logged.

The default is set to Yes, or the service is available:

```
available = Yes
```

Setting this parameter to No turns off the service and prevents connections:

```
available = No
```

Status

The Status button links to the Server Status page. The functions on this page start, stop, and display daemons. This page displays active connections, shares, and open files. It can be set to autorefresh the display, which is set in seconds.

View

The view button links to a page that displays the essential pieces of your active configuration. It also has a button for a full view of the smb.conf file when you need it.

Password

The Password button links to the Password Management page. This page has two sections: Server Password Management and Client/Server Password Management. The Server Password Management section is where you set the username and password for your admin users. The Client/Server Password Management section is where you set the username and password for all other users.

Server password management

Server Password Management is where you can change passwords for smb users, add new smb users, disable smb users, and enable smb users.

Username

This is the name of the smb user you want to add, disable, or enable, or change passwords for

Old password

This is the Old Password field, if you are changing a password.

New password

This is the new password, if you are changing a password or adding a user.

Re-type new password

The new password must be retyped here, and they must match for the change to take place.

Change password

This button changes the smb password for the supplied user.

Add new user

This button adds a new user to the smbpasswd file.

Disable user

This button disables the given smb user.

Enable user

This button enables the given smb user.

Client/Server password management

The fields in the Client/Server Password Management section are identical to the ones in the Server Password Management section above, with the addition of a Remote Machine name field

Remote machine name

The remote machine that you are attempting to change the user's password on.

Change password

You are only allowed to change the password for the user on the remote machine.

Chapter 4

Basic Operating System Configuration

Because Samba runs on so many different operating systems, a good Samba administrator needs to know how to do the basic tasks of adding users and printers to the system at hand. This chapter is for the system administrator who knows how to add users in UNIX but isn't sure of the exact syntax to add users in FreeBSD. Or, you might know how to add printers for Linux machines but now find yourself administering a Solaris box with which you are unfamiliar. For an in-depth treatment of the commands, check the man pages for each command. This chapter, however, addresses the majority of situations.

Adding Users and Groups at the OS Level

Most UNIX-like operating systems have a graphical way to add users and groups in addition to the command line. Most systems enable you to add users by editing the /etc/passwd file, but some discourage this method.

Adding users and groups in Solaris

You can add users and groups to the Solaris operating system graphically, using either admintool or the command line.

Adding groups with admintool

Admintool is the graphical tool used to add users, groups, and printers to a Solaris workstation. Use it in Open Windows or another X Window environment. To launch admintool in Open Windows:

1. Open a command tool.
2. Log on as the root user using the su command.
3. Type **admintool &** at the # prompt.

After admintool opens, add a group with these steps:

1. Click Browse; select Groups.
2. Click Edit; select Add Entry (the default).
3. Fill out the Group Name and Group ID (GID) fields.
4. Click Add to create the new group with this information.

Adding users with admintool

Admintool is the graphical tool for adding users, groups, and printers to a Solaris workstation. Use it in Open Windows or another X Windows enironment.

To launch admintool in Open Windows:

1. Open a command tool.
2. Log on as the root user using the su command.
3. Type **admintool &** at the # prompt.

After the admintool opens, add a user as follows:

1. Click Browse; select Users.
2. Click Edit; select Add User.
3. Fill in the username.
4. Fill in the User ID (UID).
5. Fill in the Primary Group.
6. Fill in secondary groups.
7. Fill in comments, typically the full name.
8. Choose the appropriate login shell from among Bourne, C, Korn, or other.

9. Under Account Security, choose the password options, which are:
   - Cleared until first login
   - Account is locked
   - No password — set uid only
   - Normal password

10. If you select normal password, enter and verify the password. The parameters are:
    - Minimum time between password changes;
    - Maximum time between password changes;
    - Maximum inactive time;
    - The password expiration date;
    - The password warning date, which specifies how many days before expiration the user is warned that their password is expiring.

11. Choose whether the user will have a home directory.

12. Check the Create Home Dir. box to automatically create the home directory, and fill in the home directory path.

13. Click Add to create the new user with this information.

Adding groups at the command line

Use the `groupadd` command to add a group using the command line. The following example adds the group testers with the group ID of 150.

```
# groupadd —g 150 testers
```

Adding users at the command line

You can add users at the command line or in a script with the `useradd` command. The syntax for `useradd` is:

```
useradd —u UID —g gid —c "Name" —d home_directory_path \ —m —s shell username
```

where

`-u UID`	is the user ID.
`-g GID`	is the group ID
`-c "Comments"`	is the comments field, typically the full name.
`-d "home directory"`	is the user's home directory.
`-m`	creates the user's home directory if it does not exist.
`-s shell`	is the user's default shell.
`username`	is the user's login name.

Adding users in Linux

The ways to add users that are common to RedHat Linux and Caldera OpenLinux are discussed first. Then the ways unique to each distribution are discussed.

Adding users at the command line using adduser or useradd

You can add users at the command line or in a script with the **adduser** or **useradd** commands. The **adduser** command is linked to the **useradd** command. The syntax for **useradd** is:

```
useradd option(s) name
```

where the following are the options that can be used:

`-u UID -o`	is the user ID, which must be unique unless the **-o** switch is used. The default is to use the smallest unused UID greater than 99.
`-g group`	is the GID or group name of the user's primary group, which must exist.
`-G group,...`	is a list of secondary groups, separated by commas and no white space.
`-d home`	is the user's home directory. The default is to append the username to default_home.
`-s shell`	is the user's login shell. The default is the default login shell.

`-c comment`	is the comment field, typically used for the user's full name and/or telephone number.
`-m –k dir`	is the user's home directory, which will be created if it does not exist. If the –k option is used, the files contained in dir are copied to the home directory; otherwise, the files in /etc/skel are used. The default is not to copy any files.
`-f inactive`	is the number of days after a password expires until the account is disabled. Using 0 disables the account as soon as the password expires; –1 disables the `-f inactive` feature.
`-e mm/dd/yy`	is the day the account will expire in mm/dd/yy format.
`-p passwd`	adds the encrypted password. Using this parameter adds the text typed as the encrypted password into the /etc/passwd, it is not the unencrypted (user's password).
`-n`	disables the GNU feature of creating a group with the same name as the user.
`-r`	creates a system account with a UID lower than minimum defined in `UID_MIN`.
`name`	is the username.

After creating the new user, assign a password for the new user using `passwd username`, unless you know how the desired password mapped to an encrypted password and added the encrypted password using the –p option.

Adding users by editing /etc/passwd

You can also add a user by editing the /etc/passwd file. This is a dangerous procedure, however, that should be used only when no other method can be used. This procedure may be needed when recovering from a crash or hardware failure, and there are no other utilities available on the recovery media. Each user has a separate line in the /etc/passwd file. Commas delimit the seven fields. The format of a line is:

```
Username : password : user ID : group ID : comment : home
directory : login command
```

If the /etc/shadow password file is being used, an X will be in the password field and the encrypted password will be stored in /etc/shadow.

After the user is added, create the home directory and copy the default configuration files from /etc/skel to the user's home directory. Then change the ownership and permissions for the new directory. Finally, assign a password for the new user with the **passwd** command.

Adding groups at the command line using groupadd

The syntax for using **groupadd** at the command line is:

```
# groupadd [-g gid [-o]] [-r] [-f] group
```

These are the options that can be used with the **groupadd** command:

-g   Is the numerical value of the group ID, which must be unique unless the —o flag is used. The default is to use the lowest unused GID above 500 (GIDs between 0 and 499 are reserved for the system).

-r   Is used to add a system account (GID between 0 and 499) and is unique to Red Hat Linux.

-f   Is a force flag to stop **groupadd** from exiting when you try to add a group that is already on the system.

Adding groups by editing /etc/group

You can add groups by editing the /etc/group file. Each group has a separate line in the /etc/group file. The format of the line is:

```
Group name : password : group ID : member 1, member 2,
member 3, ...
```

Adding users with Red Hat Linux-specific utilities

Linuxconf is a utility included with Red Hat Linux that adds or maintains users, groups, and printers, and to configure Samba. Linuxconf can be run at the command line, in an xterm window, or in Gnome as an X Window application. To open linuxconf in X Window as a normal user:

1. Open a new xterm window.

2. In the terminal, `su` to root.

3. Type **linuxconf** at the # prompt. The X Window linuxconf starts.

To open linuxconf running X Window as root, in Gnome click Program Menu, select Settings, and select Linuxconf.

Adding users with linuxconf

Linuxconf provides a menu-based way of adding a user by filling out the appropriate fields:

1. In linuxconf, scroll to Config ⇨ User Accounts ⇨ Normal ⇨ User Accounts. Click User Accounts under Normal.

2. Click Add.

3. Under the Base Info tab, fill out the Login name (username) the Full Name (comment), the group, the supplementary groups, the Home directory, the Command interpreter (shell), and the User ID. If you leave the group, Home directory, Command interpreter, and User ID blank, they will be filled in by the system defaults.

4. Under the Params tab, specify the password options: Must keep # days (minimum), Must change after # days, Warm # days before expiration, Account expire after # days. A value of −1 disables a feature.

5. Under the mail aliases, fill out the Redirect address and any e-mail aliases.

6. Select Privileges.

7. Select General System Control. Give the proper permissions for May use linuxconf, May activate config changes, May shutdown, May switch network mode, May view system logs, and SuperUser equivalence.

8. Select Services and give the proper permissions for Mail to Fax manager and Samba administration.

9. Select Miscellaneous and give the proper permissions for message of the day.

10. Select User Accounts and give the proper permissions for POP Accounts Manager, PPP Accounts Manager, and UUCP Manager.

11. Click Accept to create the user.

Tip

Changes for the new users need to be activated before you can quit linuxconf.

Adding groups using linuxconf

Linuxconf provides a menu-based way of adding a group by filling out the appropriate fields:

1. In linuxconf, scroll to Config ⇨ User Accounts ⇨ Normal ⇨ Group Definitions. Click on Group Definitions under Normal.

2. Click Add.

3. Under Base Info, fill out the Group Name, Group ID, and alternate members.

4. Under Directories, fill out the Home base directory and the Creation permissions.

Adding users with Caldera OpenLinux-specific utilities

Caldera has two unique utilities for user and group manipulation, COAS (Caldera open Administration System) and LISA (Linux Installation and System Administration). COAS is used in KDE, whereas LISA can be used at a command line or in an xterm window.

Adding users running KDE as root

Start the COAS administration utility by selecting COAS ⇨ System ⇨ Accounts on the KDE main menu. Then follow these steps:

1. Select Actions.

2. Select Create User.

3. Enter the login name.

4. Enter the Full Name.

5. If desired, change the following:
   - UID
   - Group ID
   - Default shell
   - Home directory

6. Click Password to add the password.

7. Click Shadow Information to add the minimum number of days to change, the maximum number of days to change, the number of days to warn before expiring, the number of days to disable, and the expiration date.

Adding users with LISA

LISA can be used to add users and groups to a system:

1. At the # prompt, type **lisa –useradm**.

2. Type **2** to add a new user.

3. Enter the login name.

4. Change the UID if desired.

5. Select the group to which you want to add the user.

6. Change the default user's home directory, if desired.

7. Choose the standard shell for the user.

8. Enter the full name for the user.

9. Enter and confirm the password.

Adding groups using LISA

LISA can be used to add groups to a system:

1. At the # prompt, type **lisa –useradm**.

2. Type **5** to create a new group.

3. Enter the new name of the group.

4. Enter the new group ID.

5. Confirm that you want to create the group.

Adding users in FreeBSD/NetBSD

You can add users in FreeBSD/NetBSD with the vipw utility. Addi-tionally, FreeBSD has an `adduser` command for adding a user.

Adding users in FreeBSD/NetBSD with vipw

You can add users in FreeBSD/NetBSD using vipw, a program that locks the password file and enables you to edit it, by following these steps:

1. Use the `vipw` command to lock the /etc/master.passwd file and begin editing it. `vipw` uses standard vi commands by default, although other editors can be selected by changing the `EDITOR` environmental variable:

   • The first field is the user's login name.

   • The second field is the password; leave it blank.

   • The third field is the user number (UID).

   • The fourth field is the user's group number (GID).

   • The fifth field is the class field; leave it empty, unless your FreeBSD system is using login classes.

   • The sixth field is the change; set it to 0. If it is not 0, it is the time in seconds after which the password must be changed. This field is not mirrored to /etc/passwd.

   • The seventh field is the expire field; set it to 0. If it is not 0, it is the time in seconds after which the user expires. This field is not mirrored to /etc/passwd.

   • The eighth field is the comment field for the user's full name, historically known as the gecos field.

   • The ninth field is the home directory field.

   • The tenth field is the desired shell.

2. Save and exit vipw.

To finish the process, do the following:

1. Once the user exists in the password files, use `passwd username` to set a password for the user.

2. Edit the /etc/group file to add the user to the desired groups. Be cautious of adding users to group 0; `su` uses this to determine root privileges.

3. Create the home directory for the user.

4. Copy the skeleton files from /usr/share/skel.

Adding users in FreeBSD with adduser

FreeBSD also comes with the adduser program, which enables you to add a user without invoking an editor:

1. As superuser, type **adduser** at the command line.

2. Enter the username.

3. Enter the full name.

4. Enter the shell or accept the default.

5. Enter the home directory or accept the default.

6. Enter the UID or accept the default.

7. Enter the login class or accept the default.

8. Enter the login group or accept the default.

9. Enter other groups.

10. Enter the password.

11. Reenter the password.

12. Confirm everything.

13. Decide whether you want to send a message to user.

The defaults for the `adduser` script are kept in /etc/adduser.conf and can be changed there.

User Account Maintenance at the OS Level

Even after all your users have been added, you still need to maintain their accounts. You may need to change their password, lock their accounts, or even delete their accounts.

Maintaining users in Solaris

Admintool is the primary tool used to maintain users in Solaris, although account maintenance can also be done via the command line in a command tool or via a telnet session.

Modifying an account using admintool

To launch admintool while in Open Windows, follow these steps:

1. Open a command tool.
2. Log on as the root user using the su command.
3. Type admintool & at the # prompt.

After the admintool is open, add a user by following these steps:

1. Click Browse and select Users.
2. Click Edit and select Modify/View User.
3. The values for the user display. Change the ones you need to modify.
4. Click Apply for these changes to take effect.

Locking an account using admintool

To lock an account using admintool, follow these steps:

1. In admintool, Browse Users.
2. Select the user whose account you want to lock and select Modify User.
3. Choose Account is locked from the Password menu.
4. Select Apply.

You can verify the lock by displaying the /etc/shadow file as root: you should see *LK* in the password field for this user.

Locking an account at the command line

The superuser can lock an account with the passwd command and the −1 flag. To lock user nancy's account, type:

```
#passwd −l nancy
```

Deleting an account using admintool

To delete an account using admintool, follow these steps:

1. In admintool, Browse Users.
2. Highlight the user whose account you want to delete.
3. Choose Delete User from the edit menu.

Maintaining users in Red Hat Linux

There are several ways to maintain user accounts in Red Hat Linux. You can use graphical methods such as linuxconf, or use `usermod` at the command line.

Maintaining users with linuxconf

To use linuxconf to modify a user's accounts, follow these steps:

1. Start linuxconf by typing **linuxconf** as superuser. You can do this at the console in an xterm window or via a telnet session.
2. Scroll down to Users accounts.
3. Look under Normal and select User accounts.
4. Click the user you want to edit. The fields will be filled with the user's values. Edit the ones that must be changed.
5. After everything is filled out, Tab to Accept and press Enter.

Modifying users with usermod

The `usermod` utility enables you to modify the properties for an existing user while at a command line. The syntax is:

```
#usermod  option(s) user
```

The following options can be used:

`-c comment`	Refers to new value of users comment field, usually modified by `chfn`.
`-d home dir -m`	Is the user's new home directory. If the —m flag is included, the contents of the current home directory are moved to the new home directory.

`-e expire date`	Is the date the account will be disabled.
`-f inactive days`	Is the number of days after the password expires that the account becomes disabled. A value of −1 disables this feature.
`-g initial group`	Is the group name or ID of the user's new primary group. It must already exist.
`-G group`	Is a list of supplementary groups to which the user belongs. The groups must exist and be separated by commas with no white space. If a user is in a group that is not listed, the user will be removed from that group.
`-l login name`	Is the new login name for the user.
`-s shell`	Is the new login shell.
`-u uid −o`	Is the user's ID number, which must be unique unless the −o switch is used.
`-L`	Locks a user's account.
`-U`	Unlocks a user's account.

Locking and unlocking an account at the command line

The superuser can lock and unlock an account with the **passwd** command and the −l or −u flag. To lock user nancy's account, type:

`#passwd −l nancy`

To unlock it, type:

`#passwd −u nancy`

Deleting users with userdel

To delete a user, use the command `userdel user`. The −r switch removes the user's home directory and the files in the home directory.

Maintaining users in Caldera OpenLinux

Caldera OpenLinux provides several ways to modify a user's accounts, from the X Window-based COAS to the command line using `usermod`. Administrators familiar with other Linux distributions may prefer to use `usermod`.

Modifying users with COAS

To modify users with COAS, start the COAS administration utility by selecting COAS ⇨ System ⇨ Accounts on the KDE main menu. Then continue using these steps:

1. Select Actions.
2. Select Edit User.
3. Edit the user's fields that need to be changed.

Modifying users with usermod

The `usermod` allows you modify the properties for an existing user. The syntax is:

```
#usermod  option(s) user
```

The options are:

`-c comment`	Refers to new value of users comment field, usually modifed by `chfn`.
`-d home dir -m`	Is the user's new home directory. If the -m flag is included, the contents of the current home directory are moved to the new home directory.
`-e expire date`	Is the date that the account will be disabled.
`-f inactive days`	Is the number of days after the password expires that the account will be disabled. A value of -1 disables this feature.
`-g initial group`	Is the group name or ID of the user's new primary group. It must already exist.
`-G group`	Is a list of supplementary groups to which the user belongs. The groups must exist and are separated by commas with no white space. If a

	user is in a group that is not listed, the user is removed from that group.
`-l login name`	Is the new login name for the user.
`-s shell`	Is the new login shell.
`-u uid -o`	Is the user's ID number, which must be unique unless the —o switch is used.
`-L`	Locks a user's account.
`-U`	Unlocks a user's account.

Deleting users with userdel

To delete a user, use the command `userdel  user`. The —r switch removes the user's home directory and the files in the home directory.

Maintaining users in FreeBSD/NetBSD

FreeBSD and NetBSD have two utilities for user account maintenance. Chpass is used to change the parameters of the user's account, while passwd is used to change the user's password.

Maintaining users with chpass

chpass is the FreeBSD command that is used to maintain a user's account using vi or the environment's editor. The syntax is:

```
chpass [-a list] [-s newshell] user
```

where

`-a`	Allows the superuser to directly add a user to the password database as a colon-separated list.
`-s`	Attempts to change the user's shell to newshell.
`-p`	Allows the superuser to directly supply an encrypted password in the format specified by crypt.

User variables that may be displayed are:

Login	User's login name
Password	User's encrypted password

Uid	User's ID number
Gid	User's login group
Change	Password change time in month/day/year format
Expire	Account expiration time in month/day/year format
Class	User's general class
Shell	User's login shell
Full name	User's real name
Location	User's normal location
Home Phone	User's home phone
Office Phone	User's office phone
Other information	Other locally defined information

Changing passwords using passwd

`passwd` and `yppasswd` are the FreeBSD commands used to change the user's local or YP (NIS) password. The user is first prompted for the current password. If that is correctly supplied, then the new password must be typed twice. The password must be at least six characters long and not completely alphabetic.

The syntax is:

```
passwd [-l] [-y] [user]
yppasswd [user]
```

where

-l   Updates the password in the local field only.

-y   Changes the YP (NIS) password, which is the same as the `yppasswd` command.

Adding Printers at the OS Level

Samba is well-suited for use as a print server. Using Samba/FreeBSD (or Samba/Linux) even a 486-processor machine can serve as a useful print server. The following section explains how to add printers at the OS level for use with Samba. The printers must work at the OS level before they can be used by Samba.

Adding printers in Solaris

Printers can be added in Solaris with the Admintool GUI, or at the command line with `lpadmin`. Printers in Solaris can be local (connected to the machine) or remote. Solaris does not use an /etc/printcap file.

Using the printer manager in admintool to add local printers

Admintool is the main Solaris administration tool. The Printer Manager section of Admintool can be used to add local and remote printers:

1. In Admintool select Browse Printers.
2. Select Edit ⇨ Add Printer ⇨ Add Local Printer.
3. Fill out the appropriate fields:
   - A unique printer name, up to 14 characters.
   - A comment to help users identify the printer (optional).
   - The printer port, typically /dev/term/a or /dev/term/b
   - The printer type and file contents type.
   - Choose the fault notification (write to superuser is the default).
   - Choose whether the printer is to be the system default printer.
   - Set the Print Banner to required or not required.
   - Choose whether to register the printer with NIS+.
   - Modify the user access list if desired.
4. Click Add to add the printer.

Using the printer manager in admintool to add a remote printer

Admintool is the main Solaris administration tool. The Printer Manager section of Admintool can be used to add local and remote printers.

1. Choose Add Printer, then Add Access to Remote Printer.

2. Fill out the following fields:
   - Printer name
   - Printer Server name
   - A comment to help users identify the printer (optional)
   - Select the right operating system (BSD or System V)
   - Specify whether the printer will be the default printer

3. Click Add.

Using lpadmin to add a printer at the command line

The lpadmin command may be used with the −p flag to add a new printer. When creating a new printer, -v (the device), −U (for remote access), or −s (the remote system and printer name) must be used. The syntax is:

```
lpadmin −p options
```

The options are as follows:

-A alert-type [-W]	The -A defines an alert type to alert the administrator and resends the alert every W minutes. The alert type can be an e-mail message, a console message, shell commands, or other options.
-c class	Adds the printer to the class, which will be created if it does not exist.
-D comment	A comment to display to users to describe the printer.
-e printer1	Creates the printer using the parameters of printer1. This cannot be used with the −i or −m options.
-F fault-recovery	Defines the recovery to be used for a print request to a faulted printer.
-f allow:form-list	Allows the list of forms to be printed on the printer.

`-f deny:form-list`	Denies the list of forms from being printed on the printer.
`-h`	Indicates that the device associated with the printer is hardwired; mutually exclusive with −1.
`-I content-type-list`	Specifies the content types that the printer can handle.
`-i interface`	Creates a new interface for the printer; this cannot be used with the −e or −m command.
`-l`	Indicates that the device associated with the printer is a login terminal; mutually exclusive with −h.

`-M -f form-name`
`[-a [-o filebreak]]`
`[-t tray-number]]`
	Mounts the form of **form-name** on the printer. −a prints the alignment pattern. −o inserts a form feed between each copy of the alignment pattern. −t specifies a tray on the printer.

`-M -S print-wheel`	Mounts the print wheel on the printer.
`-m model`	Selects the model interface program for the printer. This cannot be used with −i or −e.
`-o option`	Specifies an option for the printer for length, width, cpi, lpi, and stty.
`-o nobanner`	Allows print requests without banners.
`-o banner`	Forces a banner with all print requests.
`-P paper-name`	Specifies a paper that the printer supports.
`-r class`	Removes the printer from the specified class.
`-S list`	Sets a list of print wheels and aliases that can be used for the printer.

`-s system-name` `[!printer-name]`	Adds a remote printer. The remote printer is on `system-name` and is called `printer-name`.
`-T printer-type-list`	Specifies the printer as being one or more printer types.
`-t number of trays`	Specifies the number of trays on the printer.
`-u allow:login-ID-list`	Enables the users in the list to access the printer. The default is to enable all users to access the system.
`-u deny:login-ID-list`	Denies the users in the list access to the printer.
`-U dial-info`	Gives your print service access to a remote printer.
`-v device`	Specifies the device that `lp` uses to access the printer.
`-x dest-option`	Removes the printer `dest-option` from the `lp` print service.
`-d dest-option`	Makes the printer `dest-option` the new default printer for the system.

Adding printers in Red Hat Linux

You can add printers in RedHat Linux by using the included printtool utility, or by editing the /etc/printcap file.

Adding a local printer using printtool

Red Hat Linux includes the printtool utility that runs in X Window to add, modify, and delete printers. Printtool is launched from an xterm window.

1. At the # prompt, type **printtool**.
2. Click Add.
3. Select Local Printer.
4. Click OK. The port should be detected, starting with /dev/lp0 for lpt1.

5. Choose a name.

6. Specify the spool directory.

7. Specify the file size limit.

8. Specify the printer device.

9. Click Select for the Input Filter.

10. Choose the closest printer to yours under Printer Type.

11. Choose the preferred Resolution.

12. Choose the preferred Paper Size.

13. Choose the preferred Color Depth/Uniprint Mode.

14. Choose among these Printing Options of:

- Send EOF after job
- Fix stair-stepping text
- Fast text printing

15. Choose the pages per output page.

16. Set the margin.

17. Add any GhostScript options.

18. Choose to Suppress Headers.

19. Click OK.

Tip

Lpd can be conveniently restarted in printtool to make configuration changes take place. Click lpd and then restart lpd.

Adding a remote UNIX printer using printtool

Printtool can provide access to a remote printer.

1. At the # prompt, type **printtool**.

2. Click Add.

3. Select Remote Unix (lpd) Queue then Click OK.

4. Choose a name.

5. Specify the spool directory.

6. Specify the file size limit.

7. Specify the Remote Host.

8. Specify the Remote Queue.

9. Click Select for the Input Filter.

10. Choose to Suppress Headers.

11. Click OK.

Adding a remote SMB printer using printtool

Printtool can be used to give RedHat Linux access to another SMB printer, irrespective of whether it's served by another Samba server or a Windows server.

1. At the # prompt type **printtool**.

2. Click Add.

3. Select SMB/Windows 95/NT Printer.

4. Fill out the Names.

5. Fill out the Spool Directory.

6. Specify the File Limit in Kb.

7. Specify Hostname of Printer Server.

8. Fill out the IP Number of Server (optional).

9. Fill out the remote Printer Name.

10. Specify which User.

11. Specify the user's Password.

12. Specify the desired Workgroup.

13. Fill out any desired Input Filter.

14. Check the Suppress Headers if desired.

15. Click OK.

Caution

The username and password are stored locally and unencrypted. This can cause security problems.

Adding a printer by editing the /etc/printcap file

The printer database is stored in the /etc/printcap file, and printers can be added by editing this file directly to add a new entry and then creating the corresponding spool directory under /var/spool/lpd. The instructions for doing this are given at the end of the chapter.

Adding printers in Caldera OpenLinux

Printers can be added in Caldera OpenLinux by using the COAS tool, the LISA tool, or by editing the /etc/printcap file. Printers can be local or remote.

Adding a local printer using the COAS printer setup tool

To add a local printer using the COAS printer setup tool, start the COAS administration utility by selecting COAS ⇨ System ⇨ Accounts on the KDE main menu. Then follow these steps:

1. Select Peripherals.
2. Click Printer.
3. In the Printer Configuration window, click Printer and select Add.
4. In the Select printer model window, select the printer model closest to yours.
5. In the Printer Name window, type a name for the printer.
6. In the Printer Attributes window, choose the paper size, device, and speed.
7. In the Save window, choose Save.
8. In the Create Printer Queue window, click OK to create a printer queue.

Adding a remote printer using the COAS printer setup tool

To add a remote printer using the COAS printer setup tool, start the COAS administration utility by selecting COAS ⇨ System ⇨ Accounts on the KDE main menu. Then follow these steps:

1. Select Peripherals.

2. Click Printer.

3. In the Printer Configuration window, click Printer and select Add.

4. In the Select printer model window, scroll to the bottom and select Generic Remote Printer.

5. In the Printer Name window, enter a name for the remote printer.

6. In the Printer Attributes window, enter the Remote Host ID and the Remote Printer name.

7. In the Save window, choose Save.

8. In the Create Printer Queue window, click OK to create a printer queue.

Adding a local printer using LISA

The LISA administration utility can be used to add a local printer:

1. At the # prompt, type **lisa −printer**.

2. Scroll the printer closest to yours and press Enter.

3. Select the port to which the printer is connected.

4. Select the default resolution for the printer.

5. Select the default paper size for the printer.

Adding a remote printer using LISA

The LISA utility can add access to a remote printer.

1. At the # prompt, type **lisa −printer**.

2. Select the Use Network printer option 2.

3. Enter the host name of the network print server.

4. Enter the printer name.

Caution

Lisa can uncomment previously installed printers in the /etc/printcap file when used. It does make a backup file named /etc/printcap.lisasave.

Adding a printer by editing the /etc/printcap file

The printer database is stored in the /etc/printcap file, and printers can be added by directly editing this file to add a new entry and then creating the corresponding spool directory under /var/spool/lpd. See the end of the chapter for details.

Adding printers in FreeBSD/NetBSD

The FreeBsd/NetBSD branch of UNIX does not have the utilities to add printers that Solaris or Linux has. You need to add a printer by editing the /etc/printcap file. The instructions for this are at the end of the chapter.

Printer Maintenance at the OS Level

After the printers are added to the Operating System, they need to be maintained. Each OS has special tools, and most OSes have a printcap file that can be edited to maintain/modify the printer.

Maintaining/modifying printers in Solaris using print manager

Admintool's Printer Manager maintains/modifies printers in Solaris.

1. Start admintool.
2. Select Browse, then Printers.
3. Highlight the printer to modify.
4. Select Edit ➪ Modify to modify a printer using Printer Manager.

Maintaining printers in Red Hat Linux

Printers can be maintained in RedHat Linux by using the printtool or by editing the /etc/printcap file. Instructions on editing the /etc/printcap file are given at the end of the chapter.

Maintaining/modifying printers using printtool

To maintain or modify printers using printtool, follow these steps:

1. At the # prompt, type **printtool**.
2. Highlight the printer to edit.
3. Click Edit.
4. In the Edit Remote Unix (lpd) Queue Entry window, change the ßName, Spool Directory, File Limit in Kb, Remote Host, Remote Queue, Input Filter, or Suppress Headers if desired.

Tip

Lpd can be conveniently restarted from within printtool to make a configuration change. Click lpd then restart lpd.

Maintaining printers in Caldera OpenLinux

Printers can be maintained in Caldera Open Linux by using the COAS tool or by modifying the /etc/printcap file. Instructions for modifying the /etc/printcap file are at the end of the chapter.

Maintaining/modifying printers by using the COAS printer setup tool

To maintain or modify printers using the COAS printer setup tool, start the COAS administration utility by selecting COAS ➪ System ➪ Accounts on the KDE main menu. Then follow these steps:

1. Select Peripherals.
2. Click Printer.
3. In the Printer Configuration window, click the Printer to edit.
4. Printer Attributes displays the current fields filled in; change the ones you need to edit.
5. In the Save Window, choose Save.

Maintaining printers in FreeBSD/NetBSD

The FreeBsd/NetBSD branch of UNIX does not have the utilities to change printers that Solaris or Linux has. You need to modify a printer by editing the /etc/printcap file, which is discussed next.

Maintaining printers by editing the /etc/printcap file

Nearly any version of UNIX, as well as any version of Linux/FreeBSD/NEtBSD, can have a printer added or modified by editing the /etc/print file. This is the only way to add/modify a printer in FreeBsd orNetBSD. The printer database is stored in the /etc/printcap file, and printers are added by directly editing this file to add a new entry and then creating the corresponding spool directory under /var/spool/lpd.

A very simple entry in the printcap file looks like this:

```
# LOCAL djet500
 lp|dj|deskjet:\
 :sd=/var/spool/lpd/dj:\
 :mx#0:\
 :lp=/dev/lp0:\
 :sh:
```

where:

- The first line for each entry is typically a comment line describing the printer.
- The second line defines a spool with the names lp, dj, or deskjet, which means that you can print to lp, dj, or deskjet.
- The third line defines the spool directory, which is /var/spool/lpd/dj.
- The line starting with mx gives the size limitations on jobs in Kb; mx#0 indicates that there is no size limit to the job.
- The line beginning with lp indicates that the printer is attached to device /dev/lp0.

A very simple entry for a remote printer is:

```
# REMOTE djet500
```

```
lp|dj|deskjet:\
:sd=/var/spool/lpd/dj:\
:rm=machine.out.there.com:\
:rp=printername:\
:lp=/dev/null:\
:sh:
```

where:

- The third line shows that a local spool directory, managed by lpd, is still needed. Jobs wait in the local spool directory until the remote printer is available.
- The `rm` record on the fourth line indicates the remote machine name.
- The fifth line shows the `rp` field, which has the name of the remote printer.
- The sixth line shows a device of /dev/null.
- The `sh` in the seventh line suppresses headers and/or banners.

In the printcap file, lines beginning with # are assumed to be comments and ignored. Lines that start with a colon are fields in each record. Lines that are not comments and do not start with a colon or bar are assumed to start a printer-entry definition.

Other common fields are:

`:lf` The path and name of the log files.

`:if` The filter files to be applied to the print jobs.

`:ab` Always print banner.

`:af` The path and name of the accounting files.

`:br` Sets the baud rate for the port.

`:of` The path and the name of the output filter.

The easiest way to add a new printer is to copy a sample entry and then modify it.

Caution

There should be only one spool directory per printer.

Chapter 5

Other GUI
Configuration Tools

Several tools in addition to SWAT simplify the administration of Samba,
ranging from tools that run on the server, such as Linuxconf, to tools that
run on a Windows client, such as SMBEdit, to tools that run as their own
Web server, such as Webmin.

Using Linuxconf to
Configure Samba

Linuxconf is a utility that is included with Red Hat Linux and which is
used to modify and configure a Red Hat Linux system, including Samba.
It can be run at a command line as root by typing **linuxconf**. You can also
start it in Gnome running as root by selecting gnome-linuxconf from the
startup menu.

To start editing the smb.conf file, select Config ⇨ Networking ⇨ Server
Tasks ⇨ Samba File Server.

There are three working sections under linuxconf: Defaults, Default
setup for users' home, and Disk shares. (The Default setup for printers is
not working yet.)

Defaults

The Defaults section configures overall parameters for the server, as well as parameters that shares can inherit. The parameters that can be set in the default section are:

- Check the box to synchronize Linux and smb passwords. This causes the Linux password for a user to change whenever the password changes using smbpasswd.

- Fill out Server Description; for example, %v expands to the Samba version; %h expands to the host name. This is how the server is described when it appears in the Network Neighborhood.

- Fill out the Workgroup in which the server should appear.

- Fill out Guest Account, specifying a user who will have access to Public Access services.

- Check the box if encrypted passwords are required. Windows NT with Service Pack 3 and later versions of Windows 95 default to encrypted passwords.

- Fill out the Password server field if you are using server-level security. You can list several password servers in this field.

- Choose the Password level, which indicates the maximum allowed uppercase letters in the password. The higher the Password level, the longer it takes to check all permutations of the password.

- Fill out the Password program; for example, /sbin/passwd %u.

- Check the box for a preferred master if you want the Samba server to be the preferred master browser for this workgroup.

- Fill out the OS level for determining browsing elections. Setting this to 33 enables the Samba server to always win the browser election, setting it to 0 causes the Samba server to always lose the election. Windows NT Server has an OS Level of 32, while Windows NT Workstation has an OS Level of 16.

- Check the Allow null passwords account box if null passwords accounts are needed.

- Fill out the Allow hosts field to enable hosts to access the service, by name or IP number, with each additional host separated by a commas. This is analogous to /etc/hosts.allow at the OS level.

- Fill out the Deny hosts field to enable hosts to access the service, by name or IP number, with each additional host separated by a commas. This is analogous to /etc/hosts.deny at the OS level.

- Fill out the Dead time field to set the numbers of minutes of inactivity allowed before Samba disconnects the user.

- Fill out the Debug Level field. This is also known as the log level, and determines what events get logged. The higher the number, the more events get logged, and the slower the performance. The default is 2, and it can be increased when debugging a server problem.

- Fill out the Default Service field, which is typically a public, read-only service.

- Check the Domain master box if you want the Samba server to be a browser for the whole WAN.

- Fill out the Remote announce field if you want your Samba server to announce itself to workgroups to where browsing would not propagate, such as routing smb packets across subnets.

- Check to Show all available printers in the printcap file.

- Fill out the WinPopup command to deliver any WinPopup messages received. The default is to discard the message, but it can be configured to bring the message up in an xterm window or to mail it to root. Useful parameters are:

  %s   The name of the file containing the message.

  %t   The destination name to which the message was sent, typically the server name.

  %f   The name of the client sending the message.

Default setup for user's home

This section modifies the user's home. Your options are:

- Fill out the Comment/Description for the share.

- Check the box if the share is enabled and to be viewed from the browse list automatically.

- Check the box if Public access is desired; no password will be needed and the privileges will be the same as the guest account.

- Check the box if the share is Writable.

- Check the box if the share is Browseable.

- Fill out the Write list for users who will be given read-write access.

- Fill out the Setup Command, which is to execute whenever a user connects to the service. This is also known as the `preexec` parameter.

- Fill out any Setup commands to be run as root, which are to execute as root whenever a user connects to the service. This is also known as the root `preexec` parameter.

- Fill out the Cleanup command, which is to be run when the user disconnects from the service. This is also known as the `postexec` parameter.

- Fill out any Cleanup commands, which are to be run as root when the user disconnects from the service. This is also known as the root `postexec` parameter.

- Fill out the Allow hosts field to enable hosts to access the service, by name or IP number, with each additional host separated by a commas This is analogous to /etc/hosts.allow at the OS level.

- Fill out the Deny hosts field to allow hosts to access the service, by name or IP number, with each additional host separated by a comma. This is analogous to /etc/hosts.deny at the OS level.

- Fill out the Valid users field.

- Fill out the Invalid users field.

- Fill out the max connections field to specify the maximum allowed connections per service; 0 means unlimited connections.

- Fill out the User list field for clients who cannot supply a user name, such as Windows for Workgroups.

- Fill out the Read only user list field.

- Check the Only user may connect box if you want to restrict access to only users in the User's list.

Default setup for printers

This section is not yet working.

Select disk shares

This section helps you setup a specific share. You can:

- Select Add.
- Fill out the Share name field.
- Fill out the Comment/description field.

- Check the box to enable the share.

- Fill out the field to Inherit settings to copy an existing share.

- Fill out the Directory to export field for the share.

- Check the Public Access box if you want the share to be accessible without a password.

- Check the Guest Access only box if you want this share to be only accessed as guest.

- Check the Writable box if you want to allow the share to be written to.

- Check the Browseable box if you want the share in the browse lists.

- Fill out the Write list field for users who will be given read-write access.

- Fill out the Setup command field, which is to execute whenever a user connects to the service. This is also known as the `preexec` command.

- Fill out the Setup command for root field, which is to execute as root whenever a user connects to the service. This is also known as the root `preexec` command.

- Fill out the Cleanup command field, which is to be run when the user disconnects from the service. This is also known as the `postexec` command.

- Fill out the Cleanup command for root field, which is to be run as root when the user disconnects from the service. This is also known as the root `postexec` command.

- Fill out the Force user field to specify a user name for all connections to this share.

- Fill out the Force group field to specify a group for all connections to this share.

- Fill out the Admin users field to list the users who will be given administrative (superuser) rights to this share.

- Fill out the hosts to allow field to enable hosts to access the service, by name or IP number, with each additional host separated by a commas. This is similar to the /etc/hosts.allow file at the OS level.

- Fill out the hosts to deny field to enable hosts to access the service, by name or IP number, with each additional host separated by a commas. This is similar to the hosts.deny field at the OS level.

- Fill out the Don't descend field to specify the directories that Samba should always show as empty.

- Fill out the Guest account for this share field.

- Fill out the Valid users field.

- Fill out the Invalid users field.

- Fill out the Magic script field to specify a script to be executed on the Samba host by the user at connect time (this is experimental).

- Fill out the Magic output field, the file that receives any output from the magic script.

- Fill out the Max connections field to specify the maximum allowed connections per service; 0 means unlimited connections.

- Fill out the user list for clients who cannot supply a user name, such as Windows for Workgroups.

- Fill out the Read only user list field.

- Check the Only user may connect box if you want to restrict access to only users in the User's list.

Using SMBEdit to Configure Samba

SMBEdit is a Windows 95/98/NT application that allows modification of the Samba configuration file (smb.conf) by enabling it as a share, and then allowing you to edit the smb.conf file directly. You can find the homepage for SMBEdit from the main Samba home page under the GUI Interfaces link: `http://us3.samba.org/samba/smbedit/intro.htm`.

SMBEdit works by setting up a share on the Samba server that shares the smb.conf file, while SMBEdit on Windows 95/98 or NT edits the share. This lets you configure any version of Samba via SMBEdit, but each server and client has to be set up.

Tip

SMBEdit is still being developed and should be considered alpha-stage software; not all the functions work. If you use SMBEdit, visit the SMBEdit homepage to stay abreast of the latest developments.

Advantages/disadvantages of SMBEdit

SMBEdit has the advantage of working with any version of Samba.

It has the disadvantage of having operating-system dependencies. The smbedit.ini might need to be edited for a specific version of UNIX/Linux/FreeBSD and might not work with others and it might need to be edited for a specific computer, depending on the parameters with which Samba was installed.

Samba server setup for SMBEdit

You need to add a share that shares the smb.conf file with the administrator and anyone else who needs to administer the server. The following example was added to a smb.conf to configure it for SMBEdit:

```
[samba]
comment = Samba dir
path = /usr/local/etc
public = no
writable = yes
printable = no
write list = root, george
```

The smb.conf file is located in the /usr/local/etc directory, and the two users authorized to administer this samba server are root and george.

The next example is the one provided with SMBEdit:

```
[samba]

comment — Samba Dir
path = /usr/local/samba
public = no
writable = yes
printable — no
write list = @staff
```

In this example, the smb.conf file is located in /usr/local/samba and the users authorized to administer this Samba server are in the group "staff."

Samba server setup for testparm

If you want to use the testparm button, you must add a testparm share to smb.conf and the samba_testparm shell script to the samba bin directory.

The following is a sample testparm share:

```
[testparm]

    comment = run testparm

    path = /tmp

    preexec = /usr/local/bin/samba_testparm > /tmp/testparm

    postexec = /bin/rm —f /tmp/testparm

    public = yes

    writable = no

    printable = no

    write list = root, george
```

The following is a sample script for samba_testparm that works with the previous share:

```
#!/bin/sh
#
# Smbedit - samba_testparm
#
echo "Samba Settings 'date'"
/usr/local/bin/testparm << EOF


EOF
```

Samba server setup for smbstatus

If you want to use the smbstatus button, you must add an smbstatus share to smb.conf and the samba_smbstatus shell script to the samba bin directory.

The following is a sample smbstatus share:

```
[smbstatus]


coment = run smbstatus
path = /tmp
preexec = /usr/local/bin/samba_smbstatus > /tmp/smbstatus
```

```
postexec = /bin/rm -f /tmp/smbstatus
public = yes
writable = no
printable = no
write list = root, george
```

The following is a sample script for samba_smbstatus to work with the previous share:

```
#!/bin/sh
#
# Smbedit - samba_smbstatus
#
echo "# Samba Status 'date' on FreeBSD server ('uname -n')"
echo ""
/usr/local/bin/smbstats -d
echo ""
echo "Samba Processers :-
foreach PID ('/usr/local/bin/smbstatus -p')

echo " $PID"

end
exit 0
```

Windows 95/98/NT setup

You will have to download and install two files: an executable named smbedit*dll.exe and a zipped file named smbedit*.zip. Their names might change in newer versions; at this writing, their full names are smbedit-1_02dll.exe and smbedit1_02alpha8.zip. Run the executable and follow the installation instructions, and then unzip the smbedit.zip file. Click the Smbedit icon to launch it.

Tip

If you want to do server maintenance from SMBEdit, you need to check the smbedit.ini file to verify that the command lists are correct for your system because the path could vary and the actual commands vary from UNIX/Linux/BSD system to system.

Using SMBEdit

SMBEdit works by connecting to the smb.conf share on your Samba server and allowing you to edit it. SMBEdit may need to be configured for your particular server, and the same configuration may not work on two separate Samba servers.

Connecting to a Samba server

You can connect to your Samba server by using the File menu or clicking the Open Folder icon.

To connect to your Samba share with the File menu, click File, select Open, and browse through Network Neighborhood. Or connect directly with the uniform resource syntax, for example, `//Terrapin/Samba`, to open the Samba share on Terrapin.

To connect to your Samba share with the Open Folder icon, double-click the Open Folder icon, and then browse through the Network Neighborhood to your Samba share.

Modifying shares

Click the plus (+) sign to open the folder.

Click the share that you want to edit, click the Enable edit button (the lock), and edit the share in the right-hand window. The lock icon is open when enable edit is on.

Tip

To edit a share, you need the appropriate rights to the directory containing smb.conf.

Proceed to edit the share's information in the right-hand window. The syntax is the same as that used to edit the smb.conf file.

Adding shares

Click the plus (+) icon to add a share.

Deleting shares

Click the wastebasket icon to remove a share.

UNIX/Linux/FreeBSD procedures

SMBEdit gives you the functionality of basic maintenance on the UNIX/Linux/BSD server.

After opening a Samba server, highlight the server and the UNIX options become available.

Changing the UNIX logon Click the tabbed folder to change your UNIX logon.

Changing the server Click the two networked computers icon to change your server.

Adding or editing a UNIX user Click the person icon, to the left of the printer, to add or edit a UNIX user.

Add or edit a UNIX printer Click the printer icon to add or edit a UNIX printer.

Running testparm Click the paper icon to run testparm. The testparm share and script must have been installed earlier for this to work.

Running smbstatus Click the balloon icon to run smbstatus for the system. The smbstatus share and script must have been installed earlier for this to work.

Webmin

Webmin is a Web-based program for administering UNIX/Linux/FreeBSD systems, including Samba administration. Webmin is a simple Web server and a number of CGI programs to update system files.

Webmin and the CGI programs are written in Perl, and you only need the Perl 5 binary to run webmin.

Webmin's homepage is `http://www.webmin.com/webmin`.

Downloading and installing webmin

First, ensure that you have Perl 5 installed on your system. Perl is usually installed in /usr/local/bin/perl or /usr/bin/perl, but if it isn't installed, it can be downloaded and compiled from `http://www.perl.com`.

Then, download the tar and gzipped version of webmin. The most current version as of this writing is webmin-0.73, which can be downloaded from `ftp://ftp.webmin.com/webmin-0.73.tar.gz`.

Copy the gzipped file to the desired parent directory and unzip it. It will create a directory named webmin-0.73. If you have gzip installed, it is as simple as typing:

```
gzip —dc webmin-0.73.tar.gz | tar xvf —
```

The webmin directory has a shell script named setup.sh. Run this script to set up webmin. You have to answer questions about the configuration of your system; if you wish, just press Enter at each question to accept the default.

Caution

There is no option for Caldera OpenLinux. The RedHat option should work in its place, however.

After the configuration completes, you should receive the URL for your browser to use webmin.

Using webmin

Access webmin by starting your browser and accessing the webmin Web server; to access the webmin server on the Samba server terrapin running on port 10,000, you would open `http://terrapin:10000`.

Caution

Webmin requires 4Mb to run and could cause performance problems on systems with insufficient RAM.

You will have to login as the user that was set up during the configuration, along with the password. After successfully logging on, you will be at the webmin main page.

Tip

The users who have access to webmin are listed in the miniserv.users file in the webmin directory.

Editing Samba

The links are displayed alphabetically. The link for Samba is near the end and is entitled Samba Windows File Sharing. Click it to go to the Samba Exports page.

The Samba Exports page has links to configure Samba at the very top, and then links for all the existing shares, followed by links for creating new file and printer shares. At the bottom are the Global Configuration links, such as defaults, authentication, and networking options.

Module config The module config link at the top of the page takes to you to the Configuration page. The properties you can change there are:

- Location of the Samba configuration file. This can be changed to use different configuration files for different uses.
- Whether Samba has a password file, and where it is located. Samba needs its own password file if encrypted Windows passwords are being used. This is the default for Windows NT with Service Pack 4, Windows 98, and later versions of Windows 95.
- The full path to the smbstatus command.
- The full path to smbpasswd utility, which is used to synchronize Samba passwords with Unix passwords.
- The full path to smbd, the Samba daemon.
- The full path to nmbd, the Samba network browsing daemon.
- Whether SWAT, the Samba Web Administrators Tool, is being used, and where it is located.
- The list of UNIX users not to add to the SMB password list.

- Whether Samba should run from inetd. Having Samba called by inetd is appropriate only when Samba is used infrequently on the server, such as on a workstation that is only accessed from Windows occasionally.

Adding/editing a file share Click the Create a new file share link to add a new file share, or click the name of the share that you want to edit. Options that can be changed are:

- The share name.
- The path to the share directory.
- Whether it is available. If available is set to no, all attempts to connect to the share will fail.
- Whether it is browseable.
- Any comments to describe the share.

There are four links for in-depth options: Security and Access Control, File Permissions, File Naming, and Miscellaneous Options.

Security and access control Under the Security and Access Control link, these options are available:

- Whether it is writable.
- Whether guest access is none, yes, or guest only. This modifies the guest only and guest okay parameters.
- Who the guest will be as a UNIX user.
- If there is a limit to possible list, which defines the only user parameter. If this is set to yes, only users listed in the user parameter will be allowed to connect.
- To allow all hosts, or allow only a list of hosts.
- To deny no hosts, or deny a list of hosts.
- Whether to revalidate users. This only applies when security equals share. It prevents having to retype passwords when the user is connecting to a second share on the same server.
- A list of valid users and groups. This is empty by default, allowing any user to access the share. If users or groups are listed, only those users and members of the group may connect to the share.

- A list of invalid users and groups, users who should not be allowed to connect to the share.

- A list of possible users and groups. This is the `user` (or `username`) parameter and is needed for share level security; it provides a list of names to test the password against.

- A list of users with read-only permissions.

- A list of groups whose users will have read-only permissions.

- A list of users with read/write permissions.

- A list of groups whose users will have read/write permissions.

File permissions   The File Permissions link has these options available:

- The new UNIX file mode for any new files created in the share.

- The new UNIX directory mode for any new directories created in the share.

- The directories not to list. This may be for security or practical reasons; there is no need to list the /proc directory as an example.

- Force UNIX user to specify a default UNIX user name for users accessing the share.

- Force UNIX group to specify a default UNIX user group for users accessing the share.

- Allow symlinks outside the share. This enables users to follow and create symbolic links outside the share directory.

- Enable deletion of read-only files.

- Force UNIX file mode to specify a certain file permission for new file creation.

- Force UNIX directory mode to specify a certain directory permission for new directory creation.

File naming   The File Naming link options are:

- Whether to mangle case to make name match the default case.

- Whether files are case sensitive.

- The default case.

- Whether to preserve case.

- Whether to short-preserve case for filenames that are DOS compatible.

- Whether to hide dot files, such as .profile or .login.
- Whether to save the DOS archive flag.
- Whether to save the DOS hidden flag.
- Whether to save the DOS system flag.

Miscellaneous options The Miscellaneous Options link options are:

- Whether to do File Locking. Unless you are a developer writing parts of Samba, this should be yes; otherwise, data corruption could result.
- Whether to have a maximum connections value or allow unlimited connections.
- Whether to use Fake Oplocks. Turning Fake Oplocks on enables clients to cache files locally, resulting in significantly increased performance.
- Whether to use share modes. This should always be yes; otherwise, some Windows applications that are accessing files on shares could fail.
- Whether to use strict locking. The best performance is with strict locking set to no; this is the default. When set to yes, the server checks every read and write access for locks, and denies access if a lock is present.
- Whether to sync after writes. This turns on the `sync always` parameter. The default is no; if yes, the disk will be synched after every write operation, which can slow down performance.
- Whether the volume name is the same as the share name, and what it is if different.
- The UNIX-DOS filename map. This is the `mangle map` parameter, used to map UNIX names to DOS names. One of the most common uses is to map UNIX html file extensions to DOS htm file extensions, for example:

```
mangled map = (*.html *.htm)
```

- The command to run on connect. This is also known as the `preexec` command.
- The command to run on disconnect. This is also known as the `postexec` command.

- The command to run on connect as root. This is also known as the root `preexec` command.

- The command to run on disconnect as root. This is also known as the root `postexec` command.

Adding/editing a printer share   Click the Create a new printer share link to add a new printer share, or click the name of the printer share you want to edit. Options that can be changed are:

- Whether it's a specific share, with name, or the All Printers share.
- The UNIX printer name.
- The spool directory.
- Whether it is available.
- Whether it is browseable.
- The share comment.

There are two links for in-depth options: the Security and Access Control link and the Printer Options link.

Security and access control   The Security and Access Control link options are:

- Whether it is writable.
- Whether guest access is none, yes, or guest only. This modifies the `guest only` and `guest okay` parameters.
- Who the guest user will be as a UNIX user.
- If there is a limit to the possible list, which defines the only `user` parameter. If this is set to yes, only users listed in the `user` parameter are enabled to connect.
- To allow all hosts or allow only a list of hosts.
- To deny no hosts or deny a list of hosts.
- Whether to revalidate users. This only applies when `security` equals `share`. It prevents having to retype passwords when the user is connecting to a second share on the same server.
- A list of valid users and groups. This is empty by default, enabling any user to access the share. If users or groups are listed, only those users and members of the group may connect to the share.

- A list of invalid users and groups, users who should not be allowed to connect to the share.

- A list of possible users and groups. This is the user (or username) parameter and is needed for share-level security. It provides a list of names to test the password against.

- A list of users with read-only permissions.

- A list of groups whose users have read-only permissions.

- A list of users who with read/write permissions.

- A list of groups whose users have read/write permissions.

Printer options   The Printer Options link options are:

- The minimum free space, which specifies the min print space parameter to tell the amount of free disk space to spool jobs.

- Whether to force PostScript printing. This is typically used when you are supporting a PostScript printer, but the clients add Ctrl+D's at the beginning of the print jobs.

- Whether to use the default print command or a different one. This sets the print command parameter.

- Whether to use the default display queue command or a different one. This is the lpq command parameter.

- Whether to use the default delete job command or a different one. This is the lprm command parameter.

- Whether to use the default pause job command or a different one. This is the lppause command parameter.

- Whether to use the default unresume job command or a different one. This is the lpresume command parameter.

- Whether to use the default printer driver or a different one. This is the printer driver parameter.

Create a new copy   The Create a new copy link takes you to the Create Copy page, where you can create a new share by copying an existing one.

View all connections   The View all connections link shows you all the connected users and enables you to disconnect specific users.

UNIX networking Clicking the UNIX Networking link brings you to the UNIX Networking Options page. This section modifies Samba in regards to UNIX networking. Options here are:

- Whether to disconnect a connection after a specified idle time. This modifies the `deadtime` parameter.
- Whether to use a trusted hosts/users file, and which one.
- Whether to get network interfaces automatically, or to use specific ones, and specific netmasks. This modifies the `interfaces` parameter.
- Whether to use Keep alive packets, and how often to send them. This is the `keep alive` parameter, which is similar to the `SO_KEEPALIVE` socket option. It sends periodic NetBIOS keep-alive packets to determine whether a client is alive and responding, and to disconnect dead clients. This can improve performance by freeing resources.
- The maximum packet size. This is the `max xmit`.
- Which addresses to listen on.
- Any socket options to use. There are 10 socket options, and every UNIX/Linux recognizes them. The two that are primarily used are `SO_KEEPALIVE` and `TCP_NODELAY`; the other eight are best used by administrators fluent with socket operations. `SO_KEEPALIVE` can improve performance by sending TCP packets to clients to determine whether they are still alive, and disconnecting them if they are not. `TCP_NODELAY` can increase performance at an increase in network traffic.

Windows networking The Windows Networking link options are:

- Whether to use the default workgroup or specify one.
- The WINS Mode for interacting with Windows naming services — whether to be a WINS server, use a WINS server, or neither.
- The Server description.
- The Server name.
- A Server alias if desired.
- The default service.
- The services to always show.
- The max reported disk size.

- The command to use for WinPopup messages. The default is to discard the message, but it can also be configured to bring the message up in an xterm window or to mail it to root. Useful parameters are:

  `%s`   The name of the file containing the message.

  `%t`   The destination name to which the message was sent, typically the server name.

  `%f`   The name of the client sending the message.

- The browser priority. This is the `OS Level` parameter. Setting this to 33 enables the Samba server to always win the browser election; setting it to 0 causes the Samba server to always lose the election. Windows NT Server has an OS level of 32, while Windows NT Workstation has an OS level of 16.

- The highest SMB network protocol, which is selected from among CORE, COREPLUS, LANMAN!, LANMAN@, and NT1. This sets the `protocol` parameter, the default of which is NT1.

- Whether to try and become the Master Browser during browser elections to provide a list of services on the network to other clients. The Samba server should only try to become the Master Browser if it also the domain master.

- The security level to use (share, user, password server, or domain).

- The password server if applicable.

- Whether to remote announce and where to remote announce, whether workgroups or IP addresses. This is the `remote announce` parameter, which enables the Samba server to appear in the browse lists of remote subnets where it wouldn't normally appear. If you are sending remote announces to IP Addresses, use the broadcast address (such as 192.168.11.255) or IP address of the local master browser in the remote subnet.

Authentication   The Authentication link options are:

- Whether to use encrypted passwords. Windows NT with Service Pack 3 and later versions of Windows 95 default to encrypted passwords.

- Whether to allow null passwords.

- The password program, for example, /sbin/passwd %u.

- The password case difference value. This is the `password level` parameter. This indicates the maximum allowed uppercase letters in the password. The higher the password level, the longer it takes to check all permutations of the password.

- The change password chat value pairs. This is the `passwd chat` parameter, and is used to change a user's UNIX password when they change their Windows password.

- Whether to use user name mapping from UNIX to Windows. This is the `username map` parameter, and has a table to fill out the user name map.

Windows to UNIX printing The Windows to UNIX printing link options are:

- The UNIX print style (such as BSD, SYSV).
- Whether to show all printers.
- The printcap file to use.
- The printer status cache time.

Miscellaneous options The Miscellaneous options link options are:

- The debug level. This is also known as the log level, and it determines which events get logged. The higher the number, the more events that are logged and the slower the performance. The default is 2, and it can be increased when debugging a server problem.

- Whether to cache `getwd()` calls. This is the `getwd cache` parameter. When set to true, directory caching occurs and performance can increase.

- The lock directory, which contains lock files.
- The log file.
- The maximum log size.
- Whether to enable raw reads. This is the `read raw` parameter, which is true by default. It enables 65535 bytes to be sent per packet and can increase performance.

- Whether to enable raw writes. This is the `read write` parameter, and is true by default. It enables 65535 bytes to be sent per packet and can increase performance.

- The overlapping read size. This is the `read size` parameter, and can provide significant performance increases by overlapping network and disk read/writes.

- The `chroot()` directory. This is the `root directory` parameter, which can be used to have Samba use a different root directory for an added level of security.

- The path to the smbrun binary, if it is installed in a different location than was specified at compile time.

- The client time offset. The `time offset` parameter is used to add minutes to the normal GMT for a local time conversion if you are using the Samba server as a time server.

- The read prediction. The `read prediction` parameter, when sent to true, attempts to improve performance by prereading data from previously opened files.

File share defaults This link sets the file share defaults.

Printer share defaults This link sets the printer share defaults.

SWAT This link enables you to connect to the SWAT server.

Other webmin uses

Webmin can also be used to administer many other functions on a UNIX/Linux/FreeBSD machine. Some of the functions that it can administer that are relevant to Samba are:

- Scheduling cron jobs to be run at regular, specific intervals.
- Creating and using custom commands.
- Startup and shutdown actions.
- User and group maintenance.
- Printer maintenance.
- Running process lists.

Using webmin to schedule cron jobs Click the Scheduled Cron Jobs link to go to the Scheduled Cron Jobs page. On the Scheduled Cron Jobs page, is a list of existing cron jobs, a link to create a new cron job, and a link to control user access to cron jobs, as well as a Module Config for Cron.

Module config for cron Click on Module Config to go the Configuration for Scheduled Cron Jobs page. The options on this page are:

- The crontab directory.
- The command to read a user's cron job.
- The command to edit a user's cron job.
- The command to accept a user's cron job on stdin.
- The command to delete a user's cron job.
- Whether cron supports input to cron jobs.
- The file listing allowed users.
- The file listing denied users.
- The permissions if there is no allow or deny file.
- Whether it supports Vixie-cron extensions.
- The path to the Vixie-cron system crontab file.
- The run parts command.

Editing existing cron jobs Click an existing cron job. The Edit cron job page options are:

- Which user to execute the cron job as.
- Whether the cron job is active.
- The cron command.
- The input to the cron command.
- When to execute the cron command.

Creating new cron jobs Click the Create a new cron job link. The Create Cron Job page options are:

- Which user to execute the cron job as.
- Whether the cron job is active.
- The cron command.
- The input to the cron command.
- When to execute the cron command.

Controlling user access to cron jobs Click the Control user access to cron jobs link. On the Control Cron Access page, choose either allow all users, or allow a list of users, or deny a list of users.

Using webmin to create custom commands Click the Custom Commands link. On the Custom Commands page, you can edit an existing custom command or create a new custom command.

Editing an existing command Click the Edit command link for the command you want to edit. The Edit Command page options are:

- Fill out the description.
- Specify the command.
- Specify which user will run the command.
- Specify any command parameters.

Creating a new command Click the Create a new command link. The Create Command page options are:

- Fill out the description.
- Specify the command.
- Specify which user will run the command.
- Specify any command parameters.

Using webmin for startup/shutdown commands Click the Bootup and Shutdown Actions link. The Bootup and Shutdown page enables you to edit the startup file for your particular system.

You also have the option of rebooting the system or shutting down the system.

The Module Config for Bootup and Shutdown has the following options to customize this section for your server, many of which will be filled out already:

- The directory in which run level directories are located.
- The directory containing the master initialization scripts.
- The link type to use for run level files, soft or hard.
- The number of digits in action order.
- The local startup commands script, if it exists.
- The command to reboot the system.
- The command to shutdown the system.
- Whether the system supports bootup/shutdown messages.

- The path to the inittab file.
- The inittab ID for bootup runlevel.

Using webmin for printer commands Click the Printer Administration link. The Printer Administration page has a module config option, an existing printers option, and an add new printer option, as well as the capability to stop the scheduler.

Module config for printer administration Click the Module Config link near the top of the Printer Administration screen to set up the default parameters for the system's printers. The Configuration page options are:

- The printer configuration style, whether Solaris, Linux, FreeBSD or HPUX.
- The directory containing any interface programs that are being used.
- The path to smbclient, if available.
- The path to Ghostscript, if available.
- The Ghostscript font directories.
- The Ghostscript library directories.
- The path to the hpnp program, if available.
- The owner of the driver script.
- The interface script parameter.

Editing existing printers Click the printer you want to edit. The Edit Printer menu editing options are:

- Specify if the printer is accepting requests.
- The description of the printer.
- Specify if printing is enabled.
- Specify whether to print a banner page.
- Specify the maximum job size.
- Specify any alternate printer names.
- The print destination; choose between a local device, a local file, a remote UNIX server, a remote Windows server, and any user names or passwords needed to access a remote printer.

- Specify the print driver: The choices are none, a program, or a webmin driver.

Adding a new printer Click the Add a new printer link. The Create Printer window's options are:

- The printer name.
- Specify if the printer is accepting requests.
- The description of the printer.
- Specify if printing is enabled.
- Specify whether to print a banner page.
- Specify the maximum job size.
- Specify any alternate printer names.
- The print destination; choose between a local device, a local file, a remote UNIX server, a remote Windows server, and any user names or passwords needed to access a remote printer.
- Specify the print driver. The choices are none, a program, or a webmin driver.

Using webmin to check processes Click the Running Processes link. In the Process Manager window, you can choose Module config or display PID, User, Memory, CPU, Search, Run.

The Process Manager initially displays all the processes. Selecting a process gives you the process information, with the option of changing the Nice Level or sending a signal to the process.

Module config for processes Click the Module Config link to go to the Module Config page, where you can change the process list style and PS command output style.

User Click the User link to sort processes by users.

Memory Click the Memory link to sort processes by memory usage.

CPU Click the CPU link to sort processes by CPU usage.

Search Click the Search link to search for processes by matching CPU usage or owner.

Run Click the Run link to run a command. Specify the run mode and any input to the command.

The Module config for users and groups The Module Config section for users and groups lets you specify parameters for adding/changing users and groups. The configurable options for users and groups are:

- Whether the password file will be generated, or it exists, where it is located.
- The group file.
- Whether the shadow password file is being used and where it is located.
- Whether the BSD master password file is being used and where it is located.
- Whether the shadow group file is being used and where it is located.
- Any command to run before making changes.
- Any command to run after making changes.
- The default permissions on new home directories.
- The lowest UID for new users.
- The lowest UID for new groups.
- The default group for new users.
- The maximum number of users to display.
- Whether to sort users and groups by name.
- The number of previous logins to display.

Using webmin to add groups Click the Users, Groups, and Passwords link to get to the Users and Groups admin page.

Click Create a new group to get to the Create Group page, or click an existing user to get to the Edit group page.

On the Create or Edit group page, you must complete these parameters:

- Specify the group name.
- Specify the group ID.
- Specify if there will be no password, an encrypted password with encrypted password typed out, or a clear text password with password typed out. Group passwords are very rarely used.
- Add the group members.

Using webmin to add/edit users Click the Users, Groups, and Passwords link to get to the Users and Groups admin page.

Click Create a new user to get to the Create User page, or click an existing user to get to the Edit user page.

On the Create or Edit user page, you must complete or you may change these parameters:

- The Username the user will log in as.
- The UserID.
- The user's Real Name displayed in the comment field.
- The user's Home Directory.
- The user's preferred Shell, typically C, Bourne, BASH, or Korn.
- Password, with the choices of No password required, No login allowed, Encrypted password with the encrypted password typed out, or Clear text password with the clear text password typed out.
- The primary group the user will belong to.
- Any secondary groups the user will belong to.
- Whether to move the home directory if it has been changed.
- Whether to change the user ID on files and to what directories it applies.
- Whether to change the group ID on files and to what directories it applies.

Part II

Advanced Configuration

Chapter 6

Naming Services, Browsing, and Domains

People understand things better in terms of names and groups, whereas computers work most efficiently on numbers. As networks have become more complex, solutions have been developed to enable administrators to work with methods they find easiest — names, groups, and hierarchies — while enabling computers to stay with numbers. An administrator of a network of four computers (such as my home network) can easily remember each client or server's IP address; this becomes more difficult, and soon becomes impossible, with the addition of more clients or servers.

This chapter details some of the solutions developed to help humans administer large networks and how Samba interacts with these solutions. NIS is a naming service that provides a central database of network information, including hosts and users. DNS is an IP translation solution, translating IP name addresses into IP numbers. WINS is similar in function to DNS, but translates NetBIOS names and addresses. Browsing is how a Windows network displays resources, and domains are how a Windows network is arranged for easier administration.

NIS

Network Information Systems (NIS) is a name service that provides a central lookup for network resources, such as host names and addresses, users, services, automount maps, and other key files.

The biggest task in making Samba work with NIS is ensuring that NIS is working correctly in UNIX. This section covers troubleshooting NIS clients; NIS servers are beyond the scope of this book.

NIS problems often manifest themselves as connection or lookup problems.

Setting up Linux as a NIS client using traditional NIS

Linux can be set up as a NIS client using the traditional method:

1. Edit the /etc/hosts.conf file and add `nis` to the order lookup line.

2. Edit the /etc/passwd file to add the line `+::::::::` to make the system use NIS for password referrals.

Also, you can use the + or − characters to include or exclude specific users. To enable the users jerry and phil and the members of the netgroup sas while excluding jim, add:

```
+jerry:::::::
+phil:::::::
+@sas:::::::
-jim
```

The corresponding /etc/netgroup entry for sas, if the members of sas were donna, ron, and bobby, would be:

```
sas (-,donna,) (-,ron,) (-,bobby,)
```

Each member entry is of the form *hostname, username, domain name;* a blank field is a wildcard and an entry with a dash implies no valid value.

Setting up Linux as a NIS client using NYS

To set up Linux as a NIS client using NYS, follow these steps:

1. Create the /etc/yp.conf file; for example:

    ```
    domain domainname
    server nis_server
    ```

where domainname is the NIS domain containing the client and nis_server is the NIS server.

2. Add the following line to the /etc/sysconfig/network file:

   `NISDOMAIN=nisdomain`

3. Edit the /etc/nsswitch.conf file to specify the search order used by the system to find information. The following sample lines show that passwd is searched in the local passwd database first (the files entry), then in the NIS database (the NIS entry). Hostnames are searched for locally first, in the NIS database next, and then in the DNS database (the DNS entry).

   ```
   passwd:    files    nis
   hosts:     files    nis    dns
   ```

Other typical maps (databases) that can be included on the nsswitch.conf are:

automount

aliases

bootparams

ethers

group

netgroup

networks

netmasks

publickey

rpc

services

aliases

Other options that can be used in nsswitch.conf are:

`[NOTFOUND=return]`	Stop searching if the information has not been found yet.
`nis+`	Use NIS+. NIS+ is not fully supported for Linux.

If you want to use the include/exclude functions for users and netgroups, you need to use `passwd: compat` and `group: compat` in nsswitch.conf.

Then run the ypbind daemon. You can make this happen at boot time by adding a symbolic link from /etc/rc.d/rc.3d/S60ypbind to /etc/rc.d/init.d/ypbind. The syntax is:

```
#ln -s /etc/rc.d/init.d/ypbind /etc/rc.d/rc3.d/S60ypbind
```

Setting up Solaris as a NIS client

To set up a Solaris machine as a NIS client, follow these steps:

1. Create the /etc/nsswitch.conf file.
2. Add the NIS servers to the /etc/hosts files.
3. Use the `domainname` command to set the domain name.
4. Add the domain name to the /etc/defaultdomain file.
5. Initialize the system with the `ypinit` command: `ypinit -c`.
6. Enter the names of the NIS master and slave servers when prompted.
7. Start the NIS software with the command `/usr/lib/netsvc/yp/ypstart`.

Setting up FreeBSD/NetBSD as a NIS client

Most of the client-side configuration for FreeBSD/NetBSD takes place in the /etc/rc.conf file. You can find a sample rc.conf file in /etc/defaults that you can use as a template. Here's what you need to do:

1. Set the NIS domain name; the following line sets the NIS domain name to georgenet:

   ```
   nisdomainname="georgenet"    # Set to NIS domain if
   using NIS (or NO).
   ```

2. Next, enable the ypbind daemon to start on boot by adding these two lines:

```
nis_client_enable="YES"      # We're an NIS client
(or NO).
nis_client_flags=""          # Flags to ypbind (if
enabled).
```

Client flags can be used for greater security. The –S flag with a list of servers causes ypbind to restrict itself to those servers. The man pages on ypbind have more information on using flags with ypbind.

3. Edit the master.passwd, passwd, group, and other files to enable them to use NIS.

For /etc/group, delete nonsystem, critical groups and add the line +::: at the end of the file.

For /etc/master.passwd and /etc/passwd, use vipw to delete all users not needed for system operation, and add the line +:::::::::: to the end of the file.

4. Edit the /etc/host.conf file to specify your desired lookup order.

5. Edit the /etc/hosts table to add the NIS servers, and then add the line +:: at the end to enable NIS.

6. Either reboot to test your rc.conf modifications and start NIS, or set the domain with the domainname command and then run ypbind.

Testing NIS

Use the ypcat command to test NIS. This command displays the NIS password file:

```
#ypcat passwd
```

Another test is to remove all external hosts from the /etc/host file and to try to telnet to one of them. If NIS is setup correctly, telnet works.

DNS

Domain Name Service (DNS) is a network service that provides IP address-to-hostname and hostname-to-IP address translation. To grossly simplify the situation, this is needed because computer networks use numbers to find other computers, whereas users use names.

Setting up Linux as a DNS client

You must configure the /etc/resolv.conf file to query the DNS servers. The first line gives the domain, and the next line(s) give the DNS servers' IP addresses, up to three. The following example is for the domain george.net, with two name servers with IP addresses of 192.168.11.1 and 192.168.12.1:

```
search george.net
nameserver 192.168.11.1
nameserver 192.168.12.1
```

Setting up FreeBSD/NetBSD as a DNS client

To set up FreeBSD/NetBSD as a DNS Client, follow these steps:

1. Verify that the named is not running by checking the following line in rc.conf:

```
named_enable="NO"    # Run named DNS server (or NO).
```

2. Edit /etc/resolv.conf, with the first line being the domain and the next line(s) being the IP addresses of the name servers. The following example is for the domain george.net, with two name servers with IP addresses of 192.168.11.1 and 192.168.12.1:

```
domain george.net
nameserver 192.168.11.1
nameserver 192.168.12.1
```

Setting up a Solaris DNS client

The first step for a Solaris machine is to modify the /etc/resolvconf file. The second step is to check the /etc/nsswitch.conf file.

Modifying the /etc/resolv.conf file

The /etc/resolv.conf file must exist. It specifies the DNS domain and DNS name servers. The following example is for the domain george.net, with two name servers with IP addresses of 192.168.11.1 and 192.168.12.1:

```
domain george.net
nameserver 192.168.11.1
nameserver 192.168.12.1
```

Checking the /etc/nsswitch.conf file

The parameters in this file determine the order of services a client uses to resolve machine names. Enter the command:

```
cat /etc/nsswitch.conf | grep hosts
```

If you are a client that is not using NIS, this command will return:

```
hosts: dns files
```

If you are a client that is using NIS, this command will return:

```
hosts: nis dns files
```

Next, check the file /etc/netconfig to ensure that it lists all three Internet Transport Protocols: UDP, TCP, and rawip.

WINS

WINS is a NetBIOS name-verification service that is used with Windows networking. It reduces network traffic by making clients register with the WINS server instead of broadcasting NetBIOS names, and it allows clients to see NetBIOS servers across subnets.

Windows NT 4.0 server comes with a WINS server, and Samba can be a WINS server also.

Making Samba use a WINS server

Samba's default is not to use a WINS server. To make Samba use a WINS server, change the `wins server = none` parameter in the smb.conf file to `wins server = IP_address`, where `IP_address` is the IP address of the WINS server.

Configuring Samba as a WINS server

To configure Samba as a WINS server, make sure that it is not looking at any other server by verifying that the wins server parameter is wins server = none.

Then enable the wins support parameter by changing it to wins support = yes and configuring the Windows 95/98 and NT clients.

Configuring Samba as a WINS proxy

You can configure your Samba server as a WINS proxy to forward requests to the WINS server specified in smb.conf (usually by the wins server parameter) with the WINS proxy setting:

```
wins proxy = yes
```

Browsing

Windows browsing finds the servers that are in the network neighborhood and which services are being provided. Rather than have each client browse on its own, a Windows network has a master browser and/or backup browsers that provide the browse list to the clients. A Samba server can become a master or backup browser.

Master/backup browser parameters

The following parameters determine whether the Samba server becomes a master or backup browser.

Announce version

This parameter specifies the version numbers that nmbd will use when announcing itself as a server. The default is 4.2. Do not change this parameter unless you have a specific need to set a Samba server as a lower-level server.

Announce as

This parameter specifies how nmbd will announce itself to the network neighborhood browse list. The default beginning with Samba 2.x is set to

Windows NT. Don't change this parameter unless you have to stop Samba from appearing as an NT server. This could prevent the Samba server from participating as a browser server correctly.

The valid options are:

NT   Acts as a server for all modern Win95 and later Windows clients

Win95   Also acts as a server for all modern Windows clients

OS level

This parameter specifies what level Samba advertises for browse elections. This parameter determines whether nmbd can become a local master browser for the workgroup. The default is set to lose elections to Windows machines.

The default is:

```
os level = 0
```

An example of a setting that will win against all Windows servers is:

```
os level = 65
```

Preferred master

This parameter specifies whether nmbd becomes a preferred master browser for its workgroup. If this parameter is set to `preferred master = yes`, nmbd forces a master browser election on startup. By default, it will have a slight advantage in winning the election. The OS-level parameter previously discussed is another spot for you to tilt the election in your Samba server's favor. If you set this parameter to `Yes`, you should also set the `domain master = yes`. Using these three settings together — `preferred master = yes`, `domain master = yes`, and `os level = 65` — ensures that nmbd can become a domain master.

This option can be a performance bottleneck if several hosts are set to be preferred master browsers on the same subnet. It doesn't matter whether the servers are Samba, NT, or Windows 95/98 machines — if they're configured to be the master browser, they periodically attempt to become the local master browser. The result is unnecessary broadcast traffic and slower browsing.

Local master

This parameter specifies whether nmbd will participate in elections to become the local master browser on a subnet. If this parameter is set to local master = no, nmbd will not attempt to become a local master browser on a subnet. The server will also lose in all browsing elections. If you set this value to local master = no, the Samba server will never become a local master browser.

Browse list

This parameter is the opposite of the domain master = parameter. This parameter specifies whether smbd will serve a browse list to a domain master browser building a wide area browse list. The Samba server receives information about other servers during this exchange.

List/Service parameters

List/Service parameters determine how the Samba server appears in the browse list, and which services are shown. Table 6-1 lists the various List/Service parameters.

Table 6-1 *List/Service Parameters*

Parameter	Function
Workgroup	This option controls which workgroup your server will appear in when queried by clients.
Netbios name	This option sets the NetBIOS name for the Samba server.
Netbios aliases	This option creates a group of NetBIOS names that nmbd will advertise as additional names by which the Samba server can provide services. This enables one machine to appear in browse lists under multiple names.
Server string	This controls what text string appears in browse lists next to the machine name.
Auto services	This global parameter specifies the list of services added to the browse list.
Load printers	This parameter controls whether all printers in the printcap are loaded for browsing.
Browseable	This parameter specifies whether the share is visible in the list of available shares in a net view and in the browse list. This parameter does not make a share unavailable, only invisible, by default.

Parameter	Function
Lm announce	This parameter specifies whether nmbd produces Lanman announce broadcasts that are needed by OS/2 clients. If this setting is set to `false`, OS/2 clients will not be capable of seeing the Samba server in their browse list.
Lm interval	If you set the parameter `lm announce` to either `true` or `auto`, this parameter, `lm interval`, sets the frequency of broadcasts. If this parameter is set to zero, then no Lanman announcements occur.

Subnet browsing

Samba needs a few more parameters if it is to be accessible across routed subnets. Table 6-2 lists the necessary additional parameters.

Table 6-2 *Subnet Browsing Parameters*

Parameter	Function
Domain master	This global parameter turns Samba into a domain master browser, providing a list of network services to NetBIOS clients.
Remote announce	This parameter specifies whether nmbd periodically announces itself to the specified IP addresses, even across subnets. It can include a workgroup name.
Remote browse sync	This parameter specifies whether nmbd requests synchronization of browse lists with the master browser of another Samba server on a remote segment.
Wins proxy	This parameter specifies whether nmbd responds to broadcast name queries on behalf of other hosts.
Wins server	This parameter specifies the IP address or DNS name of the WINS server with which nmbd is to register.
Wins support	This parameter specifies whether the nmbd process in Samba acts as a WINS server.

Samba as a Windows 95/98 Domain Controller

Samba can be set up to act as a domain controller for Windows 95/98 clients. When the Samba server acts as a Windows 95/98 domain controller, users must be verified that they are logged in correctly when they first start their PCs. This avoids misdiagnosed errors with mistyped usernames and passwords. User's can have roaming profiles so that their network mappings are always correct.

Configuring Samba to act as a Windows 95/98 domain controller

To configure Samba to act as a Windows 95/98 domain controller, follow these steps:

1. Make sure that security is user level or server level.

2. Make sure that the Samba server is the master browser for the domain. This is the same procedure as making Samba the master browser for a subnet. Add the following parameters to the global section of smb.conf to make the Samba server always win the master browser election:

```
os level = 64
domain master = yes
local master = yes
preferred master = yes
```

3. Make Samba act as a domain controller by enabling domain logons:

```
domain logons = yes
```

Finally, Samba needs a share added named [netlogon] because the Windows 95/98 clients expect this when they try to log on. It does not need any data, it just has to exist, and users must be able to connect to it. Here is a simple one:

```
[netlogon]
    path = /export/smb/netlogon
    writeable = no
    public = no
```

Configuring the Windows 95/98 client

To make a Windows 95/98 client connect to a Samba domain controller, follow these steps:

1. Open the Network control panel.

2. Highlight Client for Microsoft Networks and click Properties.

3. Select the Log on to Windows NT domain checkbox and add the name of the domain (which is the same as the Workgroup) you want to use in the Windows NT domain box.

Samba as a Member of a Windows NT Domain

Samba can easily be configured to be a member of a Windows NT domain, so as to take advantage of the centralization and authentication that comes with domains.

Configuring the primary domain controller

To enable a Samba server to join an NT domain, you must first add the NetBIOS name of the Samba server to the NT domain on the Primary Domain Controller (PDC) using Server Manager for Domains. This creates the machine account in the domain (PDC) SAM.

Samba configuration

It takes two steps on the Samba server to make it work with an NT Domain. First, you have to join the domain with smbpasswd, and then you have to make the required changes in the smb.conf file.

Joining the domain

First, the Samba server has to successfully join the domain. Stop all Samba daemons (smbd and nmbd). Next, run the following command, where freeside is the NT domain name and wintermute is the NetBIOS name of the Primary Domain Controller for the domain freeside:

```
smbpasswd -j FREESIDE -r WINTERMUTE
```

If this is successful, you should get a message similar to this:

```
smbpasswd: Joined domain FREESIDE.
```

Once the Samba server has successfully joined the domain, the password is written in a file named domainname.Sambaservername.mac located in the same directory that the smbpasswd file is stored, typically /usr/local/samba/private. In the above case, for the Samba server named Molly, the filename would be FREESIDE.MOLLY.mac.

Smb.conf changes

In the [global] section of the smb.conf file, you need to change or add four parameters — security, workgroup, encrypt passwords, and password server:

- Security must be set to domain, such as `security = domain`.
- The workgroup parameter must be set to the domain name, such as `workgroup = FREESIDE` in the above example.
- You must have the encrypt passwords parameter set to yes, such as `encrypt passwords = yes`.
- You must have the password server parameter, with a list of Primary and Backup Domain controllers. For example, in a domain with a Primary Domain Controller of WINTERMUTE, and two Backup Domain Controllers of RIO and HAL, the password server parameter would be `password server = wintermute rio hal`.

Restart the Samba daemons, and the Samba server is now a member of the NT domain.

Samba as a Windows NT Primary Domain Controller

Using Samba as a Windows NT Primary Domain Controller is not supported in the mainstream branch of Samba, but it is supported in the beta version of Samba. This functionality is planned to be folded into the 2.1 version of Samba, but if you really need this, feel free to download the beta software and implement it.

Getting Samba that supports being an NT primary domain controller

The only version of Samba that presently supports being an NT Primary Domain Controller is the development version, which must be obtained by the Concurrent Version System (CVS). This is available at samba.org and can be accessed via the Web or with the normal CVS client. For the latest information on this, go to `http://cvs.samba.org/cvs.html`.

Web access to Samba CVS

The CVS source is available on the Web at `http://cvs.samba. org/cgi-bin/cvsweb`. Here you can access the contents of the individual files and get a `diff` listing between any two versions in the repository.

CVS client access to Samba CVS

You can also get the CVS code with a specific CVS client. The CVS client lets you retrieve the CVS code from a command-line interface.

Getting the CVS client   A CVS client is needed before you can get Samba CVS code. The source code for the CVS client is available at `http://www.cyclic.com`. There you can get information on downloading the source code and using it.

Using the CVS client to get Samba   Once you have a recent CVS client, the following command retrieves the Samba CVS code:

```
cvs -d :pserver:cvs@samba.org:/cvsroot login
```

When prompted for a password, use cvs.

Next, expand the source code into a directory. The following command creates a directory containing the latest Samba source code:

```
cvs -d :pserver:cvs@samba.org:/cvsroot co samba
```

When you are ready to merge the latest changes to the code, run this command from within the Samba directory.

```
cvs update -d -P
```

Configuring Samba

Once a version of Samba that can act as a Primary Domain Controller has been compiled, it must be configured to act as a Primary Domain Controller. Samba must be set up for encrypted passwords, and accounts must be set up on the Samba server for each workstation that will access the server.

Set up encrypted passwords

Samba must be using encrypted passwords. The smb.conf file must be configured for this, and the smbpasswd file must be populated.

Configuring smb.conf The global section of the smb.conf file needs two parameters added to it: one for encrypted passwords and one for the location of the smbpasswd file. The following example is for a system with the smbpasswd file in /usr/local/etc:

```
encrypt passwords = yes
smb passwd file = /usr/local/etc/smbpasswd
```

Populating smbpasswd You can populate the smbpasswd file initially from the passwd file, using the mksmbpasswd.sh script. The following example populates the smbpasswd file in /usr/local/etc/:

```
Cat /etc/passwd | mksmbpasswd.sh > /usr/local/etc/smbpasswd
```

Caution

The smbpasswd file needs to be kept just as secure as the passwd file. Check that the directory containing the smbpasswd file is owned by root and that no other user can access it.

After encryption is setup, test it a few times by logging in from NT clients before proceeding to the next step.

For a more in-depth treatment of password encryption, including the theory, read ENCRYPTION.txt in the Samba docs.

Adding client access The Samba server that will be a Primary Domain Controller must have an account added for each workstation that will use it. Then the smb.conf file must be modified to act as a Primary Domain Controller.

Configuring the server Each workstation that needs to access the Samba PDC must be given a machine trust account, which is essentially an account on the Samba server. The username is the NetBIOS name with a $ at the end; for example, for the client stephen the username is `stephen$`. The UID must be unique, and the shell and home directories fields are not used and can be set to /bin/False and /dev/null. The following is the entry for the client stephen, giving it a UID of 1001:

```
stephen$:*:1001:800:NT STEPHEN:/dev/null:/bin/false
```

Next, add the client to the smbpasswd file. The following example adds the client stephen to the smbpasswd file.

```
smbpasswd -a -m stephen
```

Smb.conf changes

The following three parameters — security, workgroup, and domain logons — must be set up correctly in the smb.conf file:

- The security parameter must be set to user, such as `security = user`.
- The workgroup parameter must be set up with the domain name. For the domain FREESIDE, this would be `workgroup = FREESIDE`
- The domain logons parameter tells client to use the Samba server as a Primary Domain Controller. It should be set to yes, such as `domain logons = yes`.

Next, the [netlogon] share must be added. All Windows clients attempt to connect to this share when they first log on. The following is a sample [netlogon] share.

```
[netlogon]
comment = Netlogon share for Windows domain logons
path = /usr/local/samba/netlogon
public = no
writeable = no
browseable = yes
locking = no
force create mode = 0644
```

```
force directory mode = 0755
write list = root, @wheel
```

Once Samba is restarted, smbd will create a file named domainname. SID, typically in /usr/local/samba/private, with permissions rw-r--r--. The file contains the domain SID for the Samba PDC. The filename differs depending on the value of the workgroup (domain name) parameter. If the contents of this file change, domain members will be incapable of logging on, and all will need to be added to the domain again.

Other useful smb.conf parameters

You can add several other parameters in the smb.conf file to increase the usefulness of the Samba servers. There are ways to map NT users and groups to UNIX users and groups, and ways to ensure that users have the correct drive mappings.

Domain group map This parameter specifies the location of the file that contains the mappings between UNIX and NT groups. The following example sets the domain group map location to /usr/local/samba/lib/domain_group:

```
Domain group map = /usr/local/samba/lib/domain_group
```

The format of the file is very basic, the unix_group_name = NT_group_name for each mapping, one per line. The following example maps the UNIX group testers to the NT group System_Testers:

```
testers = System_Testers
```

Domain user map This parameter specifies the location of the file that contains the mappings between UNIX and NT usernames. It is similar to the domain group map parameter. The following example sets the domain user map location to /usr/local/samba/lib/domain_user:

```
domain group map = /usr/local/samba/lib/domain_user
```

The format for the domain user map file is:

```
unixusername = [\\Domainname\\]NTusername
```

Local group map This parameter lets you define local groups on the Samba PDC and how they map to local NT groups. The following example sets the local group map location to /usr/local/samba/lib/local_group:

```
domain group map = /usr/local/samba/lib/local_group
```

The format for the local group file is:

```
unixgroup = [BUILTIN]NTgroup
```

Logon script This parameter specifies the file to be downloaded and run on a machine when a client successfully logs in. This parameter accepts the standard substitutions. This enables you to have separate logon scripts for each user or machine. The file must have DOS-style line endings. Create this file on a client machine and then ftp the file to the server. The script must be placed in the path defined by netlogon service. Do not enable write access to the netlogon share. Do not grant users write permission on the batch files. The content of the file is up to you — anything from synchronizing clocks with the time server to mounting the shares for common applications. For example:

```
NET TIME \\SUGAR /SET /YES
NET USE W: \\SUGAR\workutils
NET USE Y: \\SUGAR\datafiles
NET USE z: \\SUGAR\accounts
```

The default is a blank string, or no script is called:

```
logon script script =
```

The following is an example that sets the filename to setenv.bat:

```
logon script = setenv.bat
```

An example to make use of the standard substitution %u for user follows. It is used if you've created individual user login batch files:

```
logon script = %U.bat
```

Logon path This parameter is only used when Samba is set up as a logon server and your clients use roaming profiles. This parameter specifies the home directory where roaming profiles are stored. This option takes the standard substitutions. This enables you to have separate logon scripts for each user or machine. This option also specifies the directory from which the desktop, start menu, network neighborhood, and programs folders are loaded for your Windows 95/98 client. This share and the path must be readable by the user or the preferences and directories cannot be loaded on the Windows 95/98 client. The share must be writable at least for the first login. The Windows 95/98 client will create the user.dat and other directories during the first login. After that, the directories and any of the contents can be made read-only. Do not make the user.dat file read-only as this contains the user's perferences, which the usre may want to change. Instead, rename it to user.man and set this file to read-only. This is known as the mandatory profile.

The default is:

```
logon path = \\%N\%U\profile
```

An example to set the logon path to the server deal under the home\username directory:

```
logon path = \\DEAL\HOME\%U\PROFILE
```

Logon drive This parameter is only used when Samba is set up as a logon server for NT workstations. This parameter specifies the local path for the home directory.

The default is a blank string, or no path is specified:

```
logon drive =
```

An example to set the home directory to drive H:

```
logon drive = h:
```

Logon home This parameter specifies the home directory location when a Win95/98 or NT workstation logs in to a Samba PDC. The default is set to look to the NIS maps for a NIS home directory server. This option takes the standard substitutions, allowing you to have separate logon scripts for each user or machine.

The default is set to look for the NIS maps for the session username:

```
logon home = "\\%N\%U"
```

An example to hardcode the server name but still use substitutions for the session username:

```
logon home = "\\deal\%U"
```

Client side configuration

On the NT client, go to the Network control panel then the Identification page. Click the Change button and fill out the Domain name. Click OK and you should receive confirmation that the client joined the domain.

Looking for help

Because using Samba as a Primary Domain Controller is still development software, you may run into problems that no one else has run into before. You can do several things to diagnose and solve these problems.

Using Samba to diagnose and fix PDC problems

One of the most useful debugging tools is Samba itself. Running smbd and nmbd in debug mode (with the –d switch) at a debug level of 20 generates messages of sufficient detail to correctly diagnose most NT connectivity problems.

There is also an extension to tcpdump available at the Samba Web page that enables tcpdump to read smb packets. It can be downloaded from any Samba mirror; a direct link at the us3 mirror is http://samba.isca.uiowa.edu/samba/ftp/tcpdump-smb/.

Using Windows to diagnose and fix PDC problems

You can also diagnose many problems from a Windows NT machine using Network Monitor, also known as netmon. Network Monitor is available from several sources: the Windows NT Server install CD and the System Management Server (SMS) CDs.

Installing Network Monitor on a Windows NT server machine

To install Network Monitor on a Windows NT machine, you first need to install the Network Monitor Tools and Agent from the Windows NT Server install CD.

1. Install the Network Monitor Tools and Agent by selecting Start ⇨ Settings ⇨ Control Panel ⇨ Network ⇨ Services ⇨ Add.

2. Select Network Monitor Tools and Agent. Click OK.

3. Insert the NT Server install CD when prompted.

Installing Network Monitor on a Windows NT workstation machine

To install Network Monitor on a Windows NT machine, you first need to install the Network Monitor Tools and Agent from the Windows NT Server install CD. Then you will need to copy files from an existing NT server installation of Network Monitor.

1. Install the Network Monitor Tools and Agent by selecting Start ⇨ Settings ⇨ Control Panel ⇨ Network ⇨ Services ⇨ Add.

2. Select Network Monitor Agent. Click OK.

3. Insert the NT Workstation install CD when prompted.

Next copy the files from the NT Server in %SYSTEMROOT%\System32\netmon*.* to %SYSTEMROOT%\System32\netmon*.* on the NT Workstation.

Set permissions so that you will have administrative rights on the NT box to run Network Monitor.

Installing Network Monitor on a Windows 95 machine

To install Network Monitor on a Windows 95 machine, you first need to install the Network Monitor Tools and Agent from the Windows NT Server install CD to get the files that you need to copy.

1. Install the Network Monitor Agent by selecting Start ⇨ Settings ⇨ Control Panel ⇨ Network ⇨ Add ⇨ Services ⇨ Add.

2. Choose Have Disk and install from the ADMIN\NETTOOLS\NETMON directory on the Windows 95/98 CD.

3. Then copy the files from a working netmon installation, such as from the NT Server in %SYSTEMROOT%\System32\netmon*.* to the netmon directory on the 95/98 Workstation.

Using Internet resources to diagnose and fix PDC problems

The `samba-ntdom@samba.org` mailing list is the most current source on Samba NT domain development. The actual developer may answer your tougher technical questions.

They ask that you provide the following items to help diagnose the problem:

- The date when you last used cvs to generate the code.

- The OS and version of the server that is running Samba.

- The relevant sections of your smb.conf file; at the very least, the options in the [global] share that affect PDC support.

- The relevant portions of the log files written with a debug level of at least 20.

- If you have a complete Network Monitor trace (from the opening of the pipe to the error), you can also send the *.CAP file.

Chapter 7

Best Practices

Good Samba administrators have a variety of techniques and tips to keep their Samba server running at its best. They try to find ways to make it easier for their users to get their work done. They work on keeping their Samba server secure. They have a good backup strategy for their Samba servers, so that if it fails, they can recover their users' data with a minimum of effort.

Keeping Updated with the Internet

If you want to always run the latest Samba, you can use the Concurrent Version System (CVS) to download the latest Samba source. This is available at `samba.org` and can be accessed via the Web or with the normal CVS client.

Web access to Samba CVS

The CVS source is available on the Web at `http://cvs.samba.org/cgi-bin/cvsweb`. Here you can access the contents of the individual files and get a `diff` listing between any two versions in the repository.

CVS client access to Samba CVS

You can also get the CVS code with a specific CVS client. The CVS client lets you retrieve the CVS code from a command-line interface. This approach makes scripting and remote administration much easier than using the Web.

Getting the CVS client

A CVS client is needed before you can get Samba CVS code. The source code for the CVS client is available at http://www.cyclic.com. There you can get information on downloading the source code and using it.

Using the CVS client to get Samba

Once you have a recent CVS client, the following command retrieves the Samba CVS code:

```
cvs -d :pserver:cvs@samba.org:/cvsroot login
```

When prompted for a password, use cvs.

Next, expand the source code into a directory. The following command creates a directory containing the latest Samba source code:

```
cvs -d :pserver:cvs@samba.org:/cvsroot co samba
```

When you are ready to merge the latest changes to the code, run this command from within the Samba directory:

```
cvs update -d -P
```

User Directory Mounting Schemes

If you are running NIS and all your user directories are on an NIS-enabled Samba server, you can use NIS and Samba to have your users automatically connect to the correct server, regardless of the server they are logged in to. Somewhat similarly, you can use roaming profiles to enable a user's Windows client to always have the same resources, regardless of which actual PC they log in from.

Samba configuration for NIS autohome directories

The Samba server must be configured as a login server to make this work. The two Samba parameters are homedir map and nis homedir.

homedir map

This parameter only works if you are using NIS home directories. It also requires configuring Samba as a login server and setting the `nis homedir` parameter to `Yes`.

The `homedir map` parameter specifies the NIS map that the server will use to locate the user's home directory. This parameter uses the SUN auto.home file format to extract directory information.

The default is:

```
homedir map = auto.home
```

NIS homedir

The NIS server should also be configured as a Samba server when you are integrating Samba and NIS. Doing so helps avoid possible performance bottlenecks and enables clients to talk directly with the NIS server when mapping their home directories.

The parameter specifies whether Samba will use NIS home directories, even in cases where the home directories reside on another server. Samba consults the NIS map specified in the `homedir map` parameter and returns the home directories based on the NIS map listed there.

The default is no, or NIS maps are not searched by default:

```
nis homedir = No
```

The following is an example that turns this parameter on and searches the NIS map for a client's home directory information:

```
nis homedir = Yes
```

Operating system configuration

Make sure the Samba server is using NIS and make sure that `homedir map` is working correctly in NIS. You can test this by logging in to a server with a user whose home directory is specified by the `homedir map` and verifying that the correct directory appears.

Roaming profiles

Roaming profiles enable a Windows user to connect to a Windows (Samba) server from any number of different clients, but with the same user-specific profile regardless of the client. The client pulls the user's profile and customizes the user's environment when they log in.

If a Windows client logs into a domain, it attempts to store the profile in the user's home directory for download the next time that the user connects to the domain. This ensures that the user has the same environment profile regardless of the client, giving the user freedom to use any available client. Samba does this well.

For Windows 95/98/NT, the user's profile file is named user.dat. The Samba parameter to enable Windows 95/98/NT roaming is `logon path`.

The `logon path` parameter specifies the home directory in which roaming profiles are stored. This option also specifies the directory from which the desktop, start menu, network neighborhood, and program folders are loaded for your Windows 95/98 client. This share and the path must be readable by the user or the preferences and directories cannot be loaded on the Windows 95/98 client. The share must be writable at least for the first login. The Windows 95/98 client will create the user.dat and other directories during the first login. After that, the directories and any of the contents can be made read-only. Do not make the user.dat file read-only. Instead, rename it to user.man and set this file to read-only. This is known as the mandatory profile.

This enables you to have separate logon scripts for each user or machine. The default is:

```
logon path = \\%N\%U\profile
```

An example to set the logon path to the server deal under the home\ username directory is:

```
logon path = \\DEAL\HOME\%U\PROFILE
```

Password Authentication/ Synchronization

Passwords for Windows clients and UNIX passwords are not the same, but there are several workarounds to deal with this. One way is to have Samba use Windows passwords, and when the Windows passwords are changed in Samba, have Samba change the UNIX passwords.

Samba-based authentication/ synchronization

Samba can function fine with Windows passwords by using Windows-encrypted passwords and the smbpasswd file. The smbpasswd file does first need to be populated from the /etc/passwd file with the mksmbpasswd. sh script.

Configuring smb.conf

The global section of the smb.conf file needs two parameters added to it: one for encrypted passwords and one for the location of the smbpasswd file. The following example is for a system with the smbpasswd file in /usr/local/etc:

```
encrypt passwords = yes
smb passwd file = /usr/local/etc/smbpasswd
```

Populating smbpasswd

You can populate the smbpasswd file initially from the passwd file, using the mksmbpasswd.sh script. The following example populates the smbpasswd file in /usr/local/etc/:

```
Cat /etc/passwd | mksmbpasswd.sh > /usr/local/etc/smbpasswd
```

Caution

The smbpasswd file needs to be kept just as secure as the passwd file. Check that the directory containing the smbpasswd file is owned by root and that no other user can access it.

Synchronizing Samba and UNIX passwords

After Samba passwords are encrypted and stored in smbpasswd, the UNIX passwords need to be changed to match. This can be done automatically from Samba by using a few global parameters: unix password sync, passwd chat, and passwd program.

UNIX password sync This parameter, in the global share, determines whether Samba tries to synchronize a UNIX password when a user's Windows password is being changed in the smbpasswd file. When this is true, the program specified in `passwd program` runs as root to change the user's passwd in UNIX.

Password program This is the program used to set UNIX user passwords. The %u Samba parameter is replaced with the username. The username is then checked for existence before calling the password-changing program. If the `unix password sync` parameter is set to `true`, then this program is called with superuser privileges before passing the request to UNIX when the smb password in the smbpasswd file is changed. If this UNIX password change fails, then smbd will fail to change the smb password. This is a feature, not a bug. If the `unix password sync` parameter is set, this parameter must use absolute paths for the programs called.

The default is:

```
passwd program = /bin/passwd
```

Passwd chat This global parameter details the password chat string that Samba will use to change the user's password in UNIX. This sequence is site-specific depending on what local methods are used for password control. If the expected output is not received, the password is not changed.

The string can contain the macros:

%o   old password

%n   new password

It can also contain the standard macros:

\n   line feed

\r   carriage return

\t   tab

\s   space

The string can also contain *, which matches any set of characters.

You can use double quotes to collect strings that have spaces in a single string.

The default is:

```
passwd chat = *old*password* %o\n *new*password* %n\n
*new*password* %n\n changed
```

An example of a password chat string:

```
passwd chat = "##Enter your old password##" %o\n "##Enter
your new password##" %n\n "##Re-enter your new
password##" %n\n "## Your password has been changed##"
```

Password chat debug This parameter specifies whether the passwd chat script parameter runs in debug mode. In this mode, the strings passed to and received from the passwd chat are printed in the smbd log with a debug level of 100. If you're using plain-text passwords, you can view them in the smbd log. This option is available to help Samba administrators debug their passwd chat scripts when calling the passwd program. Turn it off after you've verified your passwd chat string works as expected. This parameter is off by default.

The default is:

```
passwd chat debug = false
```

To turn password chat debug on:

```
passwd chat debug = true
```

File Security and System Security

An in-depth treatment of securing a UNIX server can fill several books, as it's a very important and complex subject. This section provides a brief overview on securing your system, and information on where to go for more detailed information. It won't tell you how to setup and secure a firewall, setup IP masquerading, or set up a virtual private intranet.

Guidelines

While most UNIX servers are very secure out of the box, there are several guidelines that should be followed to make your Samba server even more secure.

Password usage

The most important guideline is to keep the root password secret, change it frequently, and don't use an easily guessed password. Your users should also change their passwords frequently (or be forced to change them frequently, via user options), and not use easily guessed passwords.

To assist you in choosing good passwords, you can use programs such as crack or obvious-pw to check your password. They work by trying common passwords or by matching encrypted passwords against the contents of a dictionary.

Some operating systems also check passwords when being assigned/-changed, and warn against easily guessed passwords. Red Hat Linux's password checker is very stringent, warning against a password that contains a word in the dictionary.

Processes

You should go through your startup scripts and examine the processes that are being run. Each process may be a security hole, so disable any that don't need to be run by commenting them out in the startup scripts.

System V   For a System V system such as Sun's Solaris 2.*x* or Linux, the daemons are started in the startup scripts, located in the /etc/rc.d directory, in directories related to the run-levels. You can edit the files in the appropriate run-level directory; changing the starting character from an S prevents it from being run.

BSD UNIX   Some daemons may be called from /etc/default/rc.conf, but it is preferable to kill them from /etc/rc.conf instead of commenting them out in /etc/default/rc.conf.

Services

To make your system even more secure, you can disable services that you don't need. This is commonly done to rlogin and finger. Services can be prevented from starting by editing the /etc/inetd.conf file and commenting out each unneeded service. Security can also be increased by using tcpd and by having /etc/hosts.allow and /etc/hosts.deny files.

Files

The following files are logical targets for attack. The rights for these files should be set correctly and periodically checked.

/etc/passwd The passwd file should only be writable by root. If the shadow password file is not used, the encrypted passwords can be displayed, leaving the system more vulnerable to a dictionary cracking attempt.

/etc/shadow If the shadow password file is used, it should only be readable by root.

/etc/group The group file should be examined for changes to group composition.

/etc/security On Linux systems, the /etc/security file lists the ttys that root is allowed to log in on. An intruder may try to change this.

SULOG The SULOG variable is set in /etc/default/su and it gives the path to the log file that captures all su attempts. The default is /var/adm/sulog.

Suid, sgid

Suid is a way of setting the rights on a program to make it execute as if the owner of the program had started it. The canonical example is passwd: each user needs to be able to change his or her own password, but the passwd file is only writable by root. Applying suid to passwd gives it the capability to edit the passwd file for whoever called it by making ir act as if root had started it. Sgid works the same way, but with groups.

You determine whether a program has the suid or sgid set by doing a long listing on it; the relevant executable flag is **s** instead of **x**.

A security hole occurs if a program has a suid of root and was allowed to spawn a shell, such as shelling out of vi. This new shell would have the rights of the root user, and the system would be wide open.

Most security tools check for suid/sgid, but it is a good idea to list all the suid/sgids that are set at first install, and to periodically relist them, comparing them to the first list. The following command finds all the programs with suid/sgid set and stores their names in the file initsuid in the /root directory:

```
#find / -perm -200 o -perm -400 -print > /root/initsuid
```

Security tools

There is a wide variety of free security tools available and you should check your system with them, as any malicious cracker will also have them. You should also check the tools from the security tolls' Web pages periodically, as problems are found and new updates are released. Sometimes, using an old security tool is worse than using no tool at all. Satan is an example of this, it was released with great fanfare, but hasn't been updated in years. Thus, it doesn't protect against newer attacks, and known security holes in it have never been patched.

Securing services/networks

There are several ways to increase the security of your Samba server from a network/services standpoint. Secure shell (SSH) can be used to encrypt TCP/IP connections, while tcp wrappers can control access to network utilities, and tcpd can allow or deny specific IP addresses from connecting. If you need to give some users root functionality, you can use sudo to do this.

Secure shell (SSH) The SSH program is a method of encrypting TCP/IP connections over a network. Normal TCP/IP connections (such as telnet, rlogin) pass information in unencrypted format; someone with a packet snooper can easily learn your Samba server's root password this way. With SSH, connections between the client and server are encrypted, preventing a snooper from seeing passwords in plain text. Both the client and the server must be running SSH. More information is available at the SSH home page at http://www.ssh.fi.

Secure shell can also be downloaded from many sites, including these in the United States:

```
ftp://sunsite.unc.edu:/pub/packages/security/ssh
ftp://ftp.gw,com:/pub/unix/ssh
ftp://ftp.rge.com:/oub/security/ssh
```

Secure shell is available for UNIX workstations at these sites. If you need SSH for a Windows session, try `http://www.datafellows.com/f-secure`.

tcp wrappers The tcp wrappers package is a software daemon that is designed to intercept requests to network services (those listed in /etc/services), and then monitor and allow/disallow such requests. It can filter per hosts, domain, and/or services. It is available on most OS install CDs, but if you can't find it, it can be downloaded from `ftp://porcupine.org/pub/security/`, `ftp://ftp.win.tue.nl/pub/security`, or any number of other mirror sites.

Sudo Sudo is a utility that gives specified users and groups the capability to run some (or all) commands as root on a per command basis. It has timeout and logging features. Many system administrators set up sudo for their own use, so they rarely have to su to root. Sudo's home page is `http://www.courtesan.com/sudo/`, and it can be downloaded from many sites, including:

```
ftp://ftp.rge.com:/pub/admin/sudo/
ftp://coast.cs.purdue.edu:/pub/tools/unix/sudo/
ftp://ftp.uu.net:/pub/security/sudo/
```

Password checking

The following tools can be used to check that user passwords are sufficiently difficult to be guessed or determined with brute force means. Using these must complement a good password policy. If a user can change to an easily guessed password, and crack isn't run for a few days or weeks on the password, your server's security is compromised.

crack The program crack tries to decipher standard UNIX-encrypted passwords by using standard guessing algorithms. It searches through the passwd file of your system and checks the encrypted passwords to determine whether they are easily guessed. Because it can take a fair amount of CPU work to run crack, it is best configured to run unattended. crack 5.0 and more information are available at `ftp://ftp.cert.org/pub/tools/crack` and `ftp://coast.cs.purdue.edu/pub/tools/unix/crack/`.

obvious-pw obvious-pw is what its name implies, an obvious password detector. It looks at the passwords as three-letter long segments, and compares their randomness to known three-letter word segments in English. More information is available at `ftp://isgate.is/pub/unix/sec7/obvious-pw.tar.Z`. and `http://ciac.llnl.gov/ciac/ToolsUnixAuth.html#Obvious`

Security probing

The following programs can be used to check for security holes on your system. You can assume anyone with computer knowledge who wants to get in your system will have these programs.

COPS COPS (Computer Oracle and Password System) is a collection of programs that check various security aspects of your system. COPS checks for common holes and known problems, and then reports its findings. Version 1.04 is the latest, although it is several years old. More information is available at `ftp://ftp.cert.org/pub/tools/cops` and `ftp://coast.cs.purdue.edu/pub/tools/unix/cops/`

Tiger Tiger is a set of scripts that will scan a system and look for potential holes. It is similar to COPS, but more current. The latest version is 2.2.4. Tiger can be downloaded from `http://wuarchive.wustl.edu/packages/security/TAMU/` and `ftp://net.tamu.edu/pub/security/TAMU`.

SAINT SAINT, the Security Administrator's Integrated Network Tool, is an evolution of the SATAN program and is used to probe an entire network for security holes. Because it is so rapidly developing, it has not been tested on many UNIX systems, but it should work on Solaris and FreeBSD/NetBSD and will probably work on Linux with some tweaking. SAINT's home page is `http://www.wwdsi.com/saint/`.

SATAN SATAN is a well-known network probing tool that is the precursor of SAINT. It has several known security holes that have not been addressed, and it is best not to use it. Use SAINT instead.

security This is a script on FreeBSD in the /etc directory. It can be run to check for security holes on your system.

Intruder detection

These programs are used to monitor your server for signs of change or intrusion. They work by taking a picture of your system before it has been hacked, and then they take periodic pictures, comparing crucial file sizes, dates, and contents.

Gabriel and Courtney Gabriel and Courtney are two programs that watch for network probing by SATAN and SAINT. They look for excessive amounts of network probing. Gabriel's home page is `http://www.lat.com/gabe.htm`. Gabriel can be downloaded from `ftp://ftp.lat.com/gabriel-1.0.tar.Z`. Courtney can be downloaded from `ftp://ftp.lat.com/courtney-1.3.tar.Z` or `ftp://ciac.llnl.gov/pub/ciac/sectools/unix`.

Tripwire Tripwire monitors clients and servers on a network for break-in attempts by detecting changes to critical system or data files. The newest versions are available from Tripwire's home page (`http://www.tripwiresecurity.com`); older versions are available in public ftp directories, such as `http://wuarchive.wustl.edu/packages/security/tripwire/`.

Back Up Your Samba Server

All servers crash and all servers lose data, so a backup strategy is essential. Backup devices range from a floppy drive holding 1MB to DAT drives holding many gigabytes of data. Several basic commands are available for backing up servers that are common to all forms of UNIX, as well as some unique commands.

Many systems can be backed up safely by calling the appropriate commands through cron, but there are many utilities available that make backing up easier.

Backup devices

Backup devices can range from floppies to automatically changing tape drives with gigabytes of capacity. The following section is an overview of the various backup devices available.

Floppies

Don't use floppies for backups, they are far too small and inefficient. They can be used to boot or rescue a system or to exchange small files when it is too difficult to use a network.

Mounting floppies in Solaris In Solaris 2, you use `volcheck` to mount floppies. The floppy will then be accessible under /floppy, in it's own volume, or floppy0, after a successful `volcheck`.

To unmount and eject a floppy, use `umount` and `eject`.

Mounting floppies in Linux To mount a floppy in Linux, use the `mount` command. The following example mounts a DOS-formatted floppy to /mnt/floppy:

```
mount —t msdos /dev/fd0 /mnt/floppy
```

Use `umount` to unmount the floppy.

Mounting floppies in FreeBSD/NetBSD You can use the `mount` and `umount` command to manipulate UNIX-formatted floppies.

Using floppies with mtools You can use the mtools collection to manipulate DOS-formatted floppies. Commands in the mtools suite are similar to the DOS commands, but prefaced with an m, for example, `mcd`, `mdir`, `mcopy`, and `mtype`.

The mtools collection comes with Linux and FreeBSD/NetBSD, and can be downloaded from `http://sunfreeware.com/` for Solaris.

Floppy-controller tape drives

Floppy-controller tape drives are common and cheap, but not reliable enough for daily use. They may find use for occasional backups of workstations. There is no support for them in Solaris, and very limited support for them in FreeBSD/NetBSD.

Using floppy-controller tape drives in Linux To access floppy-controller tape drives in Linux, you use the ftape program to set it up as a device. The Ftape-HOWTO for Linux is the canonical source of ftape information and instructions.

The ftape program also provides support for some parallel port tape drives.

Using floppy-controller tape drives in FreeBSD/NetBSD The floppy-controller tape device is /dev/ft0, although there is very limited support for such devices in FreeBSD/NetBSD.

Zip drives

Zip drives are common and have enough capacity for backing up a user's home directories and small file systems.

Linux The kernel recognizes an ATAPI/IDE CD as the system boots up as a hard drive device. Partition 4 is used to access MS_DOS-formatted ZIP drives. The following example shows how to mount a slave ZIP drive on the first IDE controller in DOS format to /mnt/zip:

```
mount -t msdos /dev/hdb4 /mtn/zip
```

Parallel port Zip drives are accessed using SCSI modules to interface the parallel port, and you may need to recompile the Linux kernel. The following example mounts a Windows 95-formatted ZIP drive on the parallel port:

```
mount -t vfat /dev/sda4 /mnt/zip
```

The ZIP-Drive mini-howto file contains the latest and most comprehensive information on using ZIP drives with Linux.

CD-R/CD-RW

CD-R/CD-RW drives are becoming common and have enough capacity to back up all but the largest file systems on one CD.

There is less support for CD-RW drives than straight CD-R drives, but cdrecord does write to CD-RW drives.

There are two stages to writing data using a CD burner: creating the data image with mkisofs and then writing the image using a utility such as cdwrite or cdrecord.

Linux Linux supports both SCSI and ATAPI CD burners. When CD burners first appeared, the SCSI burners were much more reliable than the

ATAPI versions, but today EIDE ATAPI burners have an increased RAM cache and have narrowed the quality gap. The two most common programs to write to CD's are cdwrite and cdrecord; cdwrite is much older and less useful than cdrecord.

- SCSI CD burners have good support and can be used with cdwrite or cdrecord.
- ATAPI CD burners are supported in versions of CD_record 1.7 and later.

Refer to the CD-Writing-HOWTO for the latest and most complete information.

FreeBSD/NetBSD   The wormcontrol program can be used to write to a CD-W drive. Under /usr/share/examples/worm there are two scripts, makecdfs.sh and burncd.sh that are used to create CDs.

- SCSI CD burners have good support and can also be used with cdwrite or cdrecord.
- ATAPI CD burners are supported in versions of CD_record 1.7 and later. Also, in the /usr/share/examples/atapi directory, there is an example script named burndata that can be used to burn data to a CD.

Solaris   At the moment, Solaris only supports SCSI CD burners. Cdwrite or cdrecord should work on Solaris with a CD burner.

- SCSI CD burners are easily supported on Solaris.
- Support for ATAPI CD burners is not yet available.

SCSI tape drives

SCSI tape drives are the preferred backup medium for higher end servers, and they are well supported in UNIX.

Linux   If SCSI support was not added when the system was installed, the kernel may need to be recompiled with SCSI support.

Backup hard drives

A second hard drive on the system can be used to back up a server in a manner similar to disk mirroring. The following is an example for backing up a server to a second hard drive in Linux:

1. Partition the second drive to match the first drive using `fdisk`.

2. Do a `mke2fs -c /dev/hdbn` (where *n* is the partition number) for each of these new partitions.

3. Mount the new file systems to tmp. One way to do this is `mount /dev/hdbn /mnt/tmpn`.

4. Use `cpio` to copy files to the newly mounted partition; for example, `find . -mount | cpio -pvum /mnt/tmpn`.

Other servers

Servers can be backed up to other servers. Many backup commands, such as `tar`, work across networks.

Common UNIX backup commands

The following section contains common UNIX commands used for backing up systems and manipulating backup devices. Operating system-specific commands are also mentioned.

smbclient

`smbclient` may be used to create tar (1)-compatible backups of all the files on an SMB/CIFS share. The secondary tar flags that can be used with this option are:

`c tar_file`	Creates a tar file on the UNIX host from the files on the SBM/CIFS server. Follow it with the name of a tar file, tape device, or "-" for standard output. If tarring to the standard output, you must turn the log level to its lowest value, `-d0`, to avoid corrupting your tar file. This flag is mutually exclusive with the x flag.

`x tar_file`	Extracts (restores) a local tar file back to a share. Use the –D option to restore to a different level other than the top level of the share. This must be followed by the name of the tar file, device or "-" for standard input. This option cannot be used with the c option.
`I include_expression`	Includes files and directories indicated by the expression. Use it with the r option for wildcards to match a list of files. If there are names at the end of the tar command, smbclient assumes they are files and directories to be tarred.
`X exclude_expression`	Excludes the files and directories specified by the expression. Use with the r option for wildcards (filename globbing).
`b blocksize`	Lets you specify a block size, which must be greater than zero.
`g`	Performs an incremental tar and only backs up files that have the archive bit set. This option can only be used with the c flag.
`q`	Quiet mode, which keeps tar from printing diagnostics as it works.
`r`	Specifies that the wildcards that have been compiled with smbclient should be used. If used with more than * or ?, you might experience performance problems.
`N filename`	Only files newer than the file specified are backed up to the tar file, and it only works with the c flag.
`a`	Causes the archive bit to be reset when a file is backed up. Only works with the g and c flags.

The following example backs up Nancy's home directory on the server payroll and creates a tar file named nancy.tar:

```
smbclient //payroll/nancy —Tc nancy.tar
```

This example restores from the mail.tar file into the eudora directory on the server laptop:

```
sbmclient //laptop/eudora —Tx mail.tar
```

smbtar

The smbtar command is a shell script for backing up SMB/CIFS shares directly to UNIX tape drives. Options for smbtar are:

-s server	The SMB/CIFS server that the share resides on.
-X	Exclude filenames.
-d directory	Change to initial directory before restoring/ backing up files.
-v	Verbose mode.
-p password	The password to use to access a share.
-u user	The user id to connect as.
-t tape	The device to use for back ups.
-b blocksize	Blocking factor.
-N filename	Backup only files newer than filename.
-i	Incremental mode; tar files are only backed up if they have the archive bit set.
-r	Files are restored to the share from the tar file.
-l log level	Log (debug) level.

mt

The mt command enables direct manipulation of the tape device. It is often used with tar to get to a specific file on a tape. Options for mt are:

-f tape_device	Apply mt commands to tape_device. If the —f flag is not included, use the TAPE environment variable.

status	Display the status of the tape device.
rewind	Rewind the tape.
retension	Wind and rewind the tape to smooth out the tape tension.
erase	Erase the tape.
fsf count	Forward skips count tape files.
bsf count	Backward skips count tape files.
eom	Skip to end of recorded media.

Tar

Tar is the canonical UNIX utility for backing up and restoring files. The typical syntax is tar options files. Options for tar are:

c	Create the tar file.
r	Replace. The files are appended to the tar file.
t	Table of contents. The names of the specified files are listed each time they occur in the tar file.
u	Update. The files are appended to the tar file if they are not already in the tar file or if they have been modified since last written to that tar file.
x	Extract or restore. The files are extracted from the tar file and written to the directory specified in the tar file, relative to the current directory.
b	Specify the blocking factor for the tape.
B	Block. Force tar to perform multiple reads (if necessary) to read exactly enough bytes to fill a block. This enables tar to work across Ethernet.
C directory file	Perform a chdir operation on *directory* and perform the c (create) or r (replace) operation on *file*.

e	Error. Exit immediately with a positive exit status if any unexpected errors occur.
f file	Use the tar file argument as the name of the tar file.
F	With one F argument, tar excludes all directories named SCCS and RCS. With two arguments — FF — tar excludes all directories named SCCS and RCS, all errs, core, and a.out. This is useful in UNIX software development and of limited use on a UNIX server.
h	Follow symbolic links as if they were normal files or directories.
i	Ignore directory checksum errors.
l	Output error message if unable to resolve all links to the files being archived. If l is not specified, no error messages are printed.
m	The modification time of the file is the time of extraction. This must be used with the x function.
o	Assign to the extracted files the user and group identifiers of the user running the program rather than those in the tar file.
p	Restore the files to their original modes, and ACLs if applicable, ignoring the present umask.
P	Don't add a trailing / on directory entries in the archive.
v	Verbose output.
w	Interactive mode.
X	Exclude. Use the exclude-file argument as a file containing files or directories to be excluded from the tar file when using the functions c, x, or t.

Solaris-specific options Solaris has three unique options for the `tar` command. These options are:

`-I include-file`	Open include-file, which contains a list of files, one per line, and treat as if each file appeared separately on the command line.
`[0-7]`	Select the alternative drive on which the tape is mounted. The default entries are specified in /etc/default/tar.

/Linux/FreeBSD/NetBSD-specific options The `tar` command in Linux/FreeBSD/NetBSD has a slightly different syntax: it is `tar [options] [tarfile] [other-files]`. Many common options can also be called by name. Options specific to Linux/FreeBSD/NetBSD include:

`D`	Compare the files in the tar file to the other-files and report any differences.
`A`	Concatenate a second tar file to the end of the first tar file.
`n`	Select drive *n* instead of the default in /etc/default/tar.
`[drive][density]`	Set drive (0-7) and storage density (1, m, h).
`--atime-preserve`	Don't change access time on extracted files.
`-checkpoint`	Print directory names encountered.
`--exclude = file`	Remove file from list of files.
`--force-local`	Interpret filenames in the form `hostname:filename` as local files.
`G`	Create/list/extract old GNU-format incremental backup.
`g`	Create/list/extract new GNU-format incremental backup.
`i`	Ignore zero-sized blocks.

`--ignore-failed-read`	Ignore unreadable files to be archived.
`k`	Keep old files.
`K file`	Begin at file in archive.
`l`	Do not archive files from other file systems.
`-L N`	Write a maximum of N*1024 bytes to each tape.
`M`	Create/list/extract a multivolume archive.
`N DATE`	Only store files newer than *DATE*.
`o`	Write a V7 format archive rather than ANSI format.
`O`	Extract files to standard output.
`R`	Show record number within archive with each message.
`--remove-files`	Remove files after adding them to the archive.
`s`	Sort the extracted list of names to match the archive.
`--same-owner`	Create extracted files with the same ownership.
`S`	Handle sparse files efficiently.
`--null`	Lets filenames be null-terminated with `-T` reads and disables `-C`.
`--totals`	Print total bytes written with `--create`.
`--version`	Prints tar version.
`W`	Attempts to verify the archive after writing it.
`z`	Filter the archive through `compress`; compress it for archive and decompress for extraction.
`--use-compress-program progname`	Filter the archive through *progname* (which must accept `-d`).

`--block-compress`	Block the output of compression program for tapes.

Examples of tar commands Back up the current directory to the default tar device:

```
tar c .
```

Back up the entire server to the tar device /dev/rmt/0 with verbose output:

```
tar cvf /dev/rmt/0 /
```

dd

Use the dd command to convert and copy files with various formats. It is often used to copy files to and from floppy devices. Options for the dd command are:

`if-file`	Specify input file name.
`of=file`	Specify output file name.
`bs=n`	Set input and output block size in n bytes.
`ibs=n`	Specify the input block size in n bytes.
`obs=n`	Specify the output block size in n bytes.
`cbs=n`	Specify the conversion block size for block and unblock in bytes by n.
`files=n`	Copy and concatenate n input files before ending.
`skip=n`	Skip n input blocks before starting to copy.
`iseek=n`	Seek n blocks from beginning of input file before copying.
`oseek=n`	Seek n blocks from beginning of output file before copying.
`seek=n`	Skip n blocks from beginning of output file before copying.

`count=n`	Copy only *n* input blocks.
`conv=value[,value...]`	Where *values* are comma-separated symbols detailing the conversion. Choices are `ascii` (convert from EBCDIC to ASCII); `ebcdic` (convert from ASCII to EBCDIC); `ibm` (convert from ASCII to EBCDIC); `block` (variable length records to fixed length records); `unblock` (fixed length records to variable length records); `lcase` (uppercase to lowercase); `ucase` (lowercase to uppercase); `swab` (swap all pairs of bytes); `noerror` (do not stop processing on an input error); `notrunc` (do not truncate the output file); and `sync` (pad input blocks to `ibs`).

Linux-specific options   In addition to the above commands, Linux has two unique options for `dd`:

`--help`	Print a help message.
`--version`	Print the version.

FreeBSD/NetBSD options   In addition to the above options, FreeBSD/NetBSD has a unique parameter for the conversion variable:

`conv=value[,value...]`

In addition to the values above, you can use `osync` to pad the output block to the full output block size.

Examples of the dd command   The following example creates boot disks for Linux installation:

```
# dd if=boot.img of=/dev/fd0 bs=1440k
```

This example capitalizes an input file:

```
dd if=lowerfile of=UPPERFILE conv=ucase
```

cpio

The cpio command copies files into or out of a cpio or tar file. Options for the cpio command are:

-o	Create an archive by reading names from standard input and copying those named files to standard output.
-i	Extract the archive specified by standard input.
-p	Read from standard input to get a list of file names.
-B	Set block input/output record to 5120 bytes, instead of default size of 512 bytes.
-c	Read or write header in ASCII.
-H	Read or write header in bar, crc, odc, tar, or ustar formats.
-b	Reverse the order of the bytes within each word.
-a	Reset the access times of files after reading them, so that it does not look like they have just been read.
-A	Append to an existing archive. Only works in copy-out mode.
-C bufsize	Block input/output bufsize bytes to the record.
-d	Create directories as needed.
-E file	Specify an input file that contains a list of filenames to be extracted from the archive.
-f	Copy in all files except those in patterns.
-I file	Read the contents of file as an input archive.
-k	Attempt to skip any corrupted file headers and I/O errors that may be encountered.
-l	Link files if possible, rather than copying them.
-L	Follow symbolic links.
- m	Retain previous file modification time.
-M message	Define a message to use when switching media.
-O file	Direct the output of cpio to file. If file is a character special device and the current medium is full, replace the medium and type a carriage return to continue to the next medium.

`-P`	Preserve ACLs.
`-r`	Interactively rename files. If the user types a carriage return alone, the file is skipped. If the user types a period (.), the original pathname is retained.
`-R id`	Reassign ownership and group information for each file to user ID.
`-s`	Swap bytes within each half word.
`-S`	Swap halfwords within each word.
`-t`	Print a table of contents of the input.
`-u`	Copy unconditionally, replacing newer files with older files.
`-v`	Verbose.
`-V`	Special verbose. Print a dot for each file read or written.
`-6`	Process a UNIX System Sixth Edition archive format file.

GNU/Linux/FreeBSD/NetBSD-specific cpio options Linux/ FreeBSD/NetBSD have several unique options for the `cpio` command. These options are:

`-0`	In copy-out and copy-pass modes, read a list of filenames terminated by a null character instead of a newline.
`--block-size=SIZE`	Set the I/O block size to SIZE * 512 bytes.
`--force-local`	With `-F`, `-I`, or `-O`, take the archive file name to be a local file even if it contains a colon, which would ordinarily indicate a remote host name.
`-H FORMAT`	Use archive format FORMAT. The valid formats are odc, newc, crc, tar, ustar, hpbin, cpio, and hpodc.

`-k`	Ignored; it is used for compatibility with other versions of cpio.
`-n,`	In the verbose table of contents listing, show numeric UID and GID instead of translating them to names.
`--no-absolute-filenames`	In copy-in mode, create all files relative to the current directory, even if they have an absolute file name in the archive.
`--no-preserve-owner`	In copy-in mode and copy-pass mode, do not change the ownership of the files; leave them owned by the user extracting them.
`--only-verify-crc`	When reading a CRC format archive in copy-in mode, only verify the CRCs of each file in the archive.
`--quiet`	Do not print the number of blocks copied.
`--sparse`	In copy-out and copy-pass modes, write files with large blocks of zeros as sparse files.
`--version`	Print the cpio program version number and exit.

Examples of cpio commands The following example lists the current directory and uses `cpio` to archive it to tape:

```
find . —print | cpio —ocvB > /dev/rmt/0
```

This example restores files whose filenames contain old:

```
Cpio —icdv "*old*" < /dev/rmt/0
```

Solaris-specific backup commands

Solaris comes with several backup options that are unique to Solaris. `ufs-dump` is used to back up an entire file system and `ufsrestore` is used to restore a file system.

ufsdump Use the `ufsdump` command to back up an entire file system. It can do a full or partial backup. The options for `ufsdump` are:

`0-9`	Specify the dump level, with 0 being a full dump.
`u`	Update the dump record (/etc/dumpdates) with the date and dump level of this dump.
`c`	Set the blocking factor to 126 for all cartridge tape drives.
`a`	Create an online archive of the filenames backed up to tape.
`f devname`	Specify to write the files to *devname*.
`v`	Verify data on tape against original data.
`files_to_dump`	Specify the files to dump. This can be a directory, a file system, or the raw or block file system device name.

Ufsrestore The `ufsrestore` command restores backups created by ufsdump. Options for `ufsrestore` are:

`i`	Restore interactively.
`r`	Restore the entire backup.
`t`	List the contents of the backup.
`x`	Restore only the contents listed on the command line.
`a file`	Get the table of contents information from file instead of tape.
`b factor`	Specify the blocking factor for tape drives.
`f dump_file`	Restore from dump_file instead of from the default tape drive.
`s number`	Skip to *number* dump_file from which to restore.
`v`	Display pathnames as the files are being restored.

Examples of ufsdump and ufsrestore To perform a full (level 0) dump of the /export/home file system to tape, use this command:

```
# ufsdump 0ufc /dev/rmt/0 /export/home
```

To restore the /export/home file system, type:

```
# ufsrestore r /dev/rmt/0
```

FreeBSD/NetBSD-specific backup commands

FreeBSD/NetBSD come with some unique software for performing backups. The dump command can be used to back up and entire file system, and pax can be used to manipulate archive files.

dump The dump command can be used to back up an entire file system, or to back up a partial file system depending on the dump level. The options for dump are:

-0-9	Dump levels. A level 0 full backup guarantees the entire file system is copied.
-B records	The number of 1KB blocks per volume. This option overrides the calculation of tape size based on length and density.
-a	Bypass all tape length considerations and enforce writing until an end-of-media indication is returned.
-b blocksize	The number of kilobytes per dump record.
-c	Change the defaults for use with a cartridge tape drive with a density of 8000 bpi and a length of 1700 feet.
-h level	Honor the user "nodump" flag only for dumps at or above the given level.
-d density	Set tape density to density. The default is 1600BPI.
-f file	Write the backup to file.
-k	Use Kerberos authentication to talk to remote tape servers.

-n	Whenever dump requires operator attention, notify all operators in the group "operator" by means similar to a wall(1).
-s feet	Attempt to calculate the amount of tape needed at a particular density for a length of tape feet long.
-T date	Use the specified date as the starting time for the dump instead of the time determined from looking in /etc/dumpdates.
-u	Update the file /etc/dumpdates after a successful dump.
-W	Dump tells the operator which file systems need to be dumped.
-w	Prints only those file systems that need to be dumped.

pax The pax command will read, write, and list the contents of an archive file, and will copy directories. The options for the pax command are:

-r	Read an archive file from standard input and extract the specified files.
-w	Write files to the standard output in the specified archive format.
-a	Append files to the end of an archive that was previously written.
-b blocksize	When writing an archive, block the output at an integer number of bytes per write to the archive file.
-c	Match all file or archive members except those specified by the pattern and file operands.
-d	Cause files of type directory being copied or archived, or archive members of type directory being extracted, to match only the directory file or archive member and not the file hierarchy rooted at the directory.

`-f archive`	Specify archive as the pathname of the input or output archive.
`-i`	Interactively rename files or archive members.
`-k`	Do not overwrite existing files.
`-l`	Link files. In the copy mode (`-r -w`), hard links are made between the source and destination file hierarchies whenever possible.
`-n`	Select the first archive member that matches each pattern operand.
`-o options`	Information to modify the algorithm for extracting or writing archive files, which information is specific to the archive format specified by `-x`. In general, options take the form `name=value`.
`-p string`	String option-argument is a string specifying file characteristics to be retained or discarded on extraction. The string consists of the specification characters a, e, m, o, and p. Multiple characteristics can be concatenated within the same string, and multiple `-p` options can be specified. The meanings of the specification characters are:
a	Do not preserve file access times.
e	"Preserve everything" — the user ID, group ID, file mode bits, file access time, and file modification time.
m	Do not preserve file modification times.
o	Preserve the user ID and group ID.
p	"Preserve" the file mode bits.
`-s replstr`	Substitute files operands according to the substitution expression replstr.
`-u`	Ignore files that are older than a preexisting file or archive member with the same name.
`-v`	When listing, produce a verbose table of contents.

`-x format`	Specify the output archive format, with the default format being ustar. Pax currently supports these formats: cpio, bcpio, sv4cpio, sv4crc, tar, and ustar.
`-B bytes`	Limit the number of bytes written to a single archive volume to bytes.
`-E limit`	Limit the number of consecutive read faults to limit while trying to read a flawed archive.
`-G group`	Choose files based on group name, or when starting with a #, a numeric gid.
`-H`	Follow only command-line symbolic links while performing a physical file system traversal.
`-L`	Follow all symbolic links to perform a logical file system traversal.
`-P`	Do not follow symbolic links, perform a physical file system traversal.
`-T [from_date] [,to_date] [/[c][m]]`	Allow files to be selected based on a file modification or inode change time falling within a specified time range of from_date to to_date (the dates are inclusive).
`-U user`	Select a file based on its username, or when starting with a #, a numeric uid.
`-X`	When traversing the file hierarchy specified by a pathname, do not descend into directories that have a different device ID.
`-Y`	This option is the same as the `-D` option, except that the inode change time is checked using the pathname created after all the file name modifications have completed.
`-Z`	This option is the same as the `-u` option, except that the modification time is checked using the pathname created after all the file name modifications have completed.

Backup software

Many system administrators are able to safely backup their systems with a judicious use of UNIX commands called by cron. When this process becomes unwieldy, there are many software applications available that make backups easier.

Amanda

Amanda, the Advanced Maryland Automatic Network Disk Archiver, is a backup system designed to archive many computers on a network to a single large-capacity tape drive. It is free software that is available at `http://www.amanda.org`; it may be included with your operating system disks.

Amanda is a sophisticated archiving program with features for automatic backups, encryption, error recovery, and more.

Taper

Taper is a GUI-based backup/restore included with Red Hat Linux. To launch it from the command line, type:

```
#taper <-T device> <type> <option>
```

Sample devices for taper are `-T f` for a floppy tape driver (/dev/ftape) and `-T s` for a SCSI tape driver (/dev/sda).

Rhbackup

Rhbackup is an archiving utility that is included with Red Hat Linux. The primary configuration file for rhbackup is /etc/sysconfig/tape, and the default backup table file is /etc/backuptab. These two files should be edited to match your particular system.

Log Files: Types and Uses

Samba log files

The default Samba log file is determined at compile time, but is usually overridden in the smb.conf file with the `log file` parameter. The following example is a search for the log file in the smb.conf and shows the result that it exists in /var/log/samba:

```
helena#cat smb.conf | grep "log fil"
    log file = /var/log/samba
```

The next example uses the NetBIOS name of each client to generate a separate log file for each client:

```
terrapin# cat smb.conf | grep "log file"
# tell Samba to use a separate log file for each machine
 log file = /var/log/log.%m
```

Because Samba is not immediately aware of the parameters in the smb.conf file when it first starts, some information is written to the default log before it switches to the defined log.

Nmbd log files

The nmbd daemon also has a log file, usually in the same directory as the samba log file and with nmbd in the name.

Contents of the Samba log files

The Samba log files contain the client connection information, to what it was connected, by whom, and from where.

The nmbd log files contain naming information, name query information, and browsing information.

Changing the debug logging level of a running process

You can change the debug logging level of a running process by using the USR1 signal to increase it and the USR2 signal to decrease it. The following example increases the logging level of process 5877:

```
#kill —USR1 5877
```

Operating system log files

Most important events occurring on your Samba server will get logged to the appropriate file. This is very useful in backtracking and debugging problems. Logging is most helpful when you can't sit in front of the server to watch the kernel messages. Each operating system stores different information in different log files. This section directs you to the right files.

Solaris

The main logging configuration file is /etc/syslog.conf. The usual place most kernel messages get logged in is /var/adm/messages.

The SULOG variable is set in /etc/default/su. It gives the path to the log file that captures all su attempts. The default is /var/adm/sulog.

Linux

The main configuration file for logs in Linux is /etc/syslog.conf. The usual place for logging most messages is in /var/log/messages.

FreeBSD/NetBSD

The main configuration file for logs in FreeBSD/NetBSD is /etc/syslog.conf. The usual place for logging most messages is in /var/log/messages/.

Printing errors are stored in /var/log/lpd-errs.

Using Cron for Automated Tasks

Cron is the UNIX daemon for automatically scheduling tasks. Cron reads the appropriate cron file to execute commands. Each line in the crontab file is an entry. Each entry has six fields:

- The first field is for which minute(s) of the hour the command should be executed. Valid values are between 0 and 59.
- The second field is for which hour of the day the command should be executed. Valid values are between 0 and 23.
- The third field is for which day of the month the command should be executed. Valid values are between 1 and 31.

- The fourth field is for the month of the year the command should be executed. Valid values are between 1 and 12, with January being 1.

- The fifth field is for the day of the week the command should be executed. Valid values are between 0 and 7, with Sunday being both 0 and 7.

- The sixth field is the command to be executed.

The crontab file can be viewed by using the −l flag with crontab.

Editing the crontab file

Use the crontab utility with the −e switch to edit a crontab file. The default editor is ed. If you want to use a friendlier editor such as vi, and if you are using the Bourne, Korn or Bourne-again shell, change the EDITOR environment variable in $HOME/.profile. Options for crontab are:

−e   Edit the crontab file.

−l   List the crontab file.

−r   Remove the current crontab.

Solaris-specific options

In addition to the preceding options for crontab, Solaris has a two unique options:

username   Use crontab with username's crontab.

file   Use crontab with a specific file.

Linux/FreeBSD/NetBSD-specific options

In addition to all of the preceding options for crontab, Linux/FreeBSD/ NetBSD have two unique options:

−u user file   Add a crontab file for user.

−u user   Work with user's crontab.

Examples of editing the crontab file

This is an example of modifying the superuser's crontab file to send a lunch notice:

```
# EDITOR = vi
# export EDITOR
# crontab —e
55 11 * * 1-5 /usr/bin/echo "Lunchtime!" > /dev/console
```

Crontab access

Access to the crontab file is controlled by two files: /etc/cron.d/cron.allow and /etc/cron.d/cron.deny.

If the cron.allow file exists, only the users listed there can use crontab.

If the cron.allow file does not exist, the cron.deny file is checked, and any users listed there are denied access to crontab. All other users can use crontab.

If neither file exists, only the superuser can use crontab.

Printing

Samba can be configured to automatically install the correct print drivers when a user connects to a printer on a Windows server for the first time. This functionality exists for Windows 95 clients and is in development for Windows NT clients.

Automatically installing printer drivers for Windows 95/98

Windows 95/98 can automatically install printer drivers when first connected to a Samba server. It's basically a three-step process.

First, create a directory for the printer files and make it a Samba share. The following is an example share from the Samba documentation:

```
[printer$]
path=/usr/local/samba/printer
     public=yes
```

```
writable=no
browseable=yes
```

Next, build the list of drivers required for the printer. Start with the two files msprint.inf and msprint2.inf, which are typically stored in the c:\windows\inf directory. Look in these two files for your printer. If your printer is in one of the files, copy it to your Samba server. At the Samba server, run the `make_printerdef` command with the filename and printername as parameters, and redirect the output to the file printer.def. The following example creates a printer.def for the HP LaserJet 4M:

```
make_printerdef msprint.inf "HP LaserJet 4M" > printer.def
```

If your printer is not listed and you have the inf files for it from the manufacturer, run the `make_printerdef` command as before, but use the manufacturers inf file instead of the msprint.inf file.

The `make_printerdef` command prints a list of required files to stderr. All these files must be copied to the directory that was created in the first step. They are usually stored in the c:\windows\system directory. If you have `preserve case = yes` set, the file names must match exactly.

Finally, add two new parameters to smb.conf. In the [global] section, add a parameter called `printer driver file`, pointing to the printer.def file that was created in the second step. The second parameter is called `printer driver location`. It points to where the printer files are kept and must be in each printer share that needs to provide automatic installs.

This procedure is covered in greater technical depth in the PRINTER_DRIVER.txt file provided with Samba.

Automatically installing printer drivers for Windows NT

The code for this is still being developed. For the moment, there is no easy way for printers to be automatically installed when an NT client first connects. However, the pace of Samba's development is rapid, so keep checking the Samba mailing lists for announcements of this functionality or workarounds.

Server-Side Automation

Samba can be configured to run commands and scripts on the server side when a user connects with the `preexec`, `root preexec`, `postexec`, or `root postexec` command. You can use Samba's built-in variables to create shares customized for each user who logs in.

Samba executable commands

Samba has the capability to execute scripts or commands when a user connects or disconnects from a share. These scripts can run as the user or as the superuser. They are often used to mount or dismount removable media.

Exec

This parameter specifies the name of a script or scripts to run when the client connects to a service. The script runs with the user ID of the current session user. This is the place to work magic for your clients, or you can do such simple things as generating a custom log message when a user connects.

Postexec

This parameter specifies the name of a script or scripts to run when the client disconnects from a service. The script runs with the user ID of the current session user. The command can be run as the root on some systems. This command is useful if you need to dismount file systems after terminating a connection.

Root preexec

This parameter is the root user version of `exec` and `preexec`. It enables root to run scripts necessary for the user environment. The most common use is to mount file systems.

Root postexec

This parameter is the root user version of `postexec`. It enables root to run scripts when the user disconnects from the service. The most common use is to unmount file systems.

Examples of Samba-executed commands

The following are examples of Samba-executed commands.

Mounting and dismounting a CD-ROM This example is a CD-ROM share on a Linux server that is mounted by root preexec when it first connects. It then dismounts by root postexec when the user disconnects.

```
[cdrom]
     comment = CDROM on liberty
     browsable = yes
     read only = yes
     path = /mnt/cdrom
     root prexec = /bin/mount /dev/hdb /mnt/cdrom
     root postexec = /bin/umount /mnt/cdrom
```

Mounting and dismounting a ZIP drive This example is a ZIP drive connected to a Linux server via the parallel port. It mounts using root preexec when the user connects and dismounts using root postexec when the user disconnects.

```
[zip]
     comment = parallel port ZIP drive
     browsable = yes
     read only = yes
     path = /mnt/cdrom
     root prexec = /bin/mount -t vfat /dev/sda4 /mnt/zip
     root postexec = /bin/umount —t vfat /mnt/zip
```

Chapter 8

Performance Tuning

This chapter provides suggestions on improving your Samba server's performance, and ways to measure your Samba server's performance. Hardware guidelines are very broad by necessity because the platforms Samba can run on range from Macintoshes to enterprise-level UNIX servers.

Memory

Adequate memory is always the first step in getting good performance. A server with plenty of memory but with an underpowered processor is almost always more efficient than a server with a faster processor but insufficient memory.

RAM versus swap

Having enough memory in your Samba server is the first step toward good performance. While it would be impossible to give a foolproof formula to determine your server's RAM and swap needs, the best way to run your server is with as many processes in RAM as possible because RAM is hundreds of times faster than the swap memory on the hard drive. To make a RAM needed estimate, add up the sizes of all the executables you plan to run on the server at the same time. Then use this figure, or even double it, to determine your needed swap space.

Samba memory requirements

The smbd daemon is over 700K and the nmbd daemon is over 300K. Each connecting client needs its own smbd daemon, so figure at least 1MB of RAM per client for best performance.

The SWAT daemon is almost 500K if it is running.

The webmin tool starts at about 500K and can consume more memory.

 Tip

These values are estimates and will change depending on a program's version, how it was compiled, what compiled it, and the operating system on which it is running.

Disk Drives

If you have the choice, SCSI hard drives are preferable to IDE or EIDE hard drives because they are generally more reliable and provide better performance.

If you have multiple hard drives, use the various utilities (such as iostat on Solaris) to evenly distribute the load on the hard drives or to ensure that the faster drive is doing more work than the slower drives.

Network Cards

Get the highest performance network cards you can for your server. One time-consuming way to measure performance is to copy files across the network from two servers that are identical except for the network cards. Generally, PCI cards are preferable to ISA cards on PC machines.

Directory Structure

If you have multiple hard drives, you can rearrange your directory structure (for example, put /home and /usr on separate drives or put /home on the faster drive) to improve your server's performance. To do this well, you need an intimate knowledge of what files are being requested simultaneously on your server.

Samba Configuration

This section lists several things that you can configure in Samba to increase performance.

Oplocks

Beginning with Samba 1.9.18, Samba supports oplocks, or opportunistic locking mechanisms. This is a way to enable clients to cache files locally from the Samba server, and when implemented, oplocks can improve performance up to 30 percent. Oplocks can be turned off on certain files on a per-share basis. The parameter to do this is the `veto oplock files` in the File Handling options.

The default is:

```
oplocks = Yes
```

An example to turn this option off:

```
oplocks = No
```

Fake oplocks

This parameter is outdated and should only be used if your Samba software cannot be upgraded. (Since version 1.9.18, Samba has implemented real oplocks.) One use for fake oplocks is for read-only file systems or file systems dedicated to one client. Using this option for services that are accessed by multiple clients may corrupt data. Don't take the chance — leave this option set to `No`.

This option is disabled by default:

```
fake oplocks = No
```

To turn this option on:

```
fake oplocks = Yes
```

Sync commands

Windows and UNIX have different implementations of sync commands. Setting the sync parameters incorrectly on a Samba server can cause drastic performance problems.

Strict sync

Use this parameter to compensate for the difference between what Windows clients think of as a sync and what UNIX systems believe is a sync. A UNIX sync call forcefully suspends the process until all outstanding data in the kernel disk buffers is stored in the specified storage area. This is very slow. In ancient days, it was necessary to ensure data validity. The default setting enables smbd to ignore the Windows client applications requests for a sync call. There is a possibility of losing data if your server crashes. This is a very slim chance based on typical UNIX server performance. The default parameter also fixes performance problems reported with the new Windows 98 Explorer shell file copies.

The default is no, or UNIX sync does not take place at the client's request:

```
strict sync = no
```

Setting strict sync to yes will cause performance problems for your server. Only use it as a troubleshooting tool:

```
strict sync = yes
```

Sync always

This parameter has no effect if the strict sync parameter is set to no.

This parameter specifies whether writes should always be written to disk storage before the write call returns. The default setting enables the server to be guided by the client's request with each write call. If this parameter is set to yes, every write will be followed by a fsync() call to force the data to be written to disk.

The default is:

```
sync always = no
```

To set this parameter on (this has no effect if you've set `strict sync = no`), change the default to:

```
sync always = yes
```

Socket options

This parameter specifies the socket options to be used when talking with clients. Socket options are controls on the networking layer of the operating system that enable the connection to be tuned. Use this option to tune your Samba server for optimal performance on your local network. You can combine any of the supported socket options any way you like as long as your OS allows it. However, several of the options can cause your Samba server to fail completely. If you're not a TCP/IP guru, stick with the defaults.

The socket options currently supported using this option are shown in the list that follows. Those marked with a # require an integer argument. The other options take a 1 or 0 argument to enable or disable the option. By default, they are enabled if you don't specify 1 or 0.

```
SO_KEEPALIVE
SO_REUSEADDR
SO_BROADCAST
TCP_NODELAY
IPTOS_LOWDELAY
IPTOS_THROUGHPUT
SO_SNDBUF #
SO_RCVBUF #
SO_SNDLOWAT #
SO_RCVLOWAT #
```

Here are some examples of common settings. The following setting increases the send buffers to 8K. Do not include any spaces before or after the second = sign:

```
socket options = SO_SNDBUF=8192
```

A pair of options to try if you are on a Local Area Network (LAN):

```
socket options = IPTOS_LOWDELAY TCP_NODELAY
```

An option to try if you are on a Wide Area Network (WAN):

```
socket options = IPTOS_THROUGHPUT
```

The default is:

```
socket options = TCP_NODELAY
```

Many reports state that using `socket options = TCP_NODELAY` can double the read performance of a Samba drive.

Custom compiling Samba

If you custom compile Samba, you can choose not to compile support for things your server does not need, such as NIS or Kerberos. This will make the daemon smaller and should give a modest increase in performance.

Compiling Samba 2.0 or later

After downloading Samba-latest_tar.gz to an appropriate temp directory, gzip and untar it with the following command string:

```
gzip —dc Samba-latest_tar.gz | tar xvf —
```

gzip is the GNU compression utility. If you get this error:

```
gzip: command not found
```

conduct a search for gzip; it might not be accessible from your path. If it's not installed on your system, it's a free download from the GNU Web page (`http://www.gnu.org`) or it might be on your OS CD-ROM.

To customize the compilation for performance improvements, add command-line parameters. The current list is available by typing **./configure --help.** These are the `configure` command-line parameters for Samba 2.0.3. Many of them are paired, with the default option noted. If the options have defaults, they are indicated by square brackets.

After the Samba package is uncompressed and untarred, start compiling by running the configure program by typing **./configure options** in the directory where configure was installed.

To then compile, type **make** in the configure directory, and then type **make install** to install the compiled files.

If you are upgrading Samba, save and rename the old binaries with the extension .old. The make revert command enables you to back out of the upgrade and return to your previous version of Samba.

If you get errors about make not being found, such as

```
make: command not found
```

it might not be in your search path. The installation will go easier when make is in your search path.

Custom compiling Samba 1.9

Unlike Samba 2.0, Samba 1.9 does not come with an autconf utility. Instead, it has a makefile that you can edit for custom compilation. The makefile is well documented. Review the makefile carefully, examining each set of parameters given and adjusting as necessary for your system. The beginning of the makefile deals with parameters common to all systems. Then, each different system on which Samba can be installed is represented by a different set of installation commands, which you'll find in the commented lines that begin with "WHICH OPERATING SYSTEM?," about a third of the way into the file. Be sure to uncomment only the correct lines for the operating system on which you are compiling Samba.

Measuring Performance

If you intend to fine-tune your Samba server, you need to know how effective your changes are. You need to measure the performance, and look at components of your server for bottlenecks. This section helps you do that.

Measuring Samba performance

A good way to measure Samba performance is to compare file transfer rates with a comparable TCP/IP operation, such as FTP. FTP a large file from your server to your client and record the time; then copy the same file from a Samba share on your server to your client. The times should be close.

Measuring Solaris performance

Solaris comes with a variety of tools to measure system performance.

Iostat

Use iostat to measure disk and CPU activity to ensure equal workload distribution on the server disks. The first line of output summarizes the I/O statistics since the server was first booted. Include a time interval to display more lines of statistics. Some of the options for iostat are:

-c	Show the percentage of time the system has spent in user mode, in system mode, waiting for I/O, and idling.
-d	Show the kilobytes transferred per second, the number of transfers per second, and the average service time in milliseconds per disk.
-D	Show the reads per second, writes per second, and percentage disk utilization per disk.
-I	Show the counts in each interval instead of rates (where applicable).
-t	Show the number of characters read and written to terminals per second.
-x	Show extended disk statistics per disk.
-l n	Limit the number of disks shown 1 to *n*; the default is 4 for -d and -D, and unlimited for -x.
disk	Explicitly specify the disks to be reported.
time count	Report once every *time* seconds, for *count* reports. The time value may be used without the count value.

Vmstat

Vmstat is the utility that reports certain statistics about process, virtual memory, disk, trap, and CPU activity. If used with no options, vmstat displays a one-line summary of the virtual memory activity since the system was booted. Vmstat options are:

-c	Show cache-flushing statistics.
-i	Show the number of interrupts per device.
-s	Report the total number of various system events since boot.
-S	Display swapping rather than paging activity.
disk	Give priority to display the disk specified.
count	Repeat the statistics *count* times.
Time	Summarize activity every *time* seconds.

The fields displayed by vmstat are:

proc	Report the number of processes in the run queue, the blocked queue, and the swapped queue.
memory	Report on virtual and real memory.
page	Show information on page faults and paging activity, in units per second. The columns are:

re	Page reclaims
mf	Minor faults
pi/po	Kilobytes paged in/paged out
fr	Kilobytes freed
de	Anticipated short-term memory shortfalls
sr	Pages scanned by clock algorithm

disk	Display the number of disk operations per second
faults	Show the trap/interrupt rates per second
in	(Nonclock) device interrupts
sy	System calls
cs	CPU context switches
CPU	Give a breakdown of percentage usage of CPU time
us	User time
sy	System time
id	Idle time

Sar

Sar is the system activity reporter. It can report resource utilization either interactively or through batch processing. The sar options are:

`wait count`	Measure the CPU utilization count times, separating each time by *wait* seconds.
`-o filename`	Run in batch mode and save the samples in *filename* in binary format.
`-f filename`	Replay a saved file.
`-d`	Display disk utilization.
`-g`	Monitor virtual memory usage.
`-q`	Show how many processes are queued for execution.
`-r`	Report the average number of available memory pages and swap-file disk blocks.
`-a`	Show use of file access system routines: iget/s, namei/s, dirblk/s.
`-A`	Report all data. The same as — abcdgkmpqruvwy.
`-b`	Report buffer activity.
`-c`	Show system calls.
`-k`	Show kernel memory allocation (KMA) activities.
`-m`	Report message and semaphore activities.
`-p`	Report paging activities.
`-u`	Report CPU utilization (the default).
`-v`	Report status of process, i-node, file tables.
`-w`	Show system swapping and switching activity.
`-y`	Report TTY device activity.
`-e time`	Select data up to *time*. The default is 18:00.
`-i time`	Select data at intervals as close as possible to *time* seconds.
`-s time`	Select data later than *time* in the form hh[:mm]. The default is 08:00.

Measuring Linux performance

Linux comes with several tools for measuring performance. Top is the same as the FreeBSD/NetBSD version, whereas vmstat differs from the Solaris and FreeBSD/NetBSD implementations.

Free

Free displays the amount of free and used memory in the system. Options for free are:

-b	Display the amount of memory in bytes.
-k	Display the amount of memory in kilobytes (the default).
-m	Display the amount of memory in megabytes.
-t	Display a line containing the totals.
-o	Don't display the buffer adjusted line.
-s count	Activate continuous polling *count* seconds apart.
-V	Display version information.

Top

Top is used to display information about the top CPU processes, ranked by raw CPU percentage. Options for top are:

-d count	Specify a delay of count between screen updates.
-S	Specify cumulative mode and list each process as well as its dead children.
-q	Refresh the screen with no delay.
-s	Run in secure mode, disabling interactive commands.
-I	Don't display any idle or zombie processes.
-c	Display command line instead of the command name only.
-n number	Update the display number iterations then exit.
-b	Batch mode; don't accept command-line input.

Interactive mode commands   Use these commands when running top in interactive mode:

q	Quit top.
c	Toggle display of command name or full command line.
f	Add fields to display.
F	Remove fields from display.
h, ?	Display help or status
k	Prompt for process ID to kill and signal to send to kill it (default signal is 15).
i	Toggle suppression of idle and zombie processes.
l	Toggle display of uptime information and load average.
m	Toggle display of memory information.
n, #	Prompt for number of processes to show. Entering 0 fills the screen.
o, O	Change the order of the displayed fields.
r	Apply `renice` to a process to alter its priority.
s	Change delay between refreshes.
t	Toggle display of processes and CPU state information.
^L	Redisplay screen.
M	Sort tasks by memory usage.
P	Sort tasks by CPU usage.
S	Toggle cumulative mode.
T	Sort tasks by time/cumulative time.
W	Write current setup to top configuration file ~/.toprc.

Vmstat

Vmstat can give you a picture of the state of the memory. The first report shows averages since the last reboot, while the next reports give information on a sampling period of length delay. Options for vmstat are:

delay	The time between reports is *delay* seconds.
-n	Display the header once.

count   Display *count* updates.

-v   Give version information.

FreeBSD/NetBSD memory tools

FreeBSD/NetBSD comes with several commands for measuring performance. Top is identical to the Linux version, and vmstat is very similar to the Solaris version.

Top

Use top to display information about the top CPU processes, ranked by raw CPU percentage. Top options are:

-S	Report system processes in the display.
-b	Use "batch" mode and ignore terminal input.
-i	Use "interactive" mode; any input is immediately read for processing.
-I	Do not display idle processes.
-t	Do not display the top process.
-n	Use "noninteractive" mode; this is the same as "batch" mode.
-q	Renice top to −20 so that it will run faster. This is useful when the system is sluggish to improve the possibility of discovering the problem.
-u	Do not take the time to map user id (uid) numbers to usernames.
-d count	Show only *count* displays and then exit.
-s time	Set the delay between screen updates to *time* seconds.
-o field	Sort the process display area on the specified field. Typical field values are CPU, size, res, and time.
-U user	Show only those processes owned by username.
N	Show the top *n* processes.

Both *count* and *n* fields can be specified as `infinite`, indicating that they can stretch as far as possible. This is accomplished by using any proper prefix of the keywords `infinity`, `maximum`, or `all`.

Interactive mode commands The following commands are used when running top in interactive mode:

q	Quit top.
h, ?	Display help or status.
k	Prompt for process ID to kill and signal to send to kill it (default signal is 15).
i, I	Toggle suppression of idle and zombie processes.
n, #	Prompt for number of processes to show. Entering 0 fills the screen.
r	Apply `renice` to a process to alter its priority.
s	Change delay between refreshes.
^L	Redisplay screen.
d	Change the number of displays to show.
u	Display only processes owned by a username, for which you will be prompted.
e	Display a list of any system errors generated by the `last kill` or `renice` command.

Vmstat

Vmstat displays kernel statistics about process, virtual memory, disk, trap, and CPU activity. The first display is for the time since a reboot and each subsequent report is for the time period since the last display. The options for vmstat are:

-c count	Repeat the display *count* times. If no wait time is given, the default is one second.
-i	Show the number of interrupts taken by each device since system startup.
-M core	Extract values associated with the name list from the specified core instead of the default /dev/kmem.

`-N system`	Extract the name list from the specified system instead of the default /kernel.
`-m`	Show the kernel dynamic memory usage listed first by size then by type.
`-n devs`	Change the maximum number of disks to display from the default of 3.
`-s`	Display the contents of the sum structure.
`-w wait`	Pause *wait* seconds between each display. If no repeat count is specified, the default is infinity.
`-p type, interface, pass`	Specify which types of devices to display. Three different categories of devices are: Type, Interface, and Passthrough.

Type:

`da`	Direct Access devices
`sa`	Sequential Access devices
`printer`	Printers
`proc`	Processor devices
`worm`	Write once read many (WORM) devices
`cd`	CD devices
`scanner`	Scanner devices
`optical`	Optical Memory devices
`changer`	Medium Changer devices
`comm`	Communication devices
`array`	Storage Array devices
`enclosure`	Enclosure Services devices
`floppy`	Floppy devices

Interface:

`IDE`	Integrated Drive Electronics devices
`SCSI`	Small Computer System Interface devices
`other`	Any other device interface

Passthrough:

pass   Passthrough devices

The user must specify at least one device type and may specify at most one device type from each category. Commas must separate multiple device types in a single device type statement.

Any number of –p arguments may be specified on the command line. All –p arguments are ORed together to form a matching expression against which all devices in the system are compared. Any device that fully matches any –p argument is included in the vmstat output, up to three devices or the maximum number of devices specified by the user.

Part III

Troubleshooting

Chapter 9

Basic Network Connectivity

Installing a Samba server is the easy part; the hard part is fixing it when it doesn't work. This chapter gives a detailed explanation of where the Samba connection can be broken, starting at the client and moving out to the server. It also explains how to diagnose naming service problems.

Windows 95/98

The two most-used options for diagnosing network problems in Windows 95/98 are the Network control panel and the MS-DOS prompt.

Network menu

The Network menu is used to configure networking for the Windows 95/98 client, including TCP/IP parameters for each network adapter, the client identification, and the Windows networking parameters.

Configuration tab

The Configuration tab displays the installed network cards and the network protocols running on each card. It also displays any network clients loaded.

To access Samba, one of the network adapters in the Configuration menu should use TCP/IP. IPX/SPX and NetBEUI are installed by default: the IPX/SPX is primarily used to connect to Novell 3 and 4 networks, and the NetBEUI is used for older versions on Windows networking. If you don't plan to connect to either one, delete IPX/SPX and NetBEUI.

Check the TCP/IP parameters by highlighting TCP/IP⟲ (network card) and clicking Properties.

IP address To use DHCP properly, the option Obtain an IP address automatically should be checked because this is what enables your PC to work with a DHCP server to get an IP address during boot. If it is not checked, you won't have an IP address, and any TCP/IP software (such as Windows networking) will fail. If your network is using static IP Addressing, check that the IP address is unique and the subnet mask is correct.

WINS configuration If your network is not using a WINS server, make sure Disable WINS resolution is selected.

If your network is using a WINS server, make sure Enable WINS resolution is selected and the IP address of the Primary and Secondary WINS server is correct, along with the Scope ID, if implemented. Or you can have WINS handled by DHCP (if using DHCP) by making sure Use DHCP for WINS resolution is selected.

Gateway The Gateway menu is where you add the IP Address of the machine that connects this network to other IP networks. If the client can reach local Samba servers, but has trouble with more remote ones, check the Gateway values.

DNS configuration This tab is where DNS is enabled or disabled. If DNS is enabled, verify the host name, domain of the client, the IP addresses of one or more DNS server, and the domain suffix search order.

Bindings The Bindings tab shows the network components that are using the TCP/IP protocol. Client for Microsoft Networks must be checked to enable access to a Samba server.

Advanced There is nothing to configure under the Advanced tab in TCP/IP.

NetBIOS Verify that the option I want to enable NetBIOS over TCP/IP is checked. The vast majority of Microsoft networks are configured with TCP/IP enabled. TCP/IP provides routing for NetBIOS. Samba is configured to run NBT by default.

NetBIOS is Windows networking, and by running on top of the TCP/IP network protocol, you can see Samba servers running on Unix/Linux/FreeBSD machines. If NetBIOS over TCP/IP is not enabled, you can still use Windows networking, but you would only see NetBEUI machines, which is an older protocol that only runs on Windows machines.

Client for Microsoft Networks configuration The properties for the Client for Microsoft Networks is where you define the network logon options for the Windows 95/98 client. Highlight Client for Microsoft Networks and click Properties.

If the client is logged on to an NT domain (or a Samba-emulated NT domain), verify that the Log on to Windows NT domain box is checked and the proper domain name appears.

Identification tab

In the Identification tab, the Computer Name must be a valid NetBIOS name, and the Workgroup must be the desired workgroup.

Access control tab

This should be set to User unless you have a good reason to use share-level security on your Samba server with the appropriate Workgroup name.

Tip

Windows 95/98 machines should never be configured as your master browser. Check this setting by opening the Network control panel. In the Configuration tab in the window "The following network components installed:" scroll to and highlight File and Printer Sharing for Microsoft Networks. Click Properties. In the Advanced tab, verify that the Browse Master is set to disabled. If it is set to Auto or Enabled, change it to Disabled. For Windows for Workgroups or DOS clients, the Browse Master setting is located in the system.ini file in the Network section. You will have to edit the system.ini file and change the setting to browse master = disabled.

MS-DOS prompt

There are several commands that you can run at the DOS prompt to diagnose network connectivity problems.

winipcfg

`winipcfg` displays the IP Configuration window. There, you find the Ethernet Adapter information for the system, including Adapter Address, IP Address, Subnet Mask, and Default Gateway. There are six buttons under these options: OK, Release, Renew, Release All, Renew All, and More Info. The Release All, Renew All, Release, and Renew buttons are options for DHCP connections. These options enable you to renew your DHCP lease on an IP address or release the address. The More Info button displays a new window with more details on Ethernet Adapter Information and Host Information. The Host Information section contains Host name, DNS servers, Node Type, NetBIOS scope ID, IP Routing Enabled, Win Proxy Enabled, and NetBIOS resolution uses DNS. `winipcfg` is best utilized as another method to verify that the information added in the Network menu is recognized by the system.

ping

`ping` is the DOS command for testing basic network connectivity. The basic syntax is:

`ping destination`

`Destination` can be the hostname or the IP address of the destination computer. If `ping` returns `Request timed out`, there is no TCP/IP connectivity between the client and the destination. Other options for `ping` are:

`-t`	Ping the host until interrupted
`-a`	Resolve addresses to hostname
`-n count`	Number of echo requests to send
`-f`	Set Don't Fragment flag in packet
`-I TTL`	Time to live
`-v TOS`	Type of service

`-r count`	Record route for count hops
`-s count`	Timestamp for count hops
`-j host-list`	Loose source route along host-list
`-k host-list`	Strict source route along host-list
`-w timeout`	Timeout, in milliseconds, to wait for each reply

tracert

The `tracert` command is used to diagnose routing problems. If your client cannot `ping` a Samba server and must go through a router, `tracert` could narrow the problem. The syntax is:

```
tracert address
```

Getting a `Request timed out` indicates a routing table failure. Options for `tracert` are:

`-d`	Do not resolve addresses to hostname
`-h max_hops`	Maximum number of hops to search for target
`-j host-list`	Loose source route along host-list
`-w timeout`	Timeout, in milliseconds, to wait for each reply

nbtstat

`nbtstat` displays the NetBIOS statistics. If you're having trouble accessing a server by hostname, `nbtstat -c` displays the NetBIOS naming cache. The other parameters usable with `nbtstat` are:

`-a remote_name`	Lists the remote machine's name table
`-A remote_IP`	Lists the remote machine's name table if given its IP address
`-c`	Lists the remote name cache
`-n`	Lists local NetBIOS names
`-r`	Lists names resolved by broadcast and WINS
`-R`	Purges and reloads remote name cache
`-S`	Lists sessions table with destination IP addresses
`-s`	Lists sessions table with remote names, converting via hosts table

netstat

The `netstat` command is used to display statistics for the TCP connections between the client and other computers. The options for `netstat` are:

`-a`	Displays all connections and ports
`-e`	Displays Ethernet statistics
`-n`	Displays addresses and port numbers in numerical form
`-p proto`	Shows connections for the protocol specified by proto; choices are tcp or udp
`-r`	Displays the contents of the routing table
`-s`	Displays per-protocol statistics
`Interval`	Redisplays selected statistics, pausing interval seconds between each display

Windows NT

The two most-used options for diagnosing network problems in Windows NT are the Network control panel and the MS-DOS prompt.

Network control panel

Use the Network control panel to configure networking for Windows NT clients including TCP/IP parameters for each network adapter, client identification, and the Windows networking parameters.

Identification

The Identification tab contains the NetBIOS Computer Name and the NetBIOS Domain that the computer will use.

Services

The Services tab has a window that displays the services that are active on your machine. The default services that should be displayed in the window are Computer Browser, NetBIOS Interface, RPC Configuration, Server, and Workstation. All of these services are required for Samba.

If any of these services is missing, click Add, select the service from the displayed list, click Have Disk (you need the Windows NT installation media), and click OK. Windows adds the service. If you need to add more then one service, repeat those steps. Continue with the protocol configuration.

Protocols

The TCP/IP protocol should be displayed in the window in the Protocols tab. To check the configuration, highlight the TCP/IP protocol and click Properties.

IP address If you are using DHCP, verify that Obtain an IP Address from a DHCP server is checked. If Specify IP Address is checked, you must enter the information for IP address, subnet mask, and default router gateway.

DNS The DNS tab has four option boxes. Host Name is the name of your client and should match the name you entered in the Identification field. The Domain box is where you enter the name of your DNS domain. The DNS service search order box is where you enter the IP address of your DNS server(s). The box Domain Suffix Search Order is for sites that have more than one DNS domain.

WINS address Again, if you are using DHCP, only fill in the DHCP address under the IP Address tab. Your client will get the WINS and DNS server information with the lease for the IP address. If you aren't using DHCP for server information, you can enable WINS resolution by entering the IP address of the Primary and Secondary WINS servers.

There are two checkboxes on this tab: the first, Enable DNS for Windows Resolution, is an option that you should *not* enable. This is not the same as enabling DNS; this option tells your WINS server to query your DNS server when it does not know an IP address. This seems like a good idea, but it does not work out that way. If your WINS server doesn't know about a machine, it's more likely you've made a typo or the machine is not currently on the network. The time spent querying the DNS server is wasted, network bandwidth is wasted, and the nine of ten times DNS can't help your WINS server find the address.

The other checkbox is Enable LMHOSTS Lookup. This option searches a local file called LMHOSTS for names and IP addresses. You can click the Import LMHOSTS button to import the WINS server's LMHOST file. But the question to ask yourself is, "Do I want to maintain another local file?"

Routing This option is for a machine with more then one NIC. It's beyond the scope of this book to configure a workstation as a gateway, so don't check the option Enable IP Forwarding.

Adapters

The adapters tab displays your network card and its properties. It's beyond the scope of this book to go over the adapter settings in detail.

Bindings

This tab displays bindings, which are connections between your network card and the services. The services for Samba are all bound to the WINS Client TCP/IP. These services are Server, Workstation, and NetBIOS Interface. These services were bound with your other configuration options.

MS-DOS prompt

There are several commands that you can run at the DOS prompt to diagnose network connectivity problems.

ping

The `ping` command is used for testing basic network connectivity. The basic syntax is:

```
ping destination
```

where `destination` can be the hostname or the IP address of the destination computer. If `ping` returns `Request timed out`, there is no TCP/IP connectivity between the client and the destination. Other options for `ping` are:

`-t`	Ping the host until interrupted
`-a`	Resolve addresses to hostname
`-n count`	Number of echo requests to send
`-f`	Set Don't Fragment flag in packet
`-I TTL`	Time to live
`-v TOS`	Type of service
`-r count`	Record route for count hops
`-s count`	Timestamp for count hops
`-j host-list`	Loose source route along host-list

tracert

The `tracert` command is used to diagnose routing problems. If your client cannot `ping` a Samba server and must go through a router, `tracert` could narrow the problem. The syntax is:

```
tracert address
```

Getting a `Request timed out` indicates a routing failure. Options for `tracert` are:

`-d`	Do not resolve addresses to hostname
`-h max_hops`	Maximum number of hops to search for target
`-j host-list`	Loose source route along host-list
`-w timeout`	Timeout, in milliseconds, to wait for each reply

nbtstat

`nbtstat` displays the NetBIOS statistics. If you're having trouble accessing a server by hostname, `nbtstat —c` displays the NetBIOS naming cache. The other parameters are:

`-a remote_name`	Lists the remote machine's name table
`-A remote_IP`	Lists the remote machine's name table
`-c`	Lists the remote name cache
`-n`	Lists local NetBIOS names
`-r`	Lists names resolved by broadcast and WINS

-R	Purges and reloads remote name cache
-S	Lists sessions table with destination IP addresses
-s	Lists sessions table with remote names, converting via hosts table

netstat

The `netstat` command is used to display statistics for TCP connections. The default is to display current active connections. The options are:

-a	Include server side connections
-e	Display Ethernet statistics
-n	Display numeric IP addresses and port numbers
-r	Display routing table
/-s	Display each per-protocol statistics
-p	The network protocol to be displayed in conjunction with the /s option

ipconfig

The `ipconfig` command shows the TCP/IP configuration. Adding the /all flag gives the verbose display.

The `ipconfig` command has a second use, which is to manipulate the DHCP lease for the client. The `ipconfig` command can release or renew the IP address for the client. An example of using `ipconfig` to release the lease on the IP address:

```
ipconfig release
```

An example of using `ipconfig` to renew the lease for the client DHCP-supplied IP address is:

```
ipconfig renew
```

nslookup

`nslookup` is used to test the DNS configuration. A successful forward lookup returns the IP address of a name, for example:

```
nslookup slashdot.org
```

UNIX/Linux/BSD

UNIX, Linux, FreeBSD, and NetBSD use the same commands to diagnose basic network connectivity. Differences between the operating systems are noted.

dmesg

dmesg displays the console messages from the time the system was booted or the buffer was filled. It's useful to see the status of devices during boot. The following example searches for the onboard Ethernet connection of a Sun Sparc Ultra 2:

```
#dmesg | grep hme0
```

ping

The ping command is used for testing basic network connectivity. The basic syntax is:

```
#ping destination
```

where destination can be the hostname or the IP address of the destination computer. If ping returns Request timed out, there is no TCP/IP connectivity between the client and the destination. Other options for ping are:

-c count	Stop after sending and receiving count ECHO_RESPONSE packets
-d	Set SO_DEBUG option of socket being used
-f	Flood ping-output packets as fast as they come back, or 100 times per second, whichever is greater
-i count	Wait count seconds between sending each packet
-l preload	Send preload number of packets as fast as possible
-n	Numeric output instead of hostnames
=p digits	Specify up to 16 pad bytes to fill out packets being sent. This is used to debug data dependent problems.
-q	Quiet output, only display the summary

`-r`	Bypass the normal routing tables and send directly to host
`-s size`	Specify the number of data bytes to be sent
`-v`	Verbose output
`-R`	Record IP route

Solaris-specific ping options

These ping options are specific to Solaris:

`-s`	The s flag in Solaris sends one datagram per second, and prints one line of output for every ECHO_RESPONSE it receives
`-l`	Loose source route
`-L`	Turn off loopback of multicast packets
`-i interface`	Specify the outgoing interface to use for multicast packets
`-I interval`	Specify the interval between transmissions in seconds
`-t ttl`	Specify the IP time to live

FreeBSD/NetBSD-specific ping options

These ping options are specific to FreeBSD/NetBSD:

`-a`	Audible; include a bell when output is received
`-I interface`	Source multicast packets with the given interface address
`-L`	Suppress loopback of multicast packets
`-Q`	Somewhat quiet; don't display ICMP error messages

ifconfig

The ifconfig command is used to display the TCP/IP configuration of the network interfaces.

Linux

To show the configured network interfaces, just type `ifconfig`. Some options are:

`interface`	The specific interface, typically eth0, eth1
`up`	Activate the interface
`down`	Deactivate the interface
`[-] arp`	Enable or disable the arp protocol on this interface
`[-]trailers`	Enable or disable trailers on Ethernet frames
`[-]allmulti`	Enable or disable promiscuous mode on the interface
`mtu N`	Set the maximum transfer unit for the interface
`netmask addr`	Set the IP netmask for this interface
`Irq addr`	Set the IRQ address for the interface
`[-]broadcast addr`	Set or clear the broadcast address

Solaris

To show all the configured network interfaces, use `ifconfig -a`. Other options are:

`auto-revarp`	Use the Reverse Address Resolution Protocol (RARP) to automatically acquire an address for this interface
`plumb`	Open the device associated with the physical interface name and set up the streams needed for TCP/IP to use the device
`unplumb`	Destroy any streams associated with this device and close the device
`private`	Tells the in.routed routing daemon that the interface should not be advertised (in.routed is a program that runs in the background on a Unix/Linux/FreeBSD system to do routing)

| `-private` | Specify unadvertised interfaces |
| `metric n` | Set the routing metric of the interface to *n* |

FreeBSD/NetBSD

To show all the configured network interfaces, use `ifconfig −a`. Other options are:

`address`	Set the hostname or IP address
`Address-family`	Set the `address-family`, such as inet (TCP/IP), atalk, or ipx
`Interface`	The specified interface, for example, ed0 or en0
`Alias`	Add another network address to this interface
`[-] arp`	Enable or disable the arp protocol on this interface
`up`	Activate the interface
`down`	Deactivate the interface
`broadcast addr`	Set the broadcast address
`delete`	Remove the specified network address
`media type`	Specify the media type the interface is using
`mediaopt opts`	Set the media options in a comma delimited list of options
`-mediaopt opts`	Disable the list of media options
`metric n`	Set the routing metric of the interface to *n*
`mtu N`	Set the maximum transfer unit for the interface
`netmask mask`	Specify how much of the address to reserve for subdividing networks into subnets

netstat

Use the `netstat` command to show the network status for all active sockets. Using the −a flag shows all sockets, whereas using the −o shows additional information. Other options are:

| `-c` | Display information continuously, refreshing once a second |
| `-i` | Include statistics for network devices |

`-n`	Show network addresses as numbers
`-r`	Show routing tables
`-t`	List only TCP sockets
`-u`	List only UDP sockets
`-v`	Print the version number and exit
`-w`	List only raw sockets
`-x`	List only UNIX sockets

Solaris options

`netstat` options specific to Solaris are:

`-f family`	Limit reports to a specified family, such as Inet or UNIX
`-g`	Show the multicast group memberships for all interfaces
`-i`	Show the state of the interfaces that are used for TCP/IP traffic
`-m`	Show the STREAMS statistics
`-p`	Show the address resolution tables
`-s`	Show per protocol statistics
`-v`	Verbose
`-I interface`	Show the state of a particular interface
`-M`	Show the multicast routing tables
`=P protocol`	Limit display of statistics to protocol
`interval`	Display information every interval seconds

FreeBSD/NETBSD-unique options

`netstat` options specific to FreeBSD/NetBSD are:

`-b`	Show the number of bytes in and out
`-d`	Show the number of dropped packets
`-f family`	Limit reports to a specified family, such as Inet for TCP/IP and atalk for Appletalk

`-g`	Show information related to multicast routing
`-I interface`	Include information about a specific interface
`-p protocol`	Show statistics about the protocol
`-s`	Show per protocol statistics
`-w wait`	Show statistics at intervals of wait seconds

nslookup

The `nslookup` command is used to query DNS servers. It can be used interactively or noninteractively.

Interactive mode

Interactive mode enables you to query name servers for host and domain information. Enter interactive mode by typing **nslookup** or **nslookup – hostname**. Commands available in interactive mode are:

`Exit`	Exit nslookup.
`finger [name]`	Connect with finger server on current host.
`help, ?`	Print a summary of the commands.
`host [server]`	Look up information for host, using server if specified.
`ls –[ahd] domain`	List information available for domain. The –a flag lists aliases of hosts, the –h flag lists CPU and operating system information, and the –d flag lists all contents of a zone transfer.
`lserver domain`	Change the default server to domain.
`root`	Change default server to the server of the domain name space.
`server domain`	Change the default server to domain.
`View filename`	Sort and list output of previous ls command.
`Set keyword[=value]`	Change the value of a keyword.

When using `Set keyword[=value]`, valid keywords are:

`All`	Print the current values of the keywords
`Class=name`	Set query class to IN (Internet), CHAOS, HESIOD or ANY
`Domain=name`	Change default domain to name
`[no]debug`	Turn debug mode on or off
`[n]d2`	Turn exhaustive debugging on or off
`[no]defname`	Append default domain name to every lookup
`[no]ignoretc`	Ignore truncate error
`[no]recurse`	Tell the name server to query or not query other servers if it does not have the information
`[no]search`	With `defname`, search for each name in parent domains of current domain
`[no]vc`	Always use a virtual circuit when sending requests to a server
`Port=port`	Connect to name server using port
`Querytype=value`	Same as `type=value`
`Retry=number`	Set number of retries number
`Root=host`	Change the name of root server to host
`Srchlist=domain`	Set searchlist to domain
`Timeout=number`	Change timeout interval to number seconds
`Type=value`	Change type of information returned from query.

When using `Type=value` you can change the type of information returned by a query to one of the following:

`A`	Host's Internet address
`ANY`	Any available information
`CNAME`	Canonical name for an alias
`HINFO`	Host CPU and operating system
`MD`	Mail Destination
`MG`	Mail Group member

`MINFO`	Mailbox or mail list information
`MR`	Mail rename domain name
`MX`	Mail Exchanger
`NS`	Name server for zone
`PTR`	Host name or pointer to other information.
`SQA`	Domain start of authority
`TXT`	Text information
`UINFO`	User information
`WKS`	Supported well-known services

Noninteractive mode

Noninteractive mode is used when `nslookup` is used with a hostname. For example:

```
#nslookup slashdot.org
```

traceroute

Use `traceroute` to verify that hosts that must pass through a router can be accessed. This is implemented in Linux and FreeBSD/NetBSD only. The syntax is:

```
#traceroute hostname
```

Options for the `traceroute` command are:

`-d`	Turn on socket-level debugging
`-g addr`	Enable the IP Loose Source Record Route option
`-l`	Enable the time-to-live value for each packet received
`-m max_ttl`	Set maximum time-to-live used in outgoing probe packets to max-ttl hops
`-n`	Print hop addresses numerically rather than symbolically
`-p port`	Set base UDP port number used for probe packets to port

`-q n`	Set number of probe packets for each time-to-live setting to the value *n*
`-r`	Bypass normal routing tables and send directly to a host
`-s src_add`	Use `src_add` as the IP address that will serve as the source address for outgoing probe packets
`-t tos`	Set the type-of-service in probe packets to tos
`-v`	Verbose
`-w n`	Set time to wait for a response to an outgoing probe packet to wait *n* seconds.

FreeBSD/NetBSD-unique options

FreeBSD/NetBSD has one unique option for `traceroute`:

`-S`	Print a summary of how many probes were not answered for each hop

dnsdomainname

The `dnsdomainname` prints the DNS domain name. This is a Linux-specific command.

domainname

The `domainname` command prints the name of the NIS domain, and the superuser can use `domainname` [name] to set it.

ypcat

The `ypcat` command prints values in an NIS database and confirms that NIS is working. To print the NIS password file, type

```
#ypcat passwd
```

Options for `ypcat` are:

`-d domain`	Specify a domain other than the default domain
`-k`	Display map keys
`-x`	Display the map nickname table

Linux-unique options

Linux has one unique option to `ypcat`:

-t   Inhibit translations of map nicknames to their corresponding map names

Chapter 10

Testing the Samba Configuration

This chapter tells you how to test various aspects of Samba, from testing the smb.conf file for syntax errors with testparm to checking that the daemons are running. It also explains how to tell what Samba is exporting, and whether specific clients are allowed to connect to the server.

Test the Configuration File with testparm

Each time you change Samba's configuration file, smb.conf, check it with the `testparm` command. This is a simple testing program but it does requires root access, so the first step of using testparm is to apply `su` to become a superuser. The testparm program checks for valid parameters in smb.conf. A *valid* parameter is not a guarantee that it is a *correct* parameter. You can misspell a name or type in the wrong host name or IP address, but to testparm these parameters, would appear to be correct. The `testparm` command is a useful tool if you know what you are really checking with it. The syntax of your configuration file is what testparm is checking. Don't sell this test short because configuration file errors are the most common type of error. To test the default smb.conf for a system, type **testparm** at a command prompt and press Enter. If no problems are reported, smbd loads the smb.conf file. The options for `testparm` are:

`-s`	Do not prompt for a carriage return after printing the service name and before dumping the definitions. This was added for Samba 2.0.
`configfilename`	Specify an alternate smb.conf file to check, rather than the default one.
`hostname`	If hostname and hostIP are specified, testparm checks them against `hosts allow` and `hosts deny` to determine whether the hostname with the hostIP address is allowed access to the Samba server.
`hostIP`	This is the IP address associated with the hostname in the previous parameter. It must be included if the hostname is included.

Tip

Typical output from testparm can fill several screens. You might want to redirect the output to a file by typing **testparm –s > testparm.txt**.

Checking the default smb.conf

The first line returned from `testparm` tells you what the default smb.conf is. Try this command to get the first line only:

```
#testparm —s | grep smb.conf
```

If you get an error message similar to:

```
Unable to open configuration file "/etc/smb.conf"!
```

write it down or print it out. Such a message tells you that Samba searched in the /etc directory for the configuration file smb.conf. If your error is incorrect path or permissions, you can determine what and where Samba expects the smb.conf file to be from the error message.

Checking for access for a specific client

To determine whether a specific client is allowed access to the shares on the Samba server, use the `hostname` and `hostIP` parameters. The following example determines which rights the client liberty has:

```
#testparm liberty 192.168.11.2
```

> **Tip**
>
> For a 1.9 Samba server, you must include the `configfile` parameter if you are using the `hostname` and `hostIP` options.

For a Samba 1.9 or prior server, use this syntax:

```
#testparm samba.conf liberty 192.168.11.2
```

Checking Whether Samba is Running with ps

The Samba server consists of two daemons: smbd and nmbd. The `ps` command displays all the daemons running on the system. Piping the output of the `ps` command to grep gives you a concise display. This should be a simple task, but no two UNIXs are ever quite the same. Different UNIXs have different parameters to show all the daemons.

Checking whether Samba is running with Linux

The –x flag is required to determine whether Samba is running on a Linux box. Type:

```
#ps –x | grep smbd
```

and

```
#ps –x | grep nmbd
```

You will get the grep process returned, as well as one or more smbd or nmbd processes.

Checking whether Samba is running with FreeBSD/NetBSD

The –x flag is required to determine whether Samba is running on a FreeBSD/NetBSD server. Type:

```
#ps –x | grep smbd
```

or

```
#ps –x | grep nmbd
```

You will get the grep process returned, as well as one or more smbd or nmbd processes.

Checking whether Samba is running with Solaris

The –e flag is needed to determine whether Samba is running on a Solaris box. Type:

```
#ps –e | grep smbd
```

or

```
#ps –e | grep nmbd
```

You will get the grep process returned, as well as one or more smbd or nmbd processes.

Checking How Samba Services Run

After Samba is successfully installed, two methods are available for starting the services automatically. You can run them as daemons or have them called by inetd when requested.

Running the Samba services as standalone daemons requires more UNIX system resources, but the response time is better. Running them from inetd means that they are only running when requested, but their performance is diminished.

For a dedicated server, running the Samba suite using standalone daemons makes the most sense. For a server that only occasionally provides Samba services, running it from inetd improves the UNIX server performance for other processes.

Starting Samba as a standalone daemon

Samba has two daemons that need to be launched: smbd and nmbd. System V and BSD have different startup scripts.

System V

For System V, such as Sun Solaris 2.*x* or Linux, there should be a Samba script in the init.d directory. For a Solaris 2.*x* system, the init.d directory is located in /etc. For a Red Hat or Caldera OpenLinux system, init.d is located in /etc/rc.d.

The Samba script should be called when the appropriate run-level starts. For almost all systems, run-level 3 is the one that calls Samba. If you look in the rc3.d directory, you should see a script that calls Samba; for example, S91smb.

The startup scripts are called in their numeric order. Caldera has a S99skipped script that disables services. If Samba is called with the S91smb script and is then killed with the S99 script, it won't be running when your clients attempt to connect to it.

BSD UNIX

You would need to add the following lines to the /etc/rc.local file to make Samba start on boot:

```
echo " smbd" && /usr/local/sbin/smbd -D
echo " nmbd" && /usr/local/sbin/nmbd -D
```

It is somewhat simpler than System V.

Starting Samba from inetd

Inetd is an Internet meta-daemon. It listens on various ports for calls and launches specific services when requested. For a server that gets infrequent Samba requests, inetd should work fine.

First, make sure inetd is listening for NetBIOS calls. Check the /etc/services file for these lines:

```
netbios-ns 137/udp
netbios-ssn 139/tcp
```

If they are not there, add them. Your server's Samba requests will be coming in on those ports.

 Caution

If you are using NIS or NIS+, you need to modify services at the master instead of the clients.

Next, edit /etc/inetd.conf to allow it to launch Samba when requested. The lines will be close to the following, but you might need to check your man pages for the exact syntax, or compare to other examples in the inetd.conf file.

```
Netbios-ssn stream tcp nowait root /usr/local/Samba/bin/smbd smbd

Netbios-ns dgram udp wait root /usr/local/Samba/bin/nmbd nmbd
```

 Caution

Some implementations of UNIX use `netbios_ssn` instead of `netbios-ssn`.

Finally, restart the inetd process by killing the process with –HUP. If inetd is process 3169, you kill the process by entering:

```
kill -HUP 3169
```

Starting and Stopping Samba

Once you pass the `testparm` test, start Samba to check your shares. For testing purposes, it's best to start Samba as a daemon because you might be starting and stopping it several times. System V and BSD UNIXs start Samba differently.

System V

A typical way to start Samba on System V is to type:

```
/etc/rc.d/init.d/smb start
```

which runs smbd and nmbd as daemons. You should get feedback similar to Starting SAMBA: smbd nmbd. Smbd is the service-providing daemon and nmbd is the browsing daemon.

On a Solaris 2.5 system, type:

```
/etc/init.d/Samba start
```

To stop the daemons, type the same string but the last parameter is stop instead of start.

BSD UNIX

On a BSD UNIX platform, you need to start each daemon by hand. For instance:

```
/usr/local/sbin/smbd -D
/usr/local/sbin/nmbd -D
```

Or you need to write the following script and make it executable (as the documentation suggests):

```
#!/bin/sh
/usr/local/sbin/smbd -D
/usr/local/sbin/nmbd -D
```

To stop the daemons, find their process number and kill it as the following example from a FreeBSD system shows:

```
terrapin# ps -x | grep smbd
 173 ?? Ss 1:04.68 /usr/local/sbin/smbd -D
 3373 ?? R 0:01.69 /usr/local/sbin/smbd -D
 3374 ?? R 0:00.23 /usr/local/sbin/smbd -D
 3376 p1 RV 0:00.00 grep smbd (csh)
terrapin# kill 173
terrapin# ps -x | grep nmbd
```

```
 175 ?? Ss 0:18.76 /usr/local/sbin/nmbd -D
terrapin# kill 175
terrapin# ps -x | grep smbd
 3387 p1 R+ 0:00.04 grep smbd
```

After finding the process numbers for smbd and nmbd and killing them, the only process left when grepping on smbd is the grep.

Checking Exports with Smbstatus

Smbstatus is a simple program that lists the current connections. Options for this program are:

-b	Brief output
-d	Verbose output
-L	List locks only
-p	Print a list of smbd processes
-S	List shares only
-s configfile	Use a specified configuration file
-u username	List shares for the specified user

Checking Printers with Testprns

Testprns is a program that determines the validity of a printer name for use in a Samba service. This test consists of checking the printcap file for the name of the specified printer. You can also specify a printcap file if you want to use one that is not being used by Samba at the time of the test. To test the printer laser, type

```
#testprns laser
```

The name of a desired printcap file can be included after the name of the printer. The following example checks the printcap file located under /opt/samba for the printer laser:

```
#testprns laser /opt/samba/printcap
```

Chapter 11

Accessing Samba

The Samba software suite includes some command-line smb commands. These commands can help with diagnostics for network and client configuration problems as well as a number of informative commands that can help with how to configure shares. Every Samba administrator should be familiar with these commands.

Checking the Shares on Your Server Using smbclient

After Samba is running, check what shares are available. You can check this without leaving UNIX with the `smbclient` command:

```
smbclient —L hostname
```

The `smbclient` command should list the shares available on your server, as this example shows:

```
[root@laptop col]# smbclient -L laptop

Added interface ip=192.168.11.4 bcast=192.168.11.255
nmask=255.255.255.0
Server time is Wed Jun 2 18:01:23 1999
Timezone is UTC-4.0
Password:
Domain=[WORKGROUP] OS=[UNIX] Server=[Samba 1.9.16p7]

Server=[laptop] User=[root] Workgroup=[WORKGROUP]
Domain=[WORKGROUP]
```

```
Sharename Type Comment
--------- ---- -------
IPC$ IPC IPC Service (Samba 1.9.16p7)
public Disk Public Stuff
root Disk Home Directories


This machine has a browse list:


Server Comment
--------- -------
LAPTOP Samba 1.9.16p7
PENTIUM P90
TERRAPIN Samba 1.9.18p10


This machine has a workgroup list:


Workgroup Master
--------- -------
WORKGROUP PENTIUM
```

Because this particular server is running with user-level security, a password was required to show what was available. If you want to list the shares without having to enter a password, add U%, which is a Samba variable that indicates the user.

Checking the Local Client Connection Using smbclient

Without leaving your Linux/UNIX box, you can test the local client connectivity with the smbclient command, specifically:

```
smbclient //terrapin/george
Added interface ip=192.168.11.5 bcast=192.168.11.255
nmask=255.255.255.0
Server time is Thu Jun 3 19:25:41 1999
```

```
Timezone is UTC-4.0
Password:
Domain=[WORKGROUP] OS=[UNIX] Server=[Samba 1.9.18p10]
security=share
smb: \> ls
 .cshrc H 509 Thu May 20 10:09:08 1999
 .login H 561 Thu May 20 10:09:08 1999
 .login_conf H 139 Thu May 20 10:09:08 1999
 .mailrc H 313 Thu May 20 10:09:08 1999
 .profile H 749 Thu May 20 10:09:08 1999
 .shrc H 832 Thu May 20 10:09:08 1999
 .mail_aliases H 351 Thu May 20 10:09:08 1999
 .rhosts H 257 Thu May 20 10:09:08 1999
 .history H 235 Thu Jun 3 19:05:54 1999
 libdes-4_04b_tar.gz A 142195 Sat May 29 22:17:26 1999

 33085 blocks of size 4096. 20195 blocks available
smb: \> exit
% ls -al
total 163
drwxr-xr-x 2 george wheel 512 May 31 10:39 .
drwxr-xr-x 3 root wheel 512 May 20 10:09 ..
-rw-r--r-- 1 george wheel 509 May 20 10:09 .cshrc
-rw------- 1 george wheel 235 Jun 3 19:05 .history
-rw-r--r-- 1 george wheel 561 May 20 10:09 .login
-rw-r--r-- 1 george wheel 139 May 20 10:09 .login_conf
-rw------- 1 george wheel 351 May 20 10:09 .mail_aliases
-rw-r--r-- 1 george wheel 313 May 20 10:09 .mailrc
-rw-r--r-- 1 george wheel 749 May 20 10:09 .profile
-rw------- 1 george wheel 257 May 20 10:09 .rhosts
-rw-r--r-- 1 george wheel 832 May 20 10:09 .shrc
-rwxr----- 1 george wheel 142195 May 29 22:17 libdes-4_
04b_tar.gz
```

If you get the error message "Not enough '\' characters in service," check your Samba version. Versions prior to 1.9.17 only recognized DOS backslashes. You would need to escape the backslashes in UNIX, or quote them, such as `smbclient \\\\laptop\\col` or `smbclient '\\laptop\col'`.

Other Options for smbclient

In addition to displaying shares, the `smbclient` command can let a Samba server access any smb-serving machine, including Windows servers. It provides a channel back from the UNIX server to a Windows server. The options are:

`-s smb.conf`	Specify the pathname to the Samba configuration file.
`-B IP_addr`	Specify the broadcast address.
`-O socket_ops`	TCP socket options for the client socket.
`-R name_resolve _order`	This option tells `smbclient` what order to use name-resolution services.
`-M NetBIOS_name`	This option enables you to send WinPopup messages to the specified computer.
`-i scope`	Set the NetBIOS scope.
`-N`	Suppress password request from `smbclient`.
`-n NetBIOS_name`	Specify a different hostname to connect as.
`-d debug_level`	Specify the debug level, which ranges from 0 to 10 or the letter A, with higher values logging more details. Level 0 only logs critical errors and serious warnings. Level 1 is good for daily operations. Levels 2 and 3 are good for debugging errors, and above level 3 generates a level of detail suitable for developers. Level A logs all debug messages.
`-P`	No longer used in Samba 2.0.
`-p port`	This option enables you to change the port to which `smbclient` connects. The default is the well-known port for NetBIOS Session Services, 139.

-l logfilename	This enables you to specify a logging filename other than the one specified at compile time.
-h T	This prints a usage message for the client.
-I IP_address	IP address is the address of the server to be connected to. The client normally attempts to locate a named SMB/CIFS server by looking it up via the NetBIOS name resolution mechanism described above in the name resolve order parameter above. Using this parameter will force the client to assume that the server is on the machine with the specified IP address and the NetBIOS name component of the resource being connected to will be ignored.
-E	Write messages to the standard error stream (stderr) instead of the standard output stream, which is STDOUT by default.
-U username	Specify the username that will be used by the client to make a connection, assuming your server is not using share-security levels instead of user-security levels.
-L NetBIOS_name	This option enables you to look at what services are available on a server. The -I option can be used to reach hosts on a different network or if you are having NetBIOS name resolution problems with your DNS servers.
-t terminal_code	This option tells smbclient how to translate characters in the filenames coming from the server.
-m max_protocol _level	This is ignored in Samba 2.0 and later. In versions prior to 2.0, this setting enabled you to choose the maximum protocol level to be negotiated.
-W WORKGROUP	Connect to a server in a different workgroup than the default workgroup.

smbclient Commands

After a connection is established, use FTP-like commands. The default prompt is:

```
smb:\>
```

To access filenames with spaces in them, enclose the filename in double quotes.

Optional parameters for the following commands are shown in square brackets:

```
[optional]
```

Required commands appear in angle brackets:

```
<required>
```

? [command]

If command is specified, the ? command displays a brief help message about the command. If no command is specified, the available commands are displayed.

! [shell command]

If shell command is specified, the ! command executes a shell locally and runs the specified shell command. If no command is specified, a local shell runs. For example, this can be used to examine files that have been retrieved. The following example looks at the first few lines of the retrieved file tapelabel.c:

```
smb: \> ! head tapelabel.c
```

To check whether you have sufficient disk space to retrieve a file, use this line:

```
smb: \> ! df -k
```

archive [level]

When using the `level` option, the archive level controls the behavior of the `mget` commands with respect to the archive bit on DOS/Windows files. With no level given, it returns the current value of the archive bit.

Level can be between 0 and 3, if used.

0   Retrieve all files regardless of the archive bit and do not change the archive bit.

1   Retrieve only files that have the archive bit set and do not change the archive bit.

2   Retrieve only files that have the archive bit set and reset the archive bit for those files.

3   Retrieve all files regardless of the archive bit and reset the archive bit.

blocksize *<blocksize>*

Specify the `blocksize` to be used with the tar command.

cancel *<jobid>*

Cancel the job with `jobid` in the print queue.

cd [directory name]

The `cd` command lets you change or print the current working directory. If `directory name` is specified, the current working directory on the server is changed to that directory. If no directory name is specified, the current working directory on the server is printed.

del <expression>

The client will request that the server attempt to delete all files matching `expression` from the current working directory on the server.

dir <[expression]

A list of the files matching `expression` in the current working directory on the server is retrieved from the server and displayed. `dir` with no expression displays all the files in the current working directory.

du

Show the space occupied by all files in the current directory.

exit | quit | q | Ctrl+D

Terminate the connection with the server and exit from `smbclient`.

get <remote filename> [local filename]

Copy the file called `remote filename` from the server to the machine running the client. If `local filename` was included, name the local copy `local file name`. Transfers in `smbclient` are binary by default unless you turn on translation. See also the `lowercase` command.

help [command]

If `command` is specified, the `help` command displays a brief help message about the command. If no command is specified, the available commands are displayed.

lcd [directory name]

If `directory name` is included, the current working directory on the local machine is changed to the directory specified. If no directory name was included, the name of the current working directory on the local machine is reported.

lowercase

Toggle lowercasing of filenames for the `get` and `mget` commands. This is off by default. When lowercasing is toggled on, local filenames are converted to lowercase when using the `get` and `mget` commands, which makes for better compatibility with UNIX systems where lowercase filenames are the norm.

ls <expression>

A list of the files matching `expression` in the current working directory on the server is retrieved from the server and displayed. `ls` with no expression displays all the files in the current working directory.

mask <expression>

Use `mask` to specify an expression to be used to filter files during recursive operation of the `mget` and `mput` commands. The masks specified with the `mget` and `mput` commands act as filters for directories rather than filters for files when recursion is toggled on.

The expression specified with the mask command is needed to filter files within those directories. For example, specifying an `mget` filter of `*1999` and a mask filter of `*.xls` and with recursion toggled on, the `mget` command retrieves all files matching `*.xls` in all directories prior to and including all directories matching `*1999` in the current working directory.

The default value for `mask` is blank, and after you change the value, it stays that way until it is changed to something else. To avoid unexpected results, it's wise to change the value of `mask` back to `*` after using the `mget` or `mput` commands.

md <directory name>

Create a new directory on the server with the specified directory name if your user privileges so allow.

mget <expression>

Copy all the files matching the expression from the server to the machine running `smbclient`.

When recursion is turned on, the filter supplied in the `mget` expression filters the directories and the `mask` command is used to filter the files.

mkdir <directory name>

Create a new directory on the server with the specified directory name if your user privileges so allow.

more <filename>

Retrieve the file named and display it in the smbclient session.

mput <expression>

Copy all the files matching the expression in the current working directory on the local machine to the current working directory on the server.

The mput expression acts differently when recursion is turned on. With recursion turned on, the filter supplied in the mput expression filters the directories and the mask command would be used to filter the files.

newer <filename>

This command lets you mget files that are newer than the date of the specified file.

print <filename>

This command lets you print the specified file on the local machine to the printable service to which server the smbclient is connected. This is considered obsolete and should not be used. It was retained for script compatibility. See also the printmode command.

printmode <graphics or text>

This command is considered obsolete in Samba 2.0 and later. It was retained for script compatibility. It sets the print mode to suit either binary data (such as graphical information) or text for all subsequent print commands.

prompt

This command toggles prompting for filenames during operations of the mget and mput commands.

When prompt is toggled on, the user is prompted to confirm the transfer of each file during these commands. When prompt is toggled off, all eligible files transfer without prompting.

put <local filename> [remote filename]

This copies the file called `local  file  name` in the current working directory from the machine running the `smbclient` to the current working directory on the server. If the remote file name parameter is included, name the remote copy `remote filename`. See the `lowercase` command if transferring files to a Windows server.

pwd

This command prints the current working directory.

queue

If you are connected to a printable server, this command displays the print queue, showing the job IDs, names, sizes, and current status of each print job.

quit

Terminate the connection with the server and exit from `smbclient`.

rd <directory name>

This removes the specified directory if you have sufficient rights to do so.

recurse

This lets you make `mget` and `mput` recurse to directories when getting or putting files. Recursion is off by default. When recursion is toggled on, these commands process all directories in the source directory and recurse to any directories that match the filter in the command. Only files that match the filter specified using the `mask` command are retrieved. When recursion is toggled off, only the files in the current working directory on the source machine that match the filter in the `mget` or `mput` commands are copied, and any filter specified using the `mask` command is ignored.

rm <expression>

Remove all the files matching the expression from the current working directory on the server.

rmdir <directory name>

This removes the specified directory, if you have sufficient rights to do so.

setmode <filename> <perm=[+|\-]rsha>

Similar to the DOS `attrib` command, `setmode` is used to set file permissions. For example:

```
setmode myfile +r
```

makes `myfile` read only.

Using nmblookup

The `nmblookup` utility looks up NetBIOS names. The general syntax is:

```
nmblookup [-M] [-R] [-S] [-r] [-A] [-h] [-B broadcast
address] [-U unicast address] [-d debuglevel] [-s smb
config file] [-i NetBIOS scope] [-T] NetBIOS_name
```

Options for `nmblookup` are:

-M	Searches for a master browser by looking up the NetBIOS name NetBIOS_name with a type of 0x1d. Use a NetBIOS name of − to do a lookup on the special name __MSBROWSE__.
-R	Set the recursion desired bit in the packet to do a recursive lookup. This is used to send a name query to a machine running a WINS server, when the user wants to query the names in the WINS server. If this bit is not set, the normal (broadcast responding) NetBIOS processing code on a machine is used instead. See rfc1001.txt and rfc1002.txt for details; these are available at `http://www.faqs.org/rfcs/` among other sites.
-S	After the name query has returned an IP address, do a node status query. A node status query returns the NetBIOS names registered by a host.

`-r`	Try to bind to UDP port 137 to send and receive UDP datagrams. This option is for a bug in Windows 95 where it ignores the source port of the requesting packet and only replies to UDP port 137. Unfortunately, on most UNIX systems, superuser privilege is required to bind to this port. In addition, if the nmbd daemon is running on this machine, it also binds to this port.
`-A`	Interpret <NetBIOS_name> as an IP address and do a node-status query on this address.
`-h`	Print a help (usage) message.
`-B broadcast address`	Send the query to the given broadcast address instead of adhering to the default behavior. The default behavior is to send the query to the broadcast address of the primary network interface as either autodetected or defined in the `interfaces` parameter of the smb.conf file.
`-U unicast address`	Do a unicast query to the specified address or host `unicast address`. This option (along with the `-R` option) is required to query a WINS server.
`-d debuglevel`	Debuglevel is an integer from 0 to 10. The default value is zero. The higher this value is, the more detail that is logged for the activities of `nmblookup`. At level 0, only critical errors and serious warnings are logged. Levels above 1 generate considerable amounts of log data and should only be used when investigating a problem. Levels above 3 are designed for use only by developers and generate huge amounts of data, most of which are extremely cryptic. Specifying this parameter here overrides the log-level parameter in the smb.conf file.
`-s smb.conf`	This parameter specifies the pathname to the Samba configuration file (smb.conf).

`-i scope`	This specifies a NetBIOS scope that `nmblookup` uses to communicate with when generating NetBIOS names. For details on the use of NetBIOS scopes, see rfc1001.txt and rfc1002.txt. NetBIOS scopes are very rarely used; only set this parameter if you are the system administrator in charge of all the NetBIOS systems with which you communicate.
`-T`	This causes any IP addresses found in the lookup to be looked up via a reverse DNS lookup into a DNS name and printed out before each `IP address NetBIOS name` pair, which is the normal output.
`NetBIOS_name`	This is the NetBIOS name being queried. Depending on the previous options, this could be a NetBIOS name or an IP address. If it is a NetBIOS name, then the different name types can be specified by appending `#<type>` to the name. This name can also be `*`, which returns all registered names within a broadcast area.

nmblookup Examples

To test that nmbd recognizes itself, type:

```
nmblookup hostname
```

You should get back the IP address that the host is communicating with on the net. If you find that it's trying to use the wrong IP address (for example, the loopback address, 127.0.0.0), you might need to add the correct interface in the smb.conf file with the `interfaces = IP address` parameter.

Then you can test to determine whether nmbd can see a specific PC, in this case liberty, by typing

```
nmblookup -B liberty
```

Or have `nmblookup` poll the network, with debugging on:

```
nmblookup -d 2 "*"
```

Chapter 12

Using Net Commands to Diagnose Problems

Samba versions 2.03 and later enable a UNIX host to join a Windows NT domain. It's a strange, new world for UNIX administrators, but the net commands help you understand it. All of the commands covered in this section are available in a Graphical User Interface (GUI) panel. As a UNIX administrator, you might find the GUI cumbersome because not all options are set in one panel. The Windows environment is so reliant on the GUI, that the command line is often overlooked. The net commands are useful and allow greater granular control. After you become familiar with the syntax of the net commands and their defaults, you might prefer to use the command line instead of the GUI panels. Try both to determine which is best for you. Remember that when the GUI fails, you should try the equivalent net command.

NT Server/Workstation Command-Line Net Commands

NT server domains and workgroups maintain user, file, and printer permissions. These commands also apply to NT workstations but are only applied to local resources and accounts unless there is a domain option for the command. When you use a command with a domain option, the status on the primary domain controller changes. The Primary Domain Controller (PDC) synchronizes all user, password, and share databases with all the backup domain controllers. The available net commands are discussed in the following sections.

net accounts

The net accounts command can add or delete user accounts on the PDC or the local system. When entered without options, the change applies only to the local system. This command also sets password size, life, and even synchronizes the PDC and the backup domain controllers. The net accounts command options are:

/domain	The /domain option makes a change to the PDC.
sync	The sync option forces an update of the user account database. All backup domain controllers receive the updated database. On busy networks, this can still take between 15 and 30 minutes.
/minpwlen:x	This option sets the minimum password length to x characters (the default is 0, the maximum is 14).
/maxpwage:x	This option sets the maximum password lifetime to x days (the default is 42, the maximum is 49,710). Unlimited is a valid option if you want to remove the password-aging limit.
/minpwage:x	This option sets the minimum number to x days between password changes (the default value is 0, the maximum allowed is 49,710).
/uniquepw:x	This option sets the number of previously remembered passwords to x (the default is 0, the maximum is 24).

net computer

The net computer \\computername command adds or removes a computer from the domain.

The net computer command options are:

/add	This option adds the computer to the domain.
/delete	This option deletes the computer from the domain.

net config

The net config command displays service configuration information. This command requires an option. The options are:

/server	This option displays server name, maximum users that can attach, maximum number of open files, and idle time.
/workstation	This option displays the computer name, username, and your NetBEUI connection name.

net continue

The net continue command starts a service that was paused and requires the name of a service.

net file

When entered without options, the net file command displays all open shared files and their ID numbers. If you enter the command with an ID number, then information about that file is displayed. The net file command options are:

id	ID number to display specific information.
/close	This option closes the file.

net group

The net group command displays the global groups that are available on the client or primary domain controller. The command requires options. The /domain options is always needed when net group is used on the PDC. The options are:

/domain	This option displays the groups on the PDC.
/add	This option adds groups and/or users to the group, or it can add users to an existing group.

The format to add a group is:

```
net group groupname /add /domain
```

The format to add users to a group is:

```
net group groupname users /add /domain
```

A useful option is the comment field for descriptions; the format for a comment is:

```
net group groupname /add /comment: "This group controls
the assets of the free world."
```

The format to delete a group is:

```
net group groupname /delete /domain
```

The format to delete users to a group is:

```
net group groupname users /delete /domain
```

net helpmsg

The net helpmsg command provides a detailed explanation of an error received when entering a command and includes the statement that, "More help is available by typing net helpmsg xxxx." The format is:

```
net helpmsg error xxxx(error number)
```

net localgroup

The net localgroup command displays or modifies groups on the local system. This command requires the /add option:

/add   This option adds localgroups and/or users to the localgroup, or it adds users to an existing localgroup.

The format to add a localgroup is:

```
net localgroup groupname /add
```

The format to add users to a group is:

```
net localgroup groupname users /add
```

A useful option is the comment field for descriptions; the format for a comment is:

```
net localgroup groupname /add /comment: "This group
controls the assets of the free world."
```

The following option adds the group to the PDC:

```
/domain
```

It might seem odd that localgroup can be used to add groups to a PDC, but it's another use for it. You might want to test changes for group security on a local system and then use the domain option to effect the change on the domain controller.

The format to delete from a localgroup:

```
net localgroup groupname /delete
```

The format to delete users to a localgroup:

```
net localgroup groupname users /delete
```

Again there's an option for the comment field for descriptions. The format for a comment is:

```
net localgroup groupname /delete /comment: "Deleted
accounting group"
```

net name

The net name command displays the current machine and usernames. There is one option for this command:

```
/delete
```

net pause

The net pause command pauses a service. The only option is the name of the service to be paused:

```
net pause servicename
```

net print

The `net print` command lists and manages a specified print queue. The format of the command is:

```
net print \\machine\printer
```

This option lists the queue of a printer on the machine specified.

If you need to find the name of a printer, use the `net view \\machine` command.

net send

The `net send` command sends a message to a machine, user, or users. The message text does not require quotes.

The format to send a message to a machine is:

```
net send machinename message
```

This is the format to send a message to a user:

```
net send username message
```

The format to send a message to everyone is:

```
net send * message
```

Use the `/domain` option to send a message to every user in a domain:

```
net send /domain:domainname message
```

Use the `/users` option to send a message to all users connected to a local server:

```
net send /users message
```

net session

The `net session` command displays session connections on the local machine. There is one option for the command:

```
/delete
```

This option terminates a session and closes all files associated with it.

net share

The `net share` command assigns or removes network shares. Enter this command without options to display what is shared on the local machine. The options for this command are:

`/users:x`	This option specifies the maximum number of users that can access the share; x is the placeholder for the numeric value.
`/unlimited`	This option specifies no limit for user connections.
`/remark:"text"`	This is the option for comments visible in the Network Neighborhood when the share is displayed.
`/delete`	This option deletes a share.

net start

The `net start` command starts a service. The only option is the name of the service to be started. The format of the command is:

```
net start servicename
```

netstat

The `netstat` command displays TCP/IP statistics for all active connections. Use the command options to limit output. A very useful option when testing intermittent problems is to use a number after any `netstat` command to repeat the command that number of times. The options are:

`/A`	This option includes the server-side connections with the display.
`/E`	This option displays the Ethernet connections.
`/N`	This option displays the numeric IP addresses and ports for connections.
`/R`	This option displays the routing table. The routing table is often the source of trouble when everything else has been checked and verified to be correct.

/S This option specifies statistics for the protocol determined by the /P option.

/P This is the option for protocol. The protocols are TCP, IP, or UDP.

/x This option specifies the number of times the `netstat` command is to repeat.

The format to combine those options is:

```
netstat /S /P TCP
```

net statistics

The `net statistics` command displays server session and services statistics. Its options are:

Server   The name of the server to query for statistics.

Workstation The name of the workstation to query for statistics.

net stop

The `net stop` command stops a service. The only option is the name of the service to stop. The format of the command is:

```
net stop servicename
```

net time

The `net time` command displays and or sets time. You must specify where the display occurs by using one of these options:

\\machinename   This option displays a specific machine's time.

/DOMAIN:domainname This option displays a specific domain's time.

/SET   This option sets the time, and you can specify either a machine or domain for your machine's time source.

The format of the command is:

```
net time /machinename /set
```

or

```
net time /DOMAIN:domainname /set
```

net use

The net use command maps network resources to the local machine. This is where you can make network drive and printer magic happen. Passwords might be required depending on the security you've set on your files and printers.

`/PERSISTENT:YES  |  NO`	This option can be a blessing or a curse. The default is Yes. If you mount anything with /PERSISTENT:No, then No becomes the default. Whatever the last persistent setting was becomes the default.
`/USER:domain\username`	This option sets a username for the share.
`/HOME`	This option maps the specified drive letter to your home directory.
`/DELETE`	This option removes a network share.

net user

The net user command can list, create, or modify user accounts. When used without an option, it lists all the users on the system or domain. The options for this command are:

`/ADD`	This option adds a user.
`/DELETE`	This option deletes a user.
`/ACTIVE:YES|NO`	This option sets an account to active or disables it.

`/FULLNAME:name`	This is the option to set a user's full name.
`/EXPIRES:date| NO`	This option sets a date for the account to expire, or sets it to never expire.
`/HOMEDIR:path`	This option sets the home directory location.
`/PASSWORDCHG:YES | NO`	This option sets the permission for the user to change the account password.
`/PASSWORDREQ: YES | NO`	This option sets whether a password is required.
/PROFILEPATH:path	This option sets the path to the user profile for the account.
`/SCRIPTPATH`	This option sets the path of the user account login script.
`/TIMES:ALL | times`	This option sets whether the user can log in any time or you can set specific login times.
`/WORKSTATIONS:list`	This option sets to which machine the user can log on. The default is every machine in the domain. If you set this option, the maximum number is eight workstations.
`/COMMENT:text`	This is the option for a comment about the user, or you could use `/USERCOMMENT`.
`/USERCOMMENT`	This option is for a user-specific comment.
`/COUNTRYCODE:X`	This option sets your operating system country code; 0 is the system default.

net view

The `net view` command displays the names of machines in a domain or network. Its options are:

`\\machinename`	This option specifies the name of the remote system for your resource display.
`/DOMAIN`	This option lists the machines in a domain.
`/DOMAIN:machinename`	This option lists the resources of the machine named in the domain.
`/NETWORK:NW`	This option lists all available NetWare servers and their resources.
`/NETWORK:NW \\machine`	This option lists the resources available for the one NetWare machine.

Windows 95/98 Command-Line net Commands

Windows 95 and 98 have a smaller subset of net commands. Just as with their big brother NT, these commands are overlooked for the flashy GUI versions. These commands give you greater granular control. This section summarizes all the Windows 95 and 98 client net commands and their options.

net config

The `net config` command displays your current workgroup settings. Its only option is:

`/YES`

This option executes the `net config` command without first prompting you to provide information or to confirm actions.

net diag

The net diag command executes the Microsoft Network Diagnostics program to test the hardware connection between two computers. This command also displays information about a single computer. The net diag command options are:

/NAMES This option specifies a diagnostic server name to avoid conflicts when net diag is used simultaneously by multiple users. This option works only when the network uses a NetBIOS protocol.

/STATUS This option enables you to specify the computer about which you want network diagnostics information.

net help

The net help command displays information about net commands and error messages. The net help command entered without options displays a brief description of all Microsoft net commands. The net help command options are:

NET command /? This option works with all net commands and displays the options and format for the command.

NET HELP suffix This option requires the suffix of the net command. It also displays the options and format for the command.

NET HELP errornum This option specifies the number of the error message about which you want to display information.

net init

The net init command loads protocol and network-adapter drivers without binding them to the Protocol Manager. This command might be required if you are using some third-party network-adapter drivers. This command is useful for testing new drivers. If the test is a success, you can then bind the drivers to the Protocol Manager by typing net start netbind. The option for the net init command is:

/DYNAMIC

This option loads the Protocol Manager dynamically. Loading the Protocol Manager dynamically is useful with some third-party networks when trying to resolve memory problems.

net logoff

The net logoff command breaks the connections between your computer and the shared resources to which it is connected. To break the connection without being prompted or being asked to confirm actions, use the /YES option.

net logon

The net logon command identifies you as a member of a workgroup. Its options are:

user	This option specifies the name that identifies you in your workgroup. The name you specify can contain up to 20 characters.
password	This option is where you enter the password. The password can contain up to 14 characters.
?	This option specifies that you want to be prompted for your password.
/DOMAIN	This option specifies that you want to log on to a Microsoft Windows NT or LAN Manager domain.
/DOMAIN:domainname	This option specifies the name of the Windows NT or LAN Manager domain to which you want to log on.
/YES	This option carries out the net logon command without first prompting you to provide information or confirm actions.
/SAVEPW:NO	This option carries out the net logon command without prompting you to create a password-list file.

If you would rather be prompted to type your username and password instead of specifying them in the net logon command line, type net logon without options.

net password

The net password command changes your logon password. Its options are:

\\computer	This option specifies the Windows NT or LAN Manager server on which you want to change your password.
/DOMAIN:domainname	This option specifies that you want to change your password on the Windows NT or LAN Manager domain you specified with the :domainname option.
user	This option specifies your Windows NT or LAN Manager username.
oldpassword	This option specifies your current password.
newpassword	This option specifies your new password, which can have up to 14 characters.

net print

The net print command displays information about the print queue on a shared printer, or controls your print jobs. The options are:

\\computer	This option specifies the name of the computer's print queue about which you want information.
\\computer\printer	This option specifies both the name of the printer about which you want information and the name of the server sharing the printer.
port	This option specifies the name of the parallel (LPT) port on your computer that is connected to the printer about which you want information.

`job#`	This option specifies the number assigned to a queued print job.

When specifying `job#`, you can also use these options:

`/PAUSE`	This option pauses a print job.
`/RESUME`	This option restarts a print job that has been paused.
`/DELETE`	This option cancels a print job.
`/YES`	This option carries out the `net print` command without first prompting you to provide information or to confirm actions.

To receive information about the print queues on each of the shared printers that are connected to the computer, specify only the name of a computer when using the `net print` command.

net start

The `net start` command starts services. Services cannot be started from a command prompt within Windows. To start the workgroup redirector you selected during setup, type `net start` without options. In general, you don't need to use any option. You might use them if you need to turn on NetWare when you don't normally connect to a NetWare server at startup. The options are:

`/BASIC`	This option starts the basic redirector.
`/NWREDIR`	This option starts the Microsoft Novell-compatible redirector.
`/WORKSTATION`	This option starts the default redirector.
`/NETBIND`	This option binds protocols and network-adapter drivers.
`/NETBEUI`	This option starts the NetBIOS interface.
`/NWLINK`	This option starts the IPX/SPX-compatible interface.
`/LIST`	This option displays a list of the services that are running.

/YES	This option carries out the net start command without first prompting you to provide information or to confirm actions.
/VERBOSE	This option displays information about device drivers and services as they are loaded.

net stop

The net stop command stops services. Services cannot be stopped from a command prompt within Windows. The net stop command options are:

/BASIC	This option stops the basic redirector.
/NWREDIR	This option stops the Microsoft Novell-compatible redirector.
/WORKSTATION	This option stops the default redirector.
/NETBEUI	This option stops the NetBIOS interface.
/NWLINK	This option stops the IPX/SPX-compatible interface.
/YES	This option carries out the net stop command without first prompting you to provide information or to confirm actions.

To stop the workgroup redirector, type **net stop** without options. This breaks all your connections to shared resources and removes the net commands from your computer's memory.

net time

The net time command displays the time or synchronizes your computer's clock with the shared clock on a Microsoft Windows for Workgroups, Windows NT, Windows 95, or NetWare time server. The net time command options are:

\\ computer	This option specifies the name of the computer designated as time server whose time you want to check or synchronize with your computer's clock.

`/WORKGROUP`	This option specifies that you want to use the clock on a computer designated as time server in another workgroup.
`/WORKGROUP:wgname`	This option specifies the name of the workgroup containing a computer whose clock you want to check or synchronize with your computer's clock. If there are multiple time servers in that workgroup, `net time` uses the first one it finds.
`/SET`	This option synchronizes your computer's clock with the clock on the computer or workgroup you specify.
`/YES`	This option carries out the `net time` command without first prompting you to provide information or to confirm actions.

net use

The `net use` command connects or disconnects your computer from a share resource or displays information about your connections. Its options are:

`drive`	This option specifies the drive letter you assign to a shared directory.
`*`	This option specifies the next available drive letter. If `*` is used with `/DELETE`, all your connections are disconnected.
`port`	This option specifies the parallel (LPT) port name you assign to a shared printer.
`computer`	This option specifies the name of the computer sharing the resource.
`directory`	This option specifies the name of the shared directory.
`printer`	This option specifies the name of the shared printer.
`password`	This option specifies the password for the shared resource, if any.

?	This option specifies that you want to be prompted for the password of the shared resource. You don't need to use this option unless the password is optional.
/SAVEPW:NO	This option specifies that the password you type should not be saved in your password-list file. You will still need to retype the password the next time you connect to this resource.
/YES	This option carries out the net use command without first prompting you to provide information or to confirm actions.
/DELETE	This option breaks the connection to the specified shared resource.
/NO	This option carries out the net use command, responding with NO automatically when you are prompted to confirm actions.
/HOME	This option makes a connection to your HOME directory if one has been specified in your LAN Manager or Windows NT user account.

To list all of your connections, type net use without options. For more then one screen at a time, type the following at the command prompt:

```
net use | MORE
```

To list all of the options in the command window use:

```
net use /? | MORE
```

or
```
net help use | MORE
```

net ver

The net ver command displays the type and version number of the workgroup redirector that the machine is using. There are no options for this command; it's short for *version*. This is a command to remember and use on clients running older operating systems. Always verify that the clients were upgraded to the latest versions before testing the hardware.

net view

The net view command displays a list of computers in a specified workgroup or the shared resources available on a specified computer. To display a list of computers in your workgroup that share resources, type net view without options. The net view command options are:

/WORKGROUP	This option specifies that you want to view the names of the computers in another workgroup that share resources.
/WORKGROUP:wgname	This option specifies the name of the workgroup whose computer names you want to view.
/YES	This option carries out the net view command without first prompting you to provide information or confirm actions.

Appendix A

Error Codes

This appendix lists the common Windows error codes for clients and servers when running Samba.

Windows 95/98 net command error codes

The following example is the format of the command for a detailed error message for error number one on a Windows 95/98 computer.

```
net help 1
```

Just change the number to the number of the error message you receive. Here is a list of the error codes that have help messages.

Error 1

An internal error occurred. Quit all current processes, restart your computer, and then try again. If the problem persists, contact Microsoft Product Support Services.

Error 2

The specified file does not exist in the current directory or path. Make sure you are specifying the filename and path correctly, and then try again.

Error 3

The specified path does not exist on that drive. Make sure you are specifying the path correctly, and then try again. If the path includes a network resource that is temporarily unavailable, try again later.

Error 4

The maximum number of files is open. Close one or more files or programs, and then try again.

Error 5

You do not currently have access to this file. The file might be marked read-only, or it could be part of a shared resource such as a folder, a named pipe, a queue, or a semaphore. You can use the ATTRIB command to change the read-only attribute, or try again later when the file might be available.

Error 8

There is not enough memory available. Quit all running programs, restart your computer, and then try again. You might also need to quit any terminate-and-stay-resident programs (TSRs) that start when you restart your computer.

Error 15

The specified drive letter or device is invalid. If you specified a drive letter, check the LASTDRIVE command in your config.sys file to make sure that drive letter is included. For more information, type **NET HELP 15** at the command prompt. Make sure you are specifying a drive letter that exists. If the problem persists, you may be trying to RESTORE to a redirected drive. Choose a different drive, and then try again.

Error 16

The specified directory cannot be removed. Either it has been typed incorrectly, it contains files or other folders, or it is the current directory in this command prompt or another command prompt that is in process. For more information, type **NET HELP 16** at the command prompt.

Do one of the following and then retry the command:

- Correct the directory name.
- Remove all files and subdirectories from the directory.
- Use the CHDIR command to change the current directory in all command prompts that might be using it.

Error 17

The file cannot be moved or renamed to a different disk drive. Retry the command, specifying the same drive for both the original and changed filenames, or try copying the file.

Error 19

The disk is write protected. Remove the write protection, or use a different disk, and then try again.

Error 20

Windows cannot find the device specified. Make sure you are using a correct device name, and then try again.

Error 21

The drive is not ready. You need to insert a disk in the drive, close the drive door, or wait until the drive is available.

Error 23

MS-DOS cannot read or write the data correctly. If the error occurred on a hard disk, retry the command. If the error persists, the hard disk might have to be reformatted. If the error occurred on a floppy disk, insert a formatted disk or the backup disk, and then try again.

Error 25

The drive cannot locate a specific area or track on the disk. Make sure the disk is properly inserted in the drive and that it is in a format compatible with MS-DOS. If the error persists, run ScanDisk to check the disk for damage.

Error 26

The specified disk cannot be accessed. Make sure that the disk is in a format compatible with MS-DOS. If the problem persists, make sure your CONFIG.SYS file contains the file system driver.

Error 27

The drive cannot find the sector requested. Make sure the disk is properly inserted in the drive and that it is in a format compatible with MS-DOS. If the error persists, run ScanDisk to check the disk for damage.

Error 28

The requested print job was not completed. Make sure that the printer is installed and connected properly, that it is turned on, and that there is paper in it. For more information, type **NET HELP 28** at the command prompt. If you are using a network server printer, there may not be enough disk space to create a spool file. Try deleting any unnecessary files from the disk that contains the spool directory, and then try again.

Error 29

MS-DOS detected an error while writing to this device. Make sure the device is installed and connected properly, turned on, and not in use by another process. The device may need to be in the proper receive mode. If the device is a disk, make sure it is formatted properly.

Error 30

MS-DOS detected an error while reading from this device. Make sure the device is installed and connected properly, turned on, and not in use by another process. The device may need to be in the proper send mode. If the device is a disk, make sure it is formatted properly.

Error 31

A device attached to the system is not functioning. For more information, type **NET HELP 31** at the command prompt.

Check the following, and then try again:

1. The device is connected properly and is turned on.

2. The disk and drive types are compatible.

3. The disk is properly inserted in the drive.

4. The drive door is closed.

5. The disk is properly formatted.

Error 33

One process has locked a portion of the file, and a second process has attempted to use the same portion. Try again later.

Error 35

The program could not open the requested file because the file control block (FCB) limit was exceeded. Edit your CONFIG.SYS file to increase the value in the FCBS= line. Restart your computer, and then try again.

Error 36

The maximum number of files in the sharing buffer has temporarily been exceeded. Quit one or more programs, and then try again, or try again later.

Error 37

Disk *** is write-protected. Remove the write protection or use a different disk, and then try again.

Error 38

The system cannot find the *** device. Make sure you are specifying a valid device name, and then try again.

Error 39

The *** device is not ready. Make sure there is a disk in the drive, that the drive door is properly closed, and that the drive is available.

Error 41

MS-DOS cannot read or write the data on disk *** correctly. If the error occurred on a hard disk, retry the command. If the error persists, the hard disk may have to be reformatted. If the error occurred on a floppy disk, insert a formatted disk or the backup disk, and then try again.

Error 43

Drive *** cannot locate a specific area or track on the disk. Make sure the disk is properly inserted in the drive and that it is in a format compatible with MS-DOS. If the error persists, run ScanDisk to check the disk for damage.

Error 45

Drive *** cannot find the sector requested. Make sure the disk is properly inserted in the drive and that it is in a format compatible with MS-DOS. If the error persists, run ScanDisk to check the disk for damage.

Error 46

The *** printer is out of paper. Make sure the printer is properly installed and connected, turned on, and loaded with paper.

Error 47

MS-DOS detected an error while writing to the *** device. Make sure the device is installed and connected properly, turned on, and not in use by another process. The device may need to be in the proper receive mode. If the device is a disk, make sure it is formatted properly.

Error 48

MS-DOS detected an error while reading from the *** device. Make sure the device is installed and connected properly, turned on, and not in use by another process. The device may need to be in the proper send mode. If the device is a disk, make sure it is formatted properly.

Error 49

The *** device is not functioning. For more information, type **NET HELP 49** at the command prompt.

Check the following, and then try again:

1. The device is connected properly and is turned on.
2. The disk and drive types are compatible.

3. The disk is properly inserted in the drive.

4. The drive door is closed.

5. The disk is properly formatted.

Error 50

You attempted an operation that cannot be performed from your computer or that is not supported on the specified server. Make sure you are using the correct server for the command or task that you want to perform. If the problem persists, contact your network administrator.

Error 51

The specified computer is not receiving requests. Make sure you are specifying the computer name correctly, or try again later when the remote computer is available.

Error 52

A duplicate workgroup or computer name exists on the network. Specify a unique name, and then try again.

Error 53

The computer name specified in the network path cannot be located. Make sure you are specifying the computer name correctly, or try again later when the remote computer is available.

Error 54

The network is currently busy processing other requests or is out of resources. Try again later, or verify your network configuration to be sure that enough network resources are specified.

Error 55

The specified resource is not available. The computer that shared the resource might have been turned off, or the permissions might have been changed. For more information, contact your network administrator.

Error 56

The network currently has too many NetBIOS requests waiting to be processed. Try again later. If the problem persists, contact your network administrator.

Error 57

The hardware that connects your computer to the network is experiencing a problem. Make sure that the cable on the back of your computer is properly connected. If the problem persists, contact your network administrator or the manufacturer of the network hardware.

Error 58

This operation cannot be performed by the specified server. Make sure that you have specified the correct computer name and command. If the problem persists, contact your network administrator.

Error 59

An unexpected network error has occurred. Quit all running programs, restart your computer, and then try again. If the problem persists, contact your network administrator.

Error 60

Your computer cannot communicate with the specified remote computer because their hardware adapters are not compatible. As a test, try communicating with a different computer. If the problem persists, contact your network administrator.

Error 61

The printer cannot take any additional print requests at this time. Try again later.

Error 62

There is not enough memory available on the print server for the requested print file. Try again later.

Error 63

Another user on the server deleted your print request. Contact the other user to find out why the file was deleted, or resend the print request later.

Error 64

The specified network resource is no longer available. The server that shared the resource might have been turned off, or the permissions might have been changed. For more information, contact your network administrator.

Error 65

You do not have the necessary access rights to use this network resource. Make sure you are specifying the correct name of the resource you want to use, or contact your network administrator for more information.

Error 66

You have specified an incorrect network resource type. Your possible choices are (1) drive letter A: through Z: for a shared directory path, or (2) port name LPT1: through LPT9: for a shared printer or modem path.

Error 67

The specified shared directory cannot be found. Make sure you have specified the network name correctly. If the problem persists, contact your network administrator.

Error 68

You have reached the maximum number of names allowed on the network adapter for your computer. Either disconnect from any resources not currently in use, or reconfigure the network adapter.

Error 69

You have reached the maximum number of connections that can be made. Disconnect from any resources not currently in use, and then try again.

To increase the maximum number of sessions, double-click the Network icon in Control Panel, click a protocol, click Properties, and then click the Advanced tab.

Error 70

The server you are trying to gain access to is either paused or still being started. Try again later. If the error persists, contact your network administrator.

Error 71

This request is not accepted by the network. The server may have run out of resources necessary to process your request. Try the request again. If the error persists, contact your network administrator. For more information, type **NET HELP 71** at the command prompt. If you are a network administrator, consult the server's documentation for information about configurable parameters.

Error 72

The printer or disk device that you specified has been paused. Use the NET CONTINUE command to activate the device, and then try again.

Error 82

The directory or file cannot be created. Make sure you are specifying the path correctly and that there is enough space for the new file. You may also need to make sure the disk is formatted properly, or try specifying a different name for the file or directory you want to create.

Error 84

You have reached the maximum number of requests the system can handle. Try the operation again later.

Error 85

The local device name is already in use. Try again, using a different device name. Your possible choices are (1) drive letter A: through Z: for a shared directory path, or (2) port name LPT1: through LPT9: for a shared printer or modem path.

Error 86

The specified network password is not correct. Type the correct password, or contact your network administrator for more information.

Error 123

The computer name or shared directory name in the specified network path is invalid. Make sure you are typing the name correctly, and that the computer you are trying to connect to is available.

Error 128

An unexpected network error has occurred.

Windows NT error codes

The following example is the format of the command for a detailed error message for error number one on a Windows NT computer.

```
net helpmsg 1
```

Just change the number to the number of the error message you receive. Here is a list of the error codes that have help messages.

Error 1

Incorrect function.

Error 2

The system cannot find the file specified.

Error 3

The system cannot find the path specified.

Error 4

The system cannot open the file.

Error 5

Access is denied.

Error 6

The handle is invalid.

Error 7

The storage control blocks were destroyed.

Error 8

Not enough storage is available to process this command.

Error 9

The storage control block address is invalid.

Error 10

The environment is incorrect.

Error 11

An attempt was made to load a program with an incorrect format.

Error 12

The access code is invalid.

Error 13

The data is invalid.

Error 14

Not enough storage is available to complete this operation.

Error 15

The system cannot find the drive specified.

Error 16

The directory cannot be removed.

Error 17

The system cannot move the file to a different disk drive.

Error 18

There are no more files.

Error 19

The media is write protected.

Error 20

The system cannot find the device specified.

Error 21

The device is not ready.

Error 22

The device does not recognize the command.

Error 23

Data error (cyclic redundancy check).

Error 24

The program issued a command but the command length is incorrect.

Error 25

The drive cannot locate a specific area or track on the disk.

Error 26

The specified disk or diskette cannot be accessed.

Error 27

The drive cannot find the sector requested.

Error 28

The printer is out of paper.

Error 29

The system cannot write to the specified device.

Error 30

The system cannot read from the specified device.

Error 31

A device attached to the system is not functioning.

Error 32

The process cannot access the file because it is being used by another process.

Error 33

The process cannot access the file because another process has locked a portion of the file.

Error 36

Too many files opened for sharing.

Error 38

Reached end of file.

Error 39

The disk is full.

Error 50

The network request is not supported.

Error 51

The remote computer is not available.

Error 52

A duplicate name exists on the network.

Error 53

The network path was not found.

Error 54

The network is busy.

Error 55

The specified network resource or device is no longer available.

Error 56

The network BIOS command limit has been reached.

Error 57

A network adapter hardware error occurred.

Error 58

The specified server cannot perform the requested operation.

Error 59

An unexpected network error occurred.

Error 60

The remote adapter is not compatible.

Error 61

The printer queue is full.

Error 62

Space to store the file waiting to be printed is not available on the server.

Error 63

Your file waiting to be printed was deleted.

Error 64

The specified network name is no longer available.

Error 65

Network access is denied.

Error 66

The network resource type is not correct.

Error 67

The network name cannot be found.

Error 68

The name limit for the local computer network adapter card was exceeded.

Error 69

The network BIOS session limit was exceeded.

Error 70

The remote server has been paused or is in the process of being started.

Error 71

No more connections can be made to this remote computer at this time because there are already as many connections as the computer can accept.

Error 72

The specified printer or disk device has been paused.

Error 80

The file exists.

Error 82

The directory or file cannot be created.

Error 83

Fail on INT 24.

Error 84

Storage to process this request is not available.

Error 85

The local device name is already in use.

Error 86

The specified network password is not correct.

Error 87

The parameter is incorrect.

Error 88

A write fault occurred on the network.

Error 89

The system cannot start another process at this time.

Error 100

Cannot create another system semaphore.

Error 101

The exclusive semaphore is owned by another process.

Error 102

The semaphore is set and cannot be closed.

Error 103

The semaphore cannot be set again.

Error 104

Cannot request exclusive semaphores at interrupt time.

Error 105

The previous ownership of this semaphore has ended.

Error 107

Program stopped because alternate diskette was not inserted.

Error 108

The disk is in use or locked by another process.

Error 109

The pipe has been ended.

Error 110

The system cannot open the device or file specified.

Error 111

The file name is too long.

Error 112

There is not enough space on the disk.

Error 113

No more internal file identifiers available.

Error 114

The target internal file identifier is incorrect.

Error 117

The IOCTL call made by the application program is not correct.

Error 118

The verify-on-write switch parameter value is not correct.

Error 119

The system does not support the command requested.

Error 120

This function is only valid in Windows NT mode.

Error 121

The semaphore timeout period has expired.

Error 122

The data area passed to a system call is too small.

Error 123

The filename, directory name, or volume label syntax is incorrect.

Error 124

The system call level is not correct.

Error 125

The disk has no volume label.

Error 126

The specified module could not be found.

Error 127

The specified procedure could not be found.

Error 128

There are no child processes to wait for.

Error 130

Attempt to use a file handle to an open disk partition for an operation other than raw disk I/O.

Error 131

An attempt was made to move the file pointer before the beginning of the file.

Error 132

The file pointer cannot be set on the specified device or file.

Error 133

A JOIN or SUBST command cannot be used for a drive that contains previously joined drives.

Error 134

An attempt was made to use a JOIN or SUBST command on a drive that has already been joined.

Error 135

An attempt was made to use a JOIN or SUBST command on a drive that has already been substituted.

Error 136

The system tried to delete the JOIN of a drive that is not joined.

Error 137

The system tried to delete the substitution of a drive that is not substituted.

Error 138

The system tried to join a drive to a directory on a joined drive.

Error 139

The system tried to substitute a drive to a directory on a substituted drive.

Error 140

The system tried to join a drive to a directory on a substituted drive.

Error 141

The system tried to SUBST a drive to a directory on a joined drive.

Error 142

The system cannot perform a JOIN or SUBST at this time.

Error 143

The system cannot join or substitute a drive to or for a directory on the same drive.

Error 144

The directory is not a subdirectory of the root directory.

Error 145

The directory is not empty.

Error 146

The path specified is being used in a substitute.

Error 147

Not enough resources are available to process this command.

Error 148

The path specified cannot be used at this time.

Error 149

An attempt was made to join or substitute a drive for which a directory on the drive is the target of a previous substitute.

Error 150

System trace information was not specified in your CONFIG.SYS file, or tracing is disallowed.

Error 151

The number of specified semaphore events for DosMuxSemWait is not correct.

Error 152

DosMuxSemWait did not execute; too many semaphores are already set.

Error 153

The DosMuxSemWait list is not correct.

Error 154

The volume label you entered exceeds the label character limit of the target file system.

Error 155

Cannot create another thread.

Error 156

The recipient process has refused the signal.

Error 157

The segment is already discarded and cannot be locked.

Error 158

The segment is already unlocked.

Error 159

The address for the thread ID is not correct.

Error 160

The argument string passed to DosExecPgm is not correct.

Error 161

The specified path is invalid.

Error 162

A signal is already pending.

Error 164

No more threads can be created in the system.

Error 167
Unable to lock a region of a file.

Error 170
The requested resource is in use.

Error 173
A lock request was not outstanding for the supplied cancel region.

Error 174
The file system does not support atomic changes to the lock type.

Error 180
The system detected a segment number that was not correct.

Error 183
Cannot create a file when that file already exists.

Error 186
The flag passed is not correct.

Error 187
The specified system semaphore name was not found.

Error 196
The operating system cannot run this application program.

Error 197
The operating system is not presently configured to run this application.

Error 199
The operating system cannot run this application program.

Error 200

The code segment cannot be greater than or equal to 64KB.

Error 203

The system could not find the environment option that was entered.

Error 205

No process in the command subtree has a signal handler.

Error 206

The filename or extension is too long.

Error 207

The ring 2 stack is in use.

Error 208

The global filename characters, * or ?, are entered incorrectly or too many global filename characters are specified.

Error 209

The signal being posted is not correct.

Error 210

The signal handler cannot be set.

Error 212

The segment is locked and cannot be reallocated.

Error 214

Too many dynamic link modules are attached to this program or dynamic link module.

Error 215

Can't nest calls to LoadModule.

Error 230

The pipe state is invalid.

Error 231

All pipe instances are busy.

Error 232

The pipe is being closed.

Error 233

No process is on the other end of the pipe.

Error 234

More data is available.

Error 240

The session was cancelled.

Error 254

The specified extended attribute name was invalid.

Error 255

The extended attributes are inconsistent.

Error 259

No more data is available.

Error 266

The Copy API cannot be used.

Error 267

The directory name is invalid.

Error 275

The extended attributes did not fit in the buffer.

Error 276

The extended attribute file on the mounted file system is corrupt.

Error 277

The extended attribute table file is full.

Error 278

The specified extended attribute handle is invalid.

Error 282

The mounted file system does not support extended attributes.

Error 288

Attempt to release mutex not owned by caller.

Error 298

Too many posts were made to a semaphore.

Error 299

Only part of a Read/WriteProcessMemory request was completed.

Error 994

Access to the extended attribute was denied.

Error 995

The I/O operation has been aborted because of either a thread exit or an application request.

Error 996

Overlapped I/O event is not in a signaled state.

Error 997

Overlapped I/O operation is in progress.

Error 998

Invalid access to memory location.

Error 999

Error performing in-page operation.

Error 1001

Recursion too deep, stack overflowed.

Error 1002

The window cannot act on the sent message.

Error 1003

Cannot complete this function.

Error 1004

Invalid flags.

Error 1005

The volume does not contain a recognized file system. Please make sure that all required file system drivers are loaded and that the volume is not corrupt.

Error 1006

The volume for a file has been externally altered such that the opened file is no longer valid.

Error 1007

The requested operation cannot be performed in full-screen mode.

Error 1008

An attempt was made to reference a token that does not exist.

Error 1009

The configuration registry database is corrupt.

Error 1010

The configuration registry key is invalid.

Error 1011

The configuration registry key could not be opened.

Error 1012

The configuration registry key could not be read.

Error 1013

The configuration registry key could not be written.

Error 1014

One of the files in the Registry database had to be recovered by use of a log or alternate copy. The recovery was successful.

Error 1015

The Registry is corrupt. The structure of one of the files that contains Registry data is corrupt, or the system's image of the file in memory is corrupt, or the file could not be recovered because the alternate copy or log was absent or corrupt.

Error 1016

An I/O operation initiated by the Registry failed and is unrecoverable. The Registry could not read in, or write out, or flush, one of the files that contain the system's image of the Registry.

Error 1017

The system has attempted to load or restore a file into the Registry, but the specified file is not in a Registry file format.

Error 1018

Illegal operation attempted on a Registry key, which has been marked for deletion.

Error 1019

System could not allocate the required space in a Registry log.

Error 1020

Cannot create a symbolic link in a Registry key that already has subkeys or values.

Error 1021

Cannot create a stable subkey under a volatile parent key.

Error 1022

A notify change request is being completed and the information is not being returned in the caller's buffer. The caller now needs to enumerate the files to find the changes.

Error 1051

A stop control has been sent to a service, which other running services are dependent on.

Error 1052

The requested control is not valid for this service

Error 1053

The service did not respond to the start or control request in a timely fashion.

Error 1054

A thread could not be created for the service.

Error 1055

The service database is locked.

Error 1056

An instance of the service is already running.

Error 1057

The account name is invalid or does not exist.

Error 1058

The specified service is disabled and cannot be started.

Error 1059

Circular service dependency was specified.

Error 1060

The specified service does not exist as an installed service.

Error 1061

The service cannot accept control messages at this time.

Error 1062

The service has not been started.

Error 1063

The service process could not connect to the service controller.

Error 1064

An exception occurred in the service when handling the control request.

Error 1065

The database specified does not exist.

Error 1066

The service has returned a service-specific error code.

Error 1067

The process terminated unexpectedly.

Error 1068

The dependency service or group failed to start.

Error 1069

The service did not start due to a logon failure.

Error 1070

After starting, the service hung in a start-pending state.

Error 1071

The specified service database lock is invalid.

Error 1072

The specified service has been marked for deletion.

Error 1073

The specified service already exists.

Error 1074

The system is currently running with the last-known-good configuration.

Error 1075

The dependency service does not exist or has been marked for deletion.

Error 1076

The current boot has already been accepted for use as the last-known-good control set.

Error 1077

No attempts to start the service have been made since the last boot.

Error 1078

The name is already in use as either a service name or a service display name.

Error 1079

The account specified for this service is different from the account specified for other services running in the same process.

Error 1100

The physical end of the tape has been reached.

Error 1101

A tape access reached a filemark.

Error 1102

Beginning of tape or partition was encountered.

Error 1103

A tape access reached the end of a set of files.

Error 1104

No more data is on the tape.

Error 1105

Tape could not be partitioned.

Error 1106

When accessing a new tape of a multivolume partition, the current block size is incorrect.

Error 1107

Tape partition information could not be found when loading a tape.

Error 1108

Unable to lock the media eject mechanism.

Error 1109

Unable to unload the media.

Error 1110

Media in drive may have changed.

Error 1111

The I/O bus was reset.

Error 1112

No media in drive.

Error 1113

No mapping for the Unicode character exists in the target multi-byte code page.

Error 1114

A dynamic link library (DLL) initialization routine failed.

Error 1115

A system shutdown is in progress.

Error 1116

Unable to abort the system shutdown because no shutdown was in progress.

Error 1117

The request could not be performed because of an I/O device error.

Error 1118

No serial device was successfully initialized. The serial driver will unload.

Error 1119

Unable to open a device that was sharing an interrupt request (IRQ) with other devices. At least one other device that uses that IRQ was already opened.

Error 1120

A serial I/O operation was completed by another write to the serial port. (The IOCTL_SERIAL_XOFF_COUNTER reached zero.)

Error 1121

A serial I/O operation completed because the time-out period expired. (The IOCTL_SERIAL_XOFF_COUNTER did not reach zero.)

Error 1122

No ID address mark was found on the floppy disk.

Error 1123

Mismatch between the floppy disk sector ID field and the floppy disk controller track address.

Error 1124

The floppy disk controller reported an error that is not recognized by the floppy disk driver.

Error 1125

The floppy disk controller returned inconsistent results in its registers.

Error 1126

While accessing the hard disk, a recalibrate operation failed, even after retries.

Error 1127

While accessing the hard disk, a disk operation failed even after retries.

Error 1128

While accessing the hard disk, a disk controller reset was needed, but even that failed.

Error 1129

Physical end of tape encountered.

Error 1130

Not enough server storage is available to process this command.

Error 1131

A potential deadlock condition has been detected.

Error 1132

The base address or the file offset specified does not have the proper alignment.

Error 1140

An attempt to change the system power state was vetoed by another application or driver.

Error 1141

The system BIOS failed an attempt to change the system power state.

Error 1142

An attempt was made to create more links on a file than the file system supports.

Error 1150

The specified program requires a newer version of Windows.

Error 1151

The specified program is not a Windows or MS-DOS program.

Error 1152

Cannot start more than one instance of the specified program.

Error 1153

The specified program was written for an older version of Windows.

Error 1154

One of the library files needed to run this application is damaged.

Error 1155

No application is associated with the specified file for this operation.

Error 1156

An error occurred in sending the command to the application.

Error 1157

One of the library files needed to run this application cannot be found.

Error 1200

The specified device name is invalid.

Error 1201

The device is not currently connected but it is a remembered connection.

Error 1202

An attempt was made to remember a device that had previously been remembered.

Error 1203

No network provider accepted the given network path.

Error 1204

The specified network provider name is invalid.

Error 1205

Unable to open the network connection profile.

Error 1206

The network connection profile is corrupt.

Error 1207

Cannot enumerate a non-container.

Error 1208

An extended error has occurred.

Error 1209

The format of the specified group name is invalid.

Error 1210

The format of the specified computer name is invalid.

Error 1211

The format of the specified event name is invalid.

Error 1212

The format of the specified domain name is invalid.

Error 1213

The format of the specified service name is invalid.

Error 1214

The format of the specified network name is invalid.

Error 1215

The format of the specified share name is invalid.

Error 1216

The format of the specified password is invalid.

Error 1217

The format of the specified message name is invalid.

Error 1218

The format of the specified message destination is invalid.

Error 1219

The credentials supplied conflict with an existing set of credentials.

Error 1220

An attempt was made to establish a session to a network server, but there are already too many sessions established to that server.

Error 1221

The workgroup or domain name is already in use by another computer on the network.

Error 1222

The network is not present or not started.

Error 1223

The operation was cancelled by the user.

Error 1224

The requested operation cannot be performed on a file with a user mapped section open.

Error 1225

The remote system refused the network connection.

Error 1226

The network connection was gracefully closed.

Error 1227

The network transport endpoint already has an address associated with it.

Error 1228

An address has not yet been associated with the network endpoint.

Error 1229

An operation was attempted on a non-existent network connection.

Error 1230

An invalid operation was attempted on an active network connection.

Error 1231

The remote network is not reachable by the transport.

Error 1232

The remote system is not reachable by the transport.

Error 1233

The remote system does not support the transport protocol.

Error 1234

No service is operating at the destination network endpoint on the remote system.

Error 1235

The request was aborted.

Error 1236

The network connection was aborted by the local system.

Error 1237

The operation could not be completed. A retry should be performed.

Error 1238

A connection to the server could not be made because the limit on the number of concurrent connections for this account has been reached.

Error 1239

Attempting to login during an unauthorized time of day for this account.

Error 1240

The account is not authorized to login from this station.

Error 1241

The network address could not be used for the operation requested.

Error 1242

The service is already registered.

Error 1243

The specified service does not exist.

Error 1244

The operation being requested was not performed because the user has not been authenticated.

Error 1245

The operation being requested was not performed because the user has not logged on to the network. The specified service does not exist.

Error 1246

Return that wants caller to continue with work in progress.

Error 1247

An attempt was made to perform an initialization operation when initialization has already been completed.

Error 1248

No more local devices.

Error 1300

Not all privileges referenced are assigned to the caller.

Error 1301

Some mapping between account names and security IDs was not done.

Error 1302

No system quota limits are specifically set for this account.

Error 1303

No encryption key is available. A well-known encryption key was returned.

Error 1304

The NT password is too complex to be converted to a LAN Manager password. The LAN Manager password returned is a NULL string.

Error 1305

The revision level is unknown.

Error 1306

Indicates two revision levels are incompatible.

Error 1307

This security ID may not be assigned as the owner of this object.

Error 1308

This security ID may not be assigned as the primary group of an object.

Error 1309

An attempt has been made to operate on an impersonation token by a thread that is not currently impersonating a client.

Error 1310

The group may not be disabled.

Error 1311

There are currently no logon servers available to service the logon request.

Error 1312

A specified logon session does not exist. It may already have been terminated.

Error 1313

A specified privilege does not exist.

Error 1314

A required privilege is not held by the client.

Error 1315

The name provided is not a properly formed account name.

Error 1316

The specified user already exists.

Error 1317

The specified user does not exist.

Error 1318

The specified group already exists.

Error 1319

The specified group does not exist.

Error 1320

Either the specified user account is already a member of the specified group, or the specified group cannot be deleted because it contains a member.

Error 1321

The specified user account is not a member of the specified group account.

Error 1322

The last remaining administration account cannot be disabled or deleted.

Error 1323

Unable to update the password. The value provided as the current password is incorrect.

Error 1324

Unable to update the password. The value provided for the new password contains values that are not allowed in passwords.

Error 1325

Unable to update the password because a password update rule has been violated.

Error 1326

Logon failure: unknown user name or bad password.

Error 1327

Logon failure: user account restriction.

Error 1328

Logon failure: account logon time restriction violation.

Error 1329

Logon failure: user not allowed to log on to this computer.

Error 1330

Logon failure: the specified account password has expired.

Error 1331

Logon failure: account currently disabled.

Error 1332

No mapping between account names and security IDs was done.

Error 1333

Too many local user identifiers (LUIDs) were requested at one time.

Error 1334

No more local user identifiers (LUIDs) are available.

Error 1335

The subauthority part of a security ID is invalid for this particular use.

Error 1336

The access control list (ACL) structure is invalid.

Error 1337

The security ID structure is invalid.

Error 1338

The security descriptor structure is invalid.

Error 1340

The inherited access control list (ACL) or access control entry (ACE) could not be built.

Error 1341

The server is currently disabled.

Error 1342

The server is currently enabled.

Error 1343

The value provided was an invalid value for an identifier authority.

Error 1344

No more memory is available for security information updates.

Error 1345

The specified attributes are invalid or incompatible with the attributes for the group as a whole.

Error 1346

Either a required impersonation level was not provided, or the provided impersonation level is invalid.

Error 1347

Cannot open an anonymous level security token.

Error 1348

The validation information class requested was invalid.

Error 1349

The type of the token is inappropriate for its attempted use.

Error 1350

Unable to perform a security operation on an object which has no associated security.

Error 1351

Indicates a Windows NT Server could not be contacted or that objects within the domain are protected such that necessary information could not be retrieved.

Error 1352

The security account manager (SAM) or local security authority (LSA) server was in the wrong state to perform the security operation.

Error 1353

The domain was in the wrong state to perform the security operation.

Error 1354

This operation is only allowed for the Primary Domain Controller of the domain.

Error 1355

The specified domain did not exist.

Error 1356

The specified domain already exists.

Error 1357

An attempt was made to exceed the limit on the number of domains per server.

Error 1358

Unable to complete the requested operation because of either a catastrophic media failure or a data structure corruption on the disk.

Error 1359

The security account database contains an internal inconsistency.

Error 1360

Generic access types were contained in an access mask, which should already be mapped to non-generic types.

Error 1361

A security descriptor is not in the right format (absolute or self-relative).

Error 1362

The requested action is restricted for use by logon processes only. The calling process has not registered as a logon process.

Error 1363

Cannot start a new logon session with an ID that is already in use.

Error 1364

A specified authentication package is unknown.

Error 1365

The logon session is not in a state that is consistent with the requested operation.

Error 1366

The logon session ID is already in use.

Error 1367

A logon request contained an invalid logon type value.

Error 1368

Unable to impersonate via a named pipe until data has been read from that pipe.

Error 1369

The transaction state of a Registry subtree is incompatible with the requested operation.

Error 1370

An internal security database corruption has been encountered.

Error 1371

Cannot perform this operation on built-in accounts.

Error 1372

Cannot perform this operation on this built-in special group.

Error 1373

Cannot perform this operation on this built-in special user.

Error 1374

The user cannot be removed from a group because the group is currently the user's primary group.

Error 1375

The token is already in use as a primary token.

Error 1376

The specified local group does not exist.

Error 1377

The specified account name is not a member of the local group.

Error 1378

The specified account name is already a member of the local group.

Error 1379

The specified local group already exists.

Error 1380

Logon failure: the user has not been granted the requested logon type at this computer.

Error 1381

The maximum number of secrets that may be stored in a single system has been exceeded.

Error 1382

The length of a secret exceeds the maximum length allowed.

Error 1383

The local security authority database contains an internal inconsistency.

Error 1384

During a logon attempt, the user's security context accumulated too many security IDs.

Error 1385

Logon failure: the user has not been granted the requested logon type at this computer.

Error 1386

A cross-encrypted password is necessary to change a user password.

Error 1387

A new member could not be added to a local group because the member does not exist.

Error 1388

A new member could not be added to a local group because the member has the wrong account type.

Error 1389

Too many security IDs have been specified.

Error 1390

A cross-encrypted password is necessary to change this user password.

Error 1391

Indicates an ACL contains no inheritable components

Error 1392

The file or directory is corrupt and non-readable.

Error 1393

The disk structure is corrupt and non-readable.

Error 1394

There is no user session key for the specified logon session.

Error 1395

The service being accessed is licensed for a particular number of connections. No more connections can be made to the service at this time because there are already as many connections as the service can accept.

Error 1400

Invalid window handle.

Error 1401

Invalid menu handle.

Error 1402

Invalid cursor handle.

Error 1403

Invalid accelerator table handle.

Error 1404
Invalid hook handle.

Error 1405
Invalid handle to a multiple-window position structure.

Error 1406
Cannot create a top-level child window.

Error 1407
Cannot find window class.

Error 1408
Invalid window, belongs to other thread.

Error 1409
Hot key is already registered.

Error 1410
Class already exists.

Error 1411
Class does not exist.

Error 1412
Class still has open windows.

Error 1413
Invalid index.

Error 1414
Invalid icon handle.

Error 1415
Using private DIALOG window words.

Error 1416

The listbox identifier was not found.

Error 1417

No wildcards were found.

Error 1418

Thread does not have a clipboard open.

Error 1419

Hot key is not registered.

Error 1420

The window is not a valid dialog window.

Error 1421

Control ID not found.

Error 1422

Invalid message for a combo box because it does not have an edit control.

Error 1423

The window is not a combo box.

Error 1424

Height must be less than 256.

Error 1425

Invalid device context (DC) handle.

Error 1426

Invalid hook procedure type.

Error 1427

Invalid hook procedure.

Error 1428

Cannot set non-local hook without a module handle.

Error 1429

This hook procedure can only be set globally.

Error 1430

The journal hook procedure is already installed.

Error 1431

The hook procedure is not installed.

Error 1432

Invalid message for single-selection listbox.

Error 1433

LB_SETCOUNT sent to non-lazy listbox.

Error 1434

This list box does not support tab stops.

Error 1435

Cannot destroy object created by another thread.

Error 1436

Child windows cannot have menus.

Error 1437

The window does not have a system menu.

Error 1438

Invalid message box style.

Error 1439

Invalid system-wide (SPI_*) parameter.

Error 1440

Screen already locked.

Error 1441

All handles to windows in a multiple-window position structure must have the same parent.

Error 1442

The window is not a child window.

Error 1443

Invalid GW_* command.

Error 1444

Invalid thread identifier.

Error 1445

Cannot process a message from a window that is not a multiple document interface (MDI) window.

Error 1446

Popup menu already active.

Error 1447

The window does not have scroll bars.

Error 1448

Scroll bar range cannot be greater than 0x7FFF.

Error 1449

Cannot show or remove the window in the way specified.

Error 1450

Insufficient system resources exist to complete the requested service.

Error 1451

Insufficient system resources exist to complete the requested service.

Error 1452

Insufficient system resources exist to complete the requested service.

Error 1453

Insufficient quota to complete the requested service.

Error 1454

Insufficient quota to complete the requested service.

Error 1455

The paging file is too small for this operation to complete.

Error 1456

A menu item was not found.

Error 1457

Invalid keyboard layout handle.

Error 1458

Hook type not allowed.

Error 1459

This operation requires an interactive window station.

Error 1460

This operation returned because the timeout period expired.

Error 1461

Invalid monitor handle.

Error 1500

The event log file is corrupt.

Error 1501

No event log file could be opened, so the event logging service did not start.

Error 1502

The event log file is full.

Error 1503

The event log file has changed between reads.

Error 1700

The string binding is invalid.

Error 1701

The binding handle is not the correct type.

Error 1702

The binding handle is invalid.

Error 1703

The RPC protocol sequence is not supported.

Error 1704

The RPC protocol sequence is invalid.

Error 1705

The string universal unique identifier (UUID) is invalid.

Error 1706

The endpoint format is invalid.

Error 1707

The network address is invalid.

Error 1708

No endpoint was found.

Error 1709

The timeout value is invalid.

Error 1710

The object universal unique identifier (UUID) was not found.

Error 1711

The object universal unique identifier (UUID) has already been registered.

Error 1712

The type universal unique identifier (UUID) has already been registered.

Error 1713

The RPC server is already listening.

Error 1714

No protocol sequences have been registered.

Error 1715

The RPC server is not listening.

Error 1716

The manager type is unknown.

Error 1717

The interface is unknown.

Error 1718

There are no bindings.

Error 1719

There are no protocol sequences.

Error 1720

The endpoint cannot be created.

Error 1721

Not enough resources are available to complete this operation.

Error 1722

The RPC server is unavailable.

Error 1723

The RPC server is too busy to complete this operation.

Error 1724

The network options are invalid.

Error 1725

There is not a remote procedure call active in this thread.

Error 1726

The remote procedure call failed.

Error 1727

The remote procedure call failed and did not execute.

Error 1728

A remote procedure call (RPC) protocol error occurred.

Error 1730

The transfer syntax is not supported by the RPC server.

Error 1732

The universal unique identifier (UUID) type is not supported.

Error 1733

The tag is invalid.

Error 1734

The array bounds are invalid.

Error 1735

The binding does not contain an entry name.

Error 1736

The name syntax is invalid.

Error 1737

The name syntax is not supported.

Error 1739

No network address is available to use to construct a universal unique identifier (UUID).

Error 1740

The endpoint is a duplicate.

Error 1741

The authentication type is unknown.

Error 1742

The maximum number of calls is too small.

Error 1743

The string is too long.

Error 1744

The RPC protocol sequence was not found.

Error 1745

The procedure number is out of range.

Error 1746

The binding does not contain any authentication information.

Error 1747

The authentication service is unknown.

Error 1748

The authentication level is unknown.

Error 1749

The security context is invalid.

Error 1750

The authorization service is unknown.

Error 1751

The entry is invalid.

Error 1752

The server endpoint cannot perform the operation.

Error 1753

There are no more endpoints available from the endpoint mapper.

Error 1754

No interfaces have been exported.

Error 1755

The entry name is incomplete.

Error 1756

The version option is invalid.

Error 1757

There are no more members.

Error 1758

There is nothing to unexport.

Error 1759

The interface was not found.

Error 1760

The entry already exists.

Error 1761

The entry is not found.

Error 1762

The name service is unavailable.

Error 1763

The network address family is invalid.

Error 1764

The requested operation is not supported.

Error 1765

No security context is available to allow impersonation.

Error 1766

An internal error occurred in a remote procedure call (RPC).

Error 1767

The RPC server attempted an integer division by zero.

Error 1768

An addressing error occurred in the RPC server.

Error 1769

A floating-point operation at the RPC server caused a division by zero.

Error 1770

A floating-point underflow occurred at the RPC server.

Error 1771

A floating-point overflow occurred at the RPC server.

Error 1772

The list of RPC servers available for the binding of auto handles has been exhausted.

Error 1773

Unable to open the character translation table file.

Error 1774

The file containing the character translation table has fewer than 512 bytes.

Error 1775

A null context handle was passed from the client to the host during a remote procedure call.

Error 1777

The context handle changed during a remote procedure call.

Error 1778

The binding handles passed to a remote procedure call do not match.

Error 1779

The stub is unable to get the remote procedure call handle.

Error 1780

A null reference pointer was passed to the stub.

Error 1781

The enumeration value is out of range.

Error 1782

The byte count is too small.

Error 1783

The stub received bad data.

Error 1784

The supplied user buffer is not valid for the requested operation.

Error 1785

The disk media is not recognized. It may not be formatted.

Error 1786

The workstation does not have a trust secret.

Error 1787

The SAM database on the Windows NT Server does not have a computer account for this workstation trust relationship.

Error 1788

The trust relationship between the primary domain and the trusted domain failed.

Error 1789

The trust relationship between this workstation and the primary domain failed.

Error 1790

The network logon failed.

Error 1791

A remote procedure call is already in progress for this thread.

Error 1792

An attempt was made to logon, but the network logon service was not started.

Error 1793

The user's account has expired.

Error 1794

The redirector is in use and cannot be unloaded.

Error 1795

The specified printer driver is already installed.

Error 1796

The specified port is unknown.

Error 1797

The printer driver is unknown.

Error 1798

The print processor is unknown.

Error 1799

The specified separator file is invalid.

Error 1800

The specified priority is invalid.

Error 1801

The printer name is invalid.

Error 1802

The printer already exists.

Error 1803

The printer command is invalid.

Error 1804

The specified datatype is invalid.

Error 1805

The Environment specified is invalid.

Error 1806

There are no more bindings.

Error 1807

The account used is an interdomain trust account. Use your global user account or local user account to access this server.

Error 1808

The account used is a Computer Account. Use your global user account or local user account to access this server.

Error 1809

The account used is a server trust account. Use your global user account or local user account to access this server.

Error 1810

The name or security ID (SID) of the domain specified is inconsistent with the trust information for that domain.

Error 1811

The server is in use and cannot be unloaded.

Error 1812

The specified image file did not contain a resource section.

Error 1813

The specified resource type can not be found in the image file.

Error 1814

The specified resource name can not be found in the image file.

Error 1815

The specified resource language ID cannot be found in the image file.

Error 1816

Not enough quota is available to process this command.

Error 1817

No interfaces have been registered.

Error 1818

The server was altered while processing this call.

Error 1819

The binding handle does not contain all required information.

Error 1820

Communications failure.

Error 1821

The requested authentication level is not supported.

Error 1822

No principal name registered.

Error 1823

The error specified is not a valid Windows NT RPC error code.

Error 1824

A UUID that is valid only on this computer has been allocated.

Error 1825

A security package specific error occurred.

Error 1826

Thread is not cancelled.

Error 1827

Invalid operation on the encoding/decoding handle.

Error 1828

Incompatible version of the serializing package.

Error 1829

Incompatible version of the RPC stub.

Error 1830

The idl pipe object is invalid or corrupted.

Error 1831

The operation is invalid for a given idl pipe object.

Error 1832

The idl pipe version is not supported.

Error 1900

The object universal unique identifier (UUID) is the nil UUID.

Error 1901

The specified time is invalid.

Error 1902

The specified Form name is invalid.

Error 1903

The specified Form size is invalid

Error 1904

The specified Printer handle is already being waited on

Error 1905

The specified Printer has been deleted

Error 1906

The state of the Printer is invalid

Error 1907

The user must change his password before he logs on the first time.

Error 1908

Could not find the domain controller for this domain.

Error 1909

The referenced account is currently locked out and may not be logged on to.

Error 1910

The object exporter specified was not found.

Error 1911

The object specified was not found.

Error 1912

The object resolver set specified was not found.

Error 1913

Some data remains to be sent in the request buffer.

Error 2000

The pixel format is invalid.

Error 2001

The specified driver is invalid.

Error 2002

The window style or class attribute is invalid for this operation.

Error 2003

The requested metafile operation is not supported.

Error 2004

The requested transformation operation is not supported.

Error 2005

The requested clipping operation is not supported.

Error 3000

Drive *** is nearly full. *** bytes are available.
  Please warn users and delete unneeded files.

Error 3001

*** errors were logged in the last *** minutes.
  Please review the server's error log.

Error 3002

*** network errors occurred in the last *** minutes.
  Please review the server's error log. The server and/or network hardware may need service.

Error 3003

There were *** bad password attempts in the last *** minutes.
   Please review the server's audit trail.

Error 3004

There were *** access-denied errors in the last *** minutes.
   Please review the server's audit trail.

Error 3006

The error log is full. No errors will be logged until the file is cleared or the limit is raised.

Error 3007

The error log is 80 full.

Error 3008

The audit log is full. No audit entries will be logged until the file is cleared or the limit is raised.

Error 3009

The audit log is 80 full.

Error 3010

An error occurred closing file ***.
   Please check the file to make sure it is not corrupted.

Error 3011

The administrator has closed ***.

Error 3012

There were *** access-denied errors in the last *** minutes.

Error 3020

A power failure was detected at ***. The server has been paused.

Error 3021

Power has been restored at ***. The server is no longer paused.

Error 3022

The UPS service is starting shut down at *** due to low battery.

Error 3023

There is a problem with a configuration of user specified shut down command file. The UPS service started anyway.

Error 3025

A defective sector on drive *** has been replaced (hotfixed). No data was lost. You should run CHKDSK soon to restore full performance and replenish the volume's spare sector pool. The hotfix occurred while processing a remote request.

Error 3026

A disk error occurred on the HPFS volume in drive ***. The error occurred while processing a remote request.

Error 3027

The user accounts database (NET.ACC) is corrupted. The local security system is replacing the corrupted NET.ACC with the backup made on *** at ***. Any updates made to the database after this time are lost.

Error 3028

The user accounts database (NET.ACC) is missing. The local security system is restoring the backup database made on *** at ***. Any updates made to the database after this time are lost.

Error 3029

Local security could not be started because the user accounts database (NET.ACC) was missing or corrupted, and no usable backup database was present.

The system is not secure!

Error 3030

The server cannot export directory ***, to client ***.
It is exported from another server.

Error 3031

The replication server could not update directory *** from the source on *** due to error ***.

Error 3032

Master *** did not send an update notice for directory *** at the expected time.

Error 3033

User *** has exceeded account limitation *** on server ***.

Error 3034

The primary domain controller for domain *** failed.

Error 3035

Failed to authenticate with ***, a Windows NT Domain Controller for domain ***.

Error 3036

The replicator attempted to log on at *** as *** and failed.

Error 3037

@I *LOGON HOURS

Error 3038

Replicator could not access ***on *** due to system error ***.

Error 3039

Replicator limit for files in a directory has been exceeded.

Error 3040

Replicator limit for tree depth has been exceeded.

Error 3041

The replicator cannot update directory ***. It has tree integrity and is the current directory for some process.

Error 3042

Network error *** occurred.

Error 3045

System error *** occurred.

Error 3046

Cannot log on. User is currently logged on and argument TRYUSER is set to NO.

Error 3047

IMPORT path *** cannot be found.

Error 3048

EXPORT path *** cannot be found.

Error 3049

Replicated data has changed in directory ***.

Error 3050

Replicator failed to update signal file in directory *** due to *** system error.

Error 3051

The Registry or the information you just typed includes an illegal value for "***".

EXPLANATION

You specified invalid values for one or more of the service's options.
ACTION
Retype the command with correct values, or change the values for the listed options in the configuration file.

Error 3052

The required parameter was not provided on the command line or in the configuration file.
EXPLANATION
This message should occur only on a down level computer. Any action to correct the problem should be performed on that computer. You must specify a value for the listed option.
ACTION
Define a value for the option, either from the command line or in the configuration file.

Error 3053

LAN Manager does not recognize "***" as a valid option.
EXPLANATION
This message should occur only on a down level computer. Any action to correct the problem should be performed on that computer. This option is not valid for this service.
ACTION
Check the spelling of this option. If you did not type it from the command line, check the configuration file.

Error 3054

A request for resource could not be satisfied.
EXPLANATION
The service required more of the listed resource than was available.
ACTION
Increase the amount of this resource. Stopping other services or applications may free some resources, such as memory. Also check the disk where your pagefile(s) are located. If this disk is full, delete unnecessary files and directories from it to clear space.

Error 3055

A problem exists with the system configuration.

EXPLANATION

This message should occur only on a down level computer. Any action to correct the problem should be performed on that computer.

The system is not configured correctly.

ACTION

Contact your network administrator.

Error 3056

A system error has occurred.

EXPLANATION

The system error may be an internal LAN Manager or Windows NT error.

ACTION

If the error code is Error 52, you need to delete the duplicate domain name in the [othodomains] section of your configuration file. If an error code beginning with "NET" is displayed, you can use the HELPMSG command to see more information about the error as follows:

NET HELPMSG message#

where message# is the actual error number.

If no error number was displayed, contact technical support.

Error 3057

An internal consistency error has occurred.

EXPLANATION

A software error occurred.

ACTION

Contact technical support.

Error 3058

The configuration file or the command line has an ambiguous option.

EXPLANATION

This message should occur only on a down level computer. Any action to correct the problem should be performed on that computer.

Some options can be confused with other options that start with the same letter.

ACTION

Spell out enough of the option so that it cannot be confused with other command options.

Error 3059

The configuration file or the command line has a duplicate parameter.

EXPLANATION

This message should occur only on a down level computer. Any action to correct the problem should be performed on that computer.

An option was used more than once in your command or in the configuration file.

An option can be used only once in a command and once in the configuration file. If an option is typed from the command line, it overrides the value in the configuration file.

ACTION

Do not type the same option twice in a command. Be sure not to use different abbreviations that can specify the same option, such as `wrkserv` and `wrkservices`.

If the error was not caused by a command, check the configuration file for duplicate options.

Error 3060

The service did not respond to control and was stopped with the DosKillProc function.

EXPLANATION

The service did not respond to a control signal. The service may not be running correctly or a fatal error might have occurred. Windows NT stopped the service.

ACTION

Contact technical support.

Error 3061

An error occurred when attempting to run the service program.

EXPLANATION

The service you specified could not start.

ACTION

In the [services] section of your configuration file, find the name of the program file for this service. Be sure this file exists and is an executable file with a filename extension of .EXE or .COM. If the program file exists, it may be damaged. If possible, restore the file from a backup version. Otherwise, contact technical support.

Error 3062

The sub-service failed to start.

EXPLANATION

The specified service could not be started automatically when another service was started.

ACTION

Start the service individually.

Error 3063

There is a conflict in the value or use of these options: ***.

EXPLANATION

This message should occur only on a down level computer. Any action to correct the problem should be performed on that computer.

Two command-line options or configuration file entries have conflicting values.

ACTION

Check the command you typed or the configuration file for conflicting options.

Error 3064

There is a problem with the file.

Error 3070

memory

Error 3071

disk space

Error 3072

thread

Error 3073

process

Error 3074

Security Failure.

Error 3075

Bad or missing LAN Manager root directory.

Error 3076

The network software is not installed.

Error 3077

The server is not started.

Error 3078

The server cannot access the user accounts database (NET.ACC).

Error 3079

Incompatible files are installed in the LANMAN tree.

Error 3080

The LANMAN\LOGS directory is invalid.

Error 3081

The domain specified could not be used.

Error 3082

The computer name is being used as a message alias on another computer.

Error 3083

The announcement of the server name failed.

Error 3084

The user accounts database is not configured correctly.

Error 3085

The server is not running with user-level security.

Error 3087

The workstation is not configured properly.

Error 3088

View your error log for details.

Error 3089

Unable to write to this file.

Error 3090

ADDPAK file is corrupted. Delete LANMAN\NETPROG\ADDPAK. SER and reapply all ADDPAKs.

Error 3091

The LM386 server cannot be started because CACHE.EXE is not running.

Error 3092

There is no account for this computer in the security database.

Error 3093

This computer is not a member of the group SERVERS.

Error 3094

The group SERVERS is not present in the local security database.

Error 3095

This Windows NT computer is configured as a member of a workgroup, not as a member of a domain. The Netlogon service does not need to run in this configuration.

Error 3096

The Windows NT domain controller for this domain could not be located.

Error 3097

A primary domain controller is already running in this domain.

Error 3098

The service failed to authenticate with the primary domain controller.

Error 3099

There is a problem with the security database creation date or serial number.

Error 5001

The cluster resource cannot be moved to another group because other resources are dependent on it.

Error 5002

The cluster resource dependency cannot be found.

Error 5003

The cluster resource cannot be made dependent on the specified resource because it is already dependent.

Error 5004

The cluster resource is not online.

Error 5005

A cluster node is not available for this operation.

Error 5006

The cluster resource is not available.

Error 5007

The cluster resource could not be found.

Error 5008

The cluster is being shut down.

Error 5009

A cluster node cannot be evicted from the cluster while it is online.

Error 5010

The object already exists.

Error 5011

The object is already in the list.

Error 5012

The cluster group is not available for any new requests.

Error 5013

The cluster group could not be found.

Error 5014

The operation could not be completed because the cluster group is not online.

Error 5015

The cluster node is not the owner of the resource.

Error 5016

The cluster node is not the owner of the group.

Error 5017

The cluster resource could not be created in the specified resource monitor.

Error 5018

The cluster resource could not be brought online by the resource monitor.

Error 5019

The operation could not be completed because the cluster resource is online.

Error 5020

The cluster resource could not be deleted or brought offline because it is the quorum resource.

Error 5021

The cluster could not make the specified resource a quorum resource because it is not capable of being a quorum resource.

Error 5022

The cluster software is shutting down.

Error 5023

The group or resource is not in the correct state to perform the requested operation.

Error 5024

The properties were stored but not all changes will take effect until the next time the resource is brought online.

Error 5025

The cluster could not make the specified resource a quorum resource because it does not belong to a shared storage class.

Error 5026

The cluster resource could not be deleted since it is a core resource.

Error 5027

The quorum resource failed to come online.

Error 5028

The quorum log could not be created or mounted successfully.

Error 5029

The cluster log is corrupt.

Error 5030

The record could not be written to the cluster log since it exceeds the maximum size.

Error 5031

The cluster log exceeds its maximum size.

Error 5032

No checkpoint record was found in the cluster log.

Error 5033

The minimum required disk space needed for logging is not available.

Appendix B

GNU General Public License

Version 2, June 1991

Copyright (C) 1989, 1991 Free Software Foundation, Inc.
59 Temple Place, Suite 330, Boston, MA 02111-1307, USA

Everyone is permitted to copy and distribute verbatim copies of this license document, but changing it is not allowed.

Preamble

The licenses for most software are designed to take away your freedom to share and change it. By contrast, the GNU General Public License is intended to guarantee your freedom to share and change free software — to make sure the software is free for all its users. This General Public License applies to most of the Free Software Foundation's software and to any other program whose authors commit to using it. (Some other Free Software Foundation software is covered by the GNU Library General Public License instead.) You can apply it to your programs, too.

When we speak of free software, we are referring to freedom, not price. Our General Public Licenses are designed to make sure that you have the freedom to distribute copies of free software (and charge for this service if you wish), that you receive source code or can get it if you want it, that you can change the software or use pieces of it in new free programs; and that you know you can do these things.

To protect your rights, we need to make restrictions that forbid anyone to deny you these rights or to ask you to surrender the rights. These restrictions translate to certain responsibilities for you if you distribute copies of the software, or if you modify it.

For example, if you distribute copies of such a program, whether gratis or for a fee, you must give the recipients all the rights that you have. You must make sure that they, too, receive or can get the source code. And you must show them these terms so they know their rights.

We protect your rights with two steps: (1) copyright the software, and (2) offer you this license which gives you legal permission to copy, distribute and/or modify the software.

Also, for each author's protection and ours, we want to make certain that everyone understands that there is no warranty for this free software. If the software is modified by someone else and passed on, we want its recipients to know that what they have is not the original, so that any problems introduced by others will not reflect on the original authors' reputations.

Finally, any free program is threatened constantly by software patents. We wish to avoid the danger that redistributors of a free program will individually obtain patent licenses, in effect making the program proprietary. To prevent this, we have made it clear that any patent must be licensed for everyone's free use or not licensed at all.

The precise terms and conditions for copying, distribution and modification follow.

TERMS AND CONDITIONS FOR COPYING, DISTRIBUTION AND MODIFICATION

0. This License applies to any program or other work which contains a notice placed by the copyright holder saying it may be distributed under the terms of this General Public License. The "Program", below, refers to any such program or work, and a "work based on the Program" means either the Program or any derivative work under copyright law: that is to say, a work containing the Program or a portion of it, either verbatim or with modifications and/or translated into another language. (Hereinafter, translation is included without limitation in the term "modification".) Each licensee is addressed as "you".

Activities other than copying, distribution and modification are not covered by this License; they are outside its scope. The act of running the Program is not restricted, and the output from the Program is covered only if its contents constitute a work based on the Program (independent of having been made by running the Program). Whether that is true depends on what the Program does.

1. You may copy and distribute verbatim copies of the Program's source code as you receive it, in any medium, provided that you conspicuously and appropriately publish on each copy an appropriate copyright notice and disclaimer of warranty; keep intact all the notices that refer to this License and to the absence of any warranty; and give any other recipients of the Program a copy of this License along with the Program.

   You may charge a fee for the physical act of transferring a copy, and you may at your option offer warranty protection in exchange for a fee.

2. You may modify your copy or copies of the Program or any portion of it, thus forming a work based on the Program, and copy and distribute such modifications or work under the terms of Section 1 above, provided that you also meet all of these conditions:

   a) You must cause the modified files to carry prominent notices stating that you changed the files and the date of any change.

   b) You must cause any work that you distribute or publish, that in whole or in part contains or is derived from the Program or any part thereof, to be licensed as a whole at no charge to all third parties under the terms of this License.

   c) If the modified program normally reads commands interactively when run, you must cause it, when started running for such interactive use in the most ordinary way, to print or display an announcement including an appropriate copyright notice and a notice that there is no warranty (or else, saying that you provide a warranty) and that users may redistribute the program under these conditions, and telling the user how to view a copy of this License. (Exception: if the Program itself is interactive but does not normally print such an announcement, your work based on the Program is not required to print an announcement.)

These requirements apply to the modified work as a whole. If identifiable sections of that work are not derived from the Program, and can be reasonably considered independent and separate works in themselves, then this License, and its terms, do not apply to those sections when you distribute them as separate works. But when you distribute the same sections as part of a whole which is a work based on the Program, the distribution of the whole must be on the terms of this License, whose permissions for other licensees extend to the entire whole, and thus to each and every part regardless of who wrote it.

Thus, it is not the intent of this section to claim rights or contest your rights to work written entirely by you; rather, the intent is to exercise the right to control the distribution of derivative or collective works based on the Program.

In addition, mere aggregation of another work not based on the Program with the Program (or with a work based on the Program) on a volume of a storage or distribution medium does not bring the other work under the scope of this License.

3. You may copy and distribute the Program (or a work based on it, under Section 2) in object code or executable form under the terms of Sections 1 and 2 above provided that you also do one of the following:

    a) Accompany it with the complete corresponding machine-readable source code, which must be distributed under the terms of Sections 1 and 2 above on a medium customarily used for software interchange; or,

    b) Accompany it with a written offer, valid for at least three years, to give any third party, for a charge no more than your cost of physically performing source distribution, a complete machine-readable copy of the corresponding source code, to be distributed under the terms of Sections 1 and 2 above on a medium customarily used for software interchange; or,

    c) Accompany it with the information you received as to the offer to distribute corresponding source code. (This alternative is allowed only for noncommercial distribution and only if you received the program in object code or executable form with such an offer, in accord with Subsection b above.)

The source code for a work means the preferred form of the work for making modifications to it. For an executable work, complete source code means all the source code for all modules it contains, plus any associated interface definition files, plus the scripts used to control compilation and installation of the executable. However, as a special exception, the source code distributed need not include anything that is normally distributed (in either source or binary form) with the major components (compiler, kernel, and so on) of the operating system on which the executable runs, unless that component itself accompanies the executable.

If distribution of executable or object code is made by offering access to copy from a designated place, then offering equivalent access to copy the source code from the same place counts as distribution of the source code, even though third parties are not compelled to copy the source along with the object code.

4. You may not copy, modify, sublicense, or distribute the Program except as expressly provided under this License. Any attempt otherwise to copy, modify, sublicense or distribute the Program is void, and will automatically terminate your rights under this License. However, parties who have received copies, or rights, from you under this License will not have their licenses terminated so long as such parties remain in full compliance.

5. You are not required to accept this License, since you have not signed it. However, nothing else grants you permission to modify or distribute the Program or its derivative works. These actions are prohibited by law if you do not accept this License. Therefore, by modifying or distributing the Program (or any work based on the Program), you indicate your acceptance of this License to do so, and all its terms and conditions for copying, distributing or modifying the Program or works based on it.

6. Each time you redistribute the Program (or any work based on the Program), the recipient automatically receives a license from the original licensor to copy, distribute or modify the Program subject to these terms and conditions. You may not impose any further restrictions on the recipients' exercise of the rights granted herein. You are not responsible for enforcing compliance by third parties to this License.

7. If, as a consequence of a court judgment or allegation of patent infringement or for any other reason (not limited to patent issues), conditions are imposed on you (whether by court order, agreement or otherwise) that contradict the conditions of this License, they do not excuse you from the conditions of this License. If you cannot distribute so as to satisfy simultaneously your obligations under this License and any other pertinent obligations, then as a consequence you may not distribute the Program at all. For example, if a patent license would not permit royalty-free redistribution of the Program by all those who receive copies directly or indirectly through you, then the only way you could satisfy both it and this License would be to refrain entirely from distribution of the Program.

   If any portion of this section is held invalid or unenforceable under any particular circumstance, the balance of the section is intended to apply and the section as a whole is intended to apply in other circumstances.

   It is not the purpose of this section to induce you to infringe any patents or other property right claims or to contest validity of any such claims; this section has the sole purpose of protecting the integrity of the free software distribution system, which is implemented by public license practices. Many people have made generous contributions to the wide range of software distributed through that system in reliance on consistent application of that system; it is up to the author/donor to decide if he or she is willing to distribute software through any other system and a licensee cannot impose that choice.

   This section is intended to make thoroughly clear what is believed to be a consequence of the rest of this License.

8. If the distribution and/or use of the Program is restricted in certain countries either by patents or by copyrighted interfaces, the original copyright holder who places the Program under this License may add an explicit geographical distribution limitation excluding those countries, so that distribution is permitted only in or among countries not thus excluded. In such case, this License incorporates the limitation as if written in the body of this License.

9. The Free Software Foundation may publish revised and/or new versions of the General Public License from time to time. Such new versions will be similar in spirit to the present version, but may differ in detail to address new problems or concerns.

   Each version is given a distinguishing version number. If the Program specifies a version number of this License which applies to it and "any later version", you have the option of following the terms and conditions either of that version or of any later version published by the Free Software Foundation. If the Program does not specify a version number of this License, you may choose any version ever published by the Free Software Foundation.

10. If you wish to incorporate parts of the Program into other free programs whose distribution conditions are different, write to the author to ask for permission. For software which is copyrighted by the Free Software Foundation, write to the Free Software Foundation; we sometimes make exceptions for this. Our decision will be guided by the two goals of preserving the free status of all derivatives of our free software and of promoting the sharing and reuse of software generally.

NO WARRANTY

11. BECAUSE THE PROGRAM IS LICENSED FREE OF CHARGE, THERE IS NO WARRANTY FOR THE PROGRAM, TO THE EXTENT PERMITTED BY APPLICABLE LAW. EXCEPT WHEN OTHERWISE STATED IN WRITING THE COPYRIGHT HOLDERS AND/OR OTHER PARTIES PROVIDE THE PROGRAM "AS IS" WITHOUT WARRANTY OF ANY KIND, EITHER EXPRESSED OR IMPLIED, INCLUDING, BUT NOT LIMITED TO, THE IMPLIED WARRANTIES OF MERCHANTABILITY AND FITNESS FOR A PARTICULAR PURPOSE. THE ENTIRE RISK AS TO THE QUALITY AND PERFORMANCE OF THE PROGRAM IS WITH YOU. SHOULD THE PROGRAM PROVE DEFECTIVE, YOU ASSUME THE COST OF ALL NECESSARY SERVICING, REPAIR OR CORRECTION.

12. IN NO EVENT UNLESS REQUIRED BY APPLICABLE LAW OR AGREED TO IN WRITING WILL ANY COPYRIGHT HOLDER, OR ANY OTHER PARTY WHO MAY MODIFY AND/OR REDISTRIBUTE THE PROGRAM AS PERMITTED ABOVE, BE LIABLE TO YOU FOR DAMAGES, INCLUDING ANY GENERAL, SPECIAL, INCIDENTAL OR CONSEQUENTIAL DAMAGES ARISING OUT OF THE USE OR INABILITY TO USE THE PROGRAM (INCLUDING BUT NOT LIMITED TO LOSS OF DATA OR DATA BEING RENDERED INACCURATE OR LOSSES SUSTAINED BY YOU OR THIRD PARTIES OR A FAILURE OF THE PROGRAM TO OPERATE WITH ANY OTHER PROGRAMS), EVEN IF SUCH HOLDER OR OTHER PARTY HAS BEEN ADVISED OF THE POSSIBILITY OF SUCH DAMAGES.

*****END OF TERMS AND CONDITIONS*****

How to Apply These Terms to Your New Programs

If you develop a new program, and you want it to be of the greatest possible use to the public, the best way to achieve this is to make it free software which everyone can redistribute and change under these terms.

To do so, attach the following notices to the program. It is safest to attach them to the start of each source file to most effectively convey the exclusion of warranty; and each file should have at least the "copyright" line and a pointer to where the full notice is found.

```
one line to give the program's name and an idea of what it does.
Copyright (C) yyyy  name of author


This program is free software; you can redistribute it and/or
modify it under the terms of the GNU General Public License
as published by the Free Software Foundation; either version 2
of the License, or (at your option) any later version.


This program is distributed in the hope that it will be useful,
```

```
but WITHOUT ANY WARRANTY; without even the implied warranty of
MERCHANTABILITY or FITNESS FOR A PARTICULAR PURPOSE. See the
GNU General Public License for more details.
```

```
You should have received a copy of the GNU General Public License
along with this program; if not, write to the Free Software
Foundation, Inc., 59 Temple Place - Suite 330, Boston, MA  02111-1307, USA.
Also add information on how to contact you by electronic and paper mail.
If the program is interactive, make it output a short notice like this when it
starts in an interactive mode:
Gnomovision version 69, Copyright (C) yyyy name of author
Gnomovision comes with ABSOLUTELY NO WARRANTY; for details
type 'show w'. This is free software, and you are welcome
to redistribute it under certain conditions; type 'show c'
for details.
```

The hypothetical commands `show w` and `show c` should show the appropriate parts of the General Public License. Of course, the commands you use may be called something other than `show w` and `show c`; they could even be mouse-clicks or menu items — whatever suits your program.

You should also get your employer (if you work as a programmer) or your school, if any, to sign a "copyright disclaimer" for the program, if necessary. Here is a sample; alter the names:

```
Yoyodyne, Inc., hereby disclaims all copyright
interest in the program `Gnomovision'
(which makes passes at compilers) written
by James Hacker.
```

```
signature of Ty Coon, 1 April 1989
Ty Coon, President of Vice
```

This General Public License does not permit incorporating your program into proprietary programs. If your program is a subroutine library, you may consider it more useful to permit linking proprietary applications with the library. If this is what you want to do, use the GNU Library General Public License instead of this License.

Appendix C

Online Resources

One of the biggest advantages of Samba and other open-source software is the speed in which fixes are generated. Once a problem has been identified, the fix might be written and a patch released overnight, or at least in a few days. Because of this speed, the only way to stay current on fixes, problems, and security issues is to use the Internet.

This appendix lists helpful resources such as web pages and mailing lists that are essential for a Samba administrator to monitor for current developments.

Samba sites

The main Samba web page is http://www.samba.org. The three mirrored US sites are: http://us1.Samba.org/Samba/Samba.html, http://us2.Samba.org/Samba/Samba.html, and http://us3.Samba.org/Samba/Samba.html. Go to these pages to find out what the latest version of Samba is (2.0.5 as of this writing).

Samba mailing lists

For the absolute latest information in Samba including bug reports and security problems as well as a variety of questions and answers about using Samba (some are even from the developers), use the appropriate mailing list. You can access them from one of the Samba web pages, or subscribe to them via email.

Some of the mailing lists are:

- `Samba@samba.org` – The main Samba list
- `Samba-announce@samba.org` – The announcement mailing list
- `Samba-ntdom@samba.org` – The mailing list for NT domain controller support
- `Samba-technical@samba.org` – A technical mailing list for Samba developers
- `Samba-cvs@samba.org` – A mailing list for people interested in running the current developing version; to get prereleased versions of Samba

There is a complete list at `http://lists.samba.org/`. To subscribe to one of the lists, send email to `listproc@samba.org` with no subject and a body of "subscribe *listname* Your Full Name." You should receive a welcome message within a few minutes.

Samba newsgroups

The comp newsgroup related to smb networking is comp.protocols.smb.

Sun and Solaris sites

Solaris is a Sun product, so the first place to look for help with Solaris is the Sun homepage, `http://www.sun.com`.

Patches for Solaris and an informational database are kept at Sunsolve, `http://sunsolve.sun.com`. Full access requires a contract, but recommended patches and security patches are free at `http://sunsolve.sun.com/pubpatch`

Documentation for Sun products is available at the Sun documentation web page, `http://docs.sun.com`.

Solaris Central

Solaris Central, `http://www.solariscentral.org/`, is a web page for Solaris users and administrators but is not affiliated with Sun. Solaris Central focuses on Solaris and UNIX news.

Sunfreeware

Sunfreeware, `http://www.sunfreeware.com/`, is a site sponsored by Sun that collects and distributes free software for Sun machines, both Intel and Sparc. You might find a needed utility here, and it includes the latest Samba version.

Solaris newsgroups

Two of the Usenet newsgroups related to Solaris are `comp.unix.solaris` and `comp.sys.sun.admin`.

Linux sites

Thousands of sites are devoted to Linux. The following are just a few that stand out, and any good search engine will bring up hundreds more.

Linux.org

Linux.org, `http://www.linux.org`, is a web page with a good collection of links to other Linux articles on the web.

Red Hat

One of the most common distributions of Linux is Red Hat. At their homepage, `http://www.RedHat.com`, you can find their latest version of Linux, download it for free, read all the documentation available, and browse through their tech support files and discussion areas.

Caldera

Caldera is another Linux distribution that is geared towards business use. At their homepage, `http://www.calderasystems.com`, you can also find their latest version of Linux, download it for free, read all the documentation available, and browse through their tech support files and discussion areas.

Linuxtoday

Linuxtoday, `http://www.linuxtoday.com`, is a page frequently updated with links to Linux articles in online magazines. It's geared towards an industry/business viewpoint and can be very helpful in increasing a Samba/Linux presence in an office.

Tunelinux

Tunelinux, `http://www.tunelinux.com`, is a web page devoted to increasing performance for Linux machines.

Linux Gazzette

Linux Gazette, `http://www.linuxgazette.com`, is a monthly online journal devoted to teaching people about Linux. The articles range from newbie to experienced Linux administrator with emphasis on the practical.

Linux Journal

This homepage, `http://linuxjournal.com`, is an online version of the magazine Linux Journal.

Linux Links

Linux Links, `http://www.linuxlinks.com/`, is a big collection of links to Linux homepages, well organized by categories.

Linux newsgroups

There are many Linux newsgroups in the `comp.os.linux` hierarchy. Some of the following can be useful:

- `Comp.os.linux.announce`—a moderated newsgroup with the latest announcements
- `Comp.os.linux.apps`—a newsgroup for Linux applications
- `Comp.os.linux.networking`—a newsgroup for Linux networking questions

FreeBSD sites

The main FreeBSD page is at http://www.freebsd.org. Here you will find all sorts of links for FreeBSD information including online man pages and tutorials.

FreBSD Rocks

FreeBSD Rocks, http://www.freebsdrocks.com, is a web page with links to FreeBSD articles on the web.

FreeBSD zine

FreeBsdzine, http://www.freebsdzine.org, is an online magazine devoted to FreeBSD, with articles for all experience levels, ranging from newbie to experienced network administrator.

DaemonNews

DaemonNews, http://www.daemonnews.org, is a monthly online magazine focusing on the BSD Family of software: FreeBSD, NetBSD, and OpenBSD.

FreeBSD mailing lists

Mailing lists are the primary means of communication in the FreeBSD community. A selected set of the FreeBSD mailing lists are:

- freebsd-announce – Important events and project milestones
- freebsd-bugs – Bug reports
- freebsd-newbies – New FreeBSD users activities and discussions
- freebsd-questions – User questions and technical support

To post to a specific list, just send mail to *listname*@FreeBSD.org. It will then be redistributed to mailing list members worldwide.

To subscribe to a list, send mail to `majordomo@FreeBSD.org` and include

`subscribe <listname> [<optional address>]`

in the body of the message.

Also, you can search the archives of the mailing lists at `http://www.freebsd.org`.

FreeBSD newsgroups

Mailing lists are the preferred method of communication in the FreeBSD community, but two recommended newsgroups are `comp.unix.freebsd.misc` and `comp.unix.freebsd.announce`.

NetBSD sites

The main homepage for NetBSD is `http://www.netbsd.org`. Here you will find all sorts of links for NetBSD information including online man pages and tutorials.

DaemonNews

Daemonnews, `http://www.daemonnews.org`, is a monthly online magazine focusing on the BSD Family of software: FreeBSD, NetBSD, and OpenBSD.

NetBSD mailing lists

Here's a selected set of the NetBSD mailing lists:

- `netbsd-announce`
- `netbsd-bugs`
- `netbsd-help`
- `online web form to subscribe`

NetBSD newsgroup

Here's the Usenet newsgrop devoted to NetBSD:

```
Comp.unix.bsd.freebsd
```

Open-source sites

The following sites provide information about open-source software and open-source initiatives.

GNU

GNU is a product of the Free Software Foundation. Their GNU Web site, `http://www.gnu.org`, has many benchmark utilities for UNIX/Linux/BSD including the gnu compiler (gcc), the gnu compression utility (gzip), and many others.

Slashdot

Slashdot, `http://slashdot.org`, is a web page entitled "News for Nerds." Many links to articles of a computer/technical/science/social nature are posted daily with a very lively forum to respond to the article. Many of the posters do have a strong pro-Linux/anti-Microsoft bias, but don't let that keep you from finding useful information.

Freshmeat

Freshmeat, `http://www.freshmear.org/`, is a web page devoted to open-source software including downloads. You can find useful or fun packages here.

General UNIX Links

Finally, here are a few links providing information about UNIX in general.

Unixintegration

Unixintegration's web page, at `http://www.performancecomputing.com/unixintegration/`, is focused on integrating UNIX and NT machines.

Caida network tools

The Caida network tools page, `http://www.caida.org/Tools/`, is a good resource to help you troubleshoot network problems.

DNS Resources directory

Information about DNS is available at the DNS Resources page, `http://www.dns.net/dnsrd/`.

Index

Continued

Continued

my2cents.idgbooks.com